**Publisher and
Creative Director:**
B. Martin Pedersen

Chief Visionary Officer:
Patti Judd

Design Director:
Hee Ra Kim

Designers:
B. Martin Pedersen
Hee Ra Kim
Hiewon Sohn

Associate Editor:
Colleen Boyd

Contributing Editor:
Patti Judd

**Publisher's Assistant
/Designer:**
Claire Yuan Zhuang

Interns:
Maggie Herrera
Lauren Letarte
Ella York

Japanese Advisors:
USA: Toshiaki & Kumiko Ide
Japan: Taku Satoh
Sakura Nomiyama

Chief Executive Officer:
B. Martin Pedersen

Cover Image:
"Japan Drone"
School: Texas State University
Professor: William Meek
Student: Brandy Compton

Published by:
Graphis Inc.
389 5th Ave., Suite 1105
New York, NY 10016
Phone: 212-532-9387
www.graphis.com
help@graphis.com

ISBN 13: 978-1-954632-39-4

Dear Graphis Readers,

Welcome to *Graphis Journal* 385, where creative visionaries, design disruptors, and visual storytellers converge. This issue is filled with the kind of work that makes you stop, stare, think—and then think again. From bold posters to immersive ad campaigns and forward-thinking architecture, each feature is a testament to what happens when talent meets tenacity.

DESIGN: In a heartfelt tribute from fellow designer Finn Nygaard, we remember the late **Kari Piippo** (FI), a Graphis Master whose iconic poster work embodied his mantra: "Simple, Strong, and Sharp." Kari's legacy runs deep in the Finnish design community and far beyond. **Brad Hochberg**, co-founder of **The Refinery** (US), lets us peek behind the curtain of Hollywood's entertainment marketing machine. His work sits at the intersection of collaboration and strategy, helping shape how we see the shows and films we love. On the packaging front, **Sol Benito**'s (IN) **Vishal Vora** elevates form and function with work that is as smart as it is stunning—blending art, idea, and execution in a way few can.

ADVERTISING: If you've gamed in the last decade, you've probably seen the work of **PETROL Advertising** (US). As one of the leading agencies in the video game industry, PETROL doesn't just sell games—they build worlds. Their campaigns create emotional connections, bridging cultures and languages with bold, cinematic storytelling.

PHOTOGRAPHY: Scott Lowden (US) calls his photographic approach "life-fashionography," blending documentary and fashion aesthetics to create images that are both intimate and elevated. His work is rooted in connection, shaped by serendipity, and guided by a deep respect for storytelling. **Hadley Stambaugh** (US), photographer and creative director at the Savannah College of Art & Design, champions the voices of students and alumni through sharp visual narratives that shine with confidence and clarity.

ART/ILLUSTRATION: The illustration work featured in this issue is a celebration of visual storytelling at its most expressive—from textured analog pieces to vibrant digital dreamscapes. These artists are pushing the field forward with work that is arresting, detailed, and emotionally resonant.

EDUCATION: At the **School of Visual Arts** (US), educator **Justin Colt** encourages students to leave their comfort zones behind. His teaching philosophy blends high standards with a collaborative ethos, empowering young creatives to stretch, fail, try again—and thrive.

PRODUCTS: Boats: The **Gentleman's Yacht** (IT) merges old-world elegance with future-forward propulsion systems. Meanwhile, the **Picnic Boat 37** (US) delivers performance and design in equal measure.

Cars: The **Huayra Codalunga** (IT) channels the spirit of 1960s endurance racing, while the **Super 3** (UK) brings a three-wheeled twist to retro-inspired driving. These machines don't just move—they make a statement.

ARCHITECTURE: From **The Nest** (TH), a tree-framed home that dissolves into its lush environment, to **MO.CA** (ES), a sustainable living prototype from the Institute for Advanced Architecture of Catalonia, this issue showcases architecture that doesn't just respond to its surroundings—it elevates them.

Thank you for joining us in celebrating creative excellence. We hope this issue leaves you inspired, energized, and ready to make something bold.

B. Martin Pedersen
Publisher & Creative Director

Contents

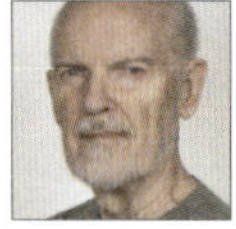

Kari began his career as a versatile poster designer in the late 1970s. In addition to posters primarily related to theater, culture, and social issues, he designed logos for institutions such as the Arts Promotion Centre Finland, the Finnish Medicines Agency, and the Ministry of the Environment. At Kari's initiative, the Mikkeli Art Museum established its Illustration Triennial, which was first held in 1987. He was also actively involved in the Lahti International Poster Triennial since the 1970s. Kari received the State Award for Applied Arts (Finland, 1988) and the Pro Finlandia Medal of the Order of the Lion of Finland (Finland, 2011). He was named Graphic Designer of the Year (Finland, 1990) and was honored with the Platinum Award in the Best of the Year competition (Finland, 1993). His major international awards include first prize in the UNICEF: A World Fit to Live In competition (France, 1970), the Chaumont Icograda Excellence Award (France, 1990), first prize in the International Poster Biennial in Mexico (1990, 2006, 2021), and the Warsaw Poster Biennale Icograda Excellence Award (Poland, 2010). He was also celebrated as a Graphis Master by Graphis (USA). Kari became a member of AGI in 1997.

Introduction by Finn Nygaard (Graphis Master)

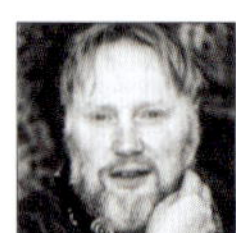

Finn Nygaard is a graphic designer, poster artist, and painter. Born in Denmark in 1955, he has created more than 1,000 posters, plus numerous illustrations and calligraphic work. More than 300 of those posters were created for jazz festivals, jazz clubs, and more. He has also created CD and LP record covers for Storyville Records. Many of his posters have received national and international awards. Finn has had several one-man shows and exhibitions all over the world in major galleries and museums such as the Museum of Printing History, the Pálffy Palace, the Danish Poster Museum, and more. Several of his posters have found their way into permanent collections.

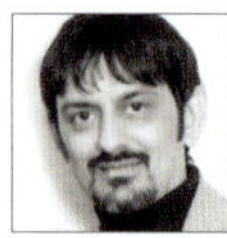

Sol Benito is an award-winning packaging design studio based in Mumbai, India, headed by founder and designer Vishal Vora. He studied graphic design at the I.S. College of Fine Arts and has over 20 years of multidisciplinary and multisector experience in design direction, management, and implementation in India and overseas. Vishal has worked for various markets in Europe, America, and the GCC. With a keen eye for quality design, he has profound experience in applying graphic principles to produce innovative designs for any media. Vishal would describe his approach to design as emotional, intuitive, and aspirational. His inclination lies in branding, packaging design, product design, and exhibition design.

Introduction by Patti Judd

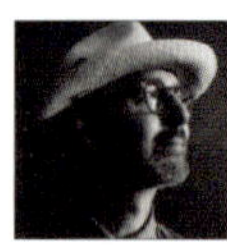

Brad Hochberg is a founding partner and creative director at The Refinery, a multi-award-winning Los Angeles-based entertainment marketing agency. Brad has worked on major campaigns for studios and streamers for two decades, starting with Seiniger Advertising, then Poetic Justice, Concept Arts, and Trailer Park, before co-founding The Refinery in 2006. Brad deeply loves "the visual" and leads his team with a historical perspective paired with a modern lens. He believes the creative's job is simple: Elicit a response, draw the eye to the message, and get an audience to connect.

Introduction by Jim Pascoe

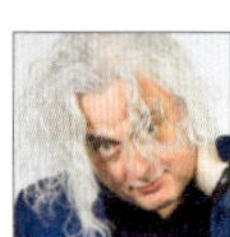

Jim Pascoe, RAVE Collective partner and creative director, weaves together a lifetime of diverse creative endeavors. As the author of more than a dozen books, he has a passion for storytelling that fuels his work and inspires all who collaborate with him. His experimental musical taste mirrors his fearless, boundary-pushing approach to creativity. In addition, Jim is a seasoned tarot reader, using the cards to unlock new perspectives and insights. With his rare blend of writing, music, and mysticism, Jim infuses each project with a unique vision, cultivating a spirit of innovation and imagination that defines the creative soul of RAVE Collective.

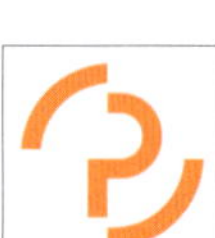

Fueled by Creativity, Informed by Intelligence, Driven by Results: PETROL offers industry-leading, integrated marketing capabilities that connect exceptional brands to the communities they inspire. For more than 22 years, PETROL has been creating rocket fuel for brands on a global scale and has pioneered iconic creative and marketing strategies that make the target market want more. PETROL is constantly developing global marketing campaigns for over 50 major brands across numerous genres and industries. Whether it be growing a brand, promoting a new title, or launching a new product, PETROL strategically brings things to life that may not exist in the real world to irresistible reality in the digital space.

Introduction by Simon Bollier

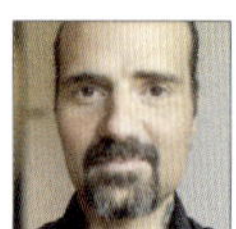

Simon is a senior creative with extensive experience in entertainment marketing and advertising. Over the last 20 years, he has developed high-impact campaigns for major studios, streaming platforms, and gaming brands, including Netflix, Apple, Paramount Pictures, and Activision. With a keen eye for storytelling, branding, and visual innovation, he excels in crafting compelling narratives across multiple platforms. Passionate about pushing creative boundaries, Simon delivers bold, immersive, and culturally resonant designs in fast-paced, dynamic environments.

(Opposite page) Western Digital by PETROL Advertising

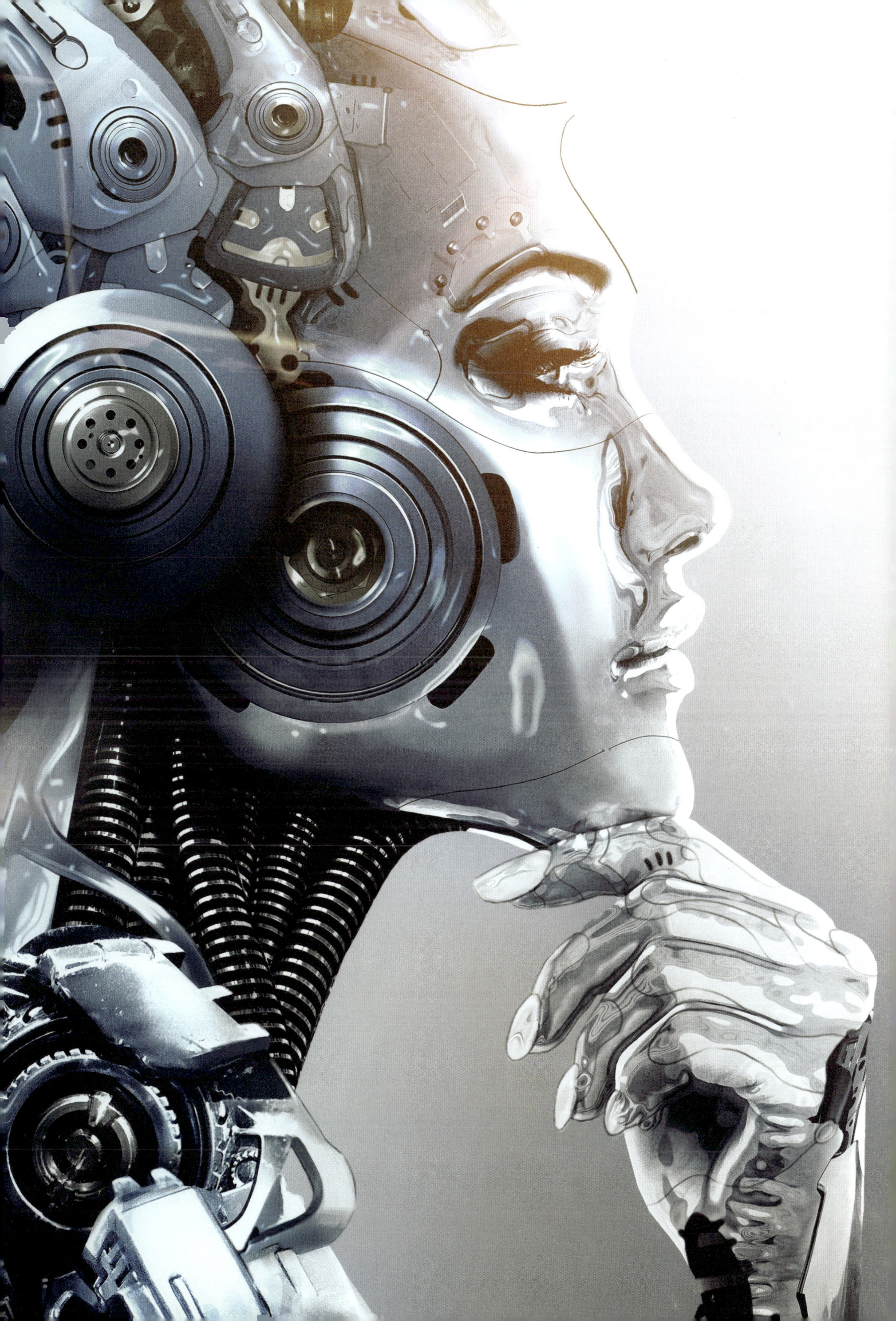

(Opposite page) AHS Snakes by The Refinery

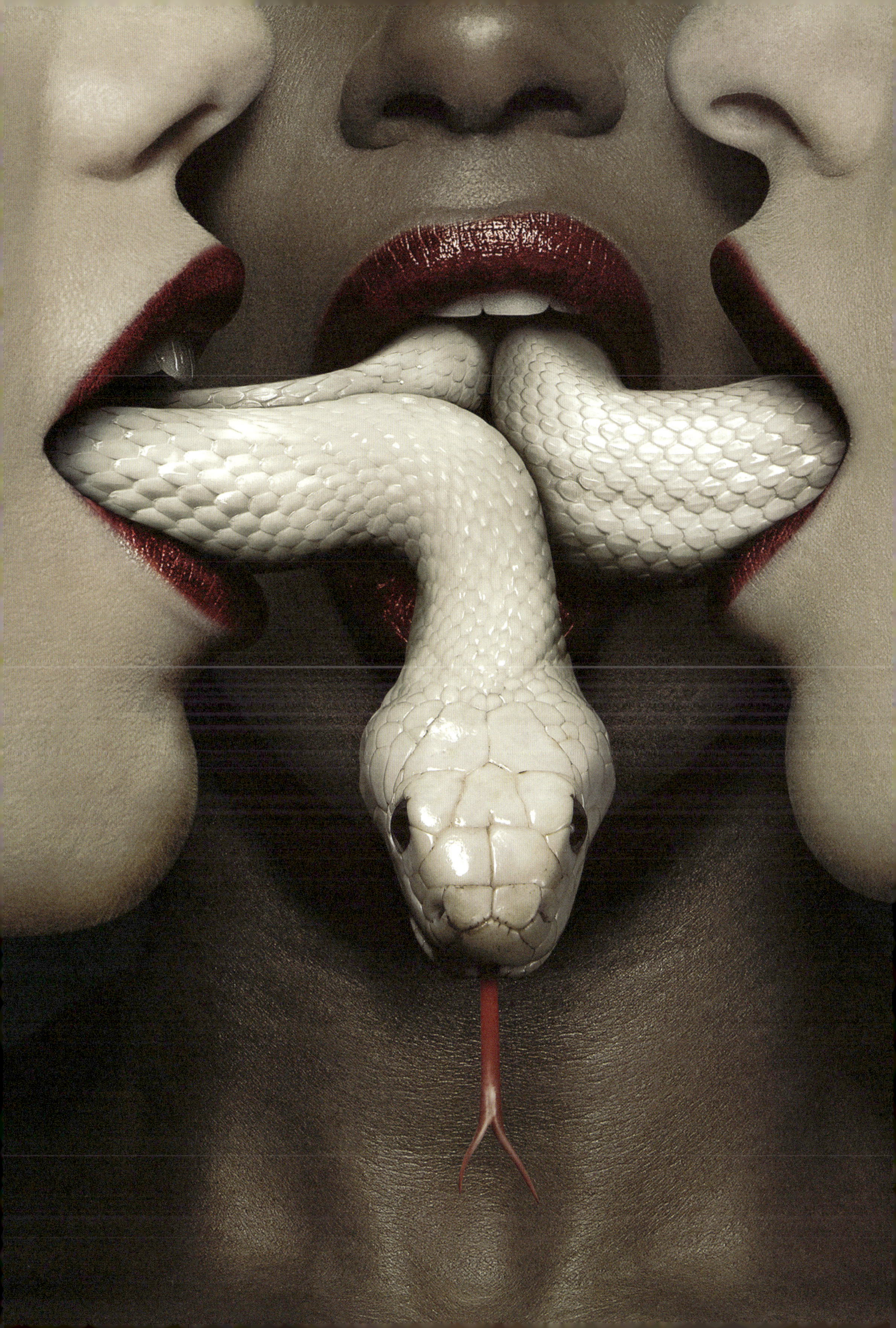

(Opposite page) Super 3 by Morgan Motor Company

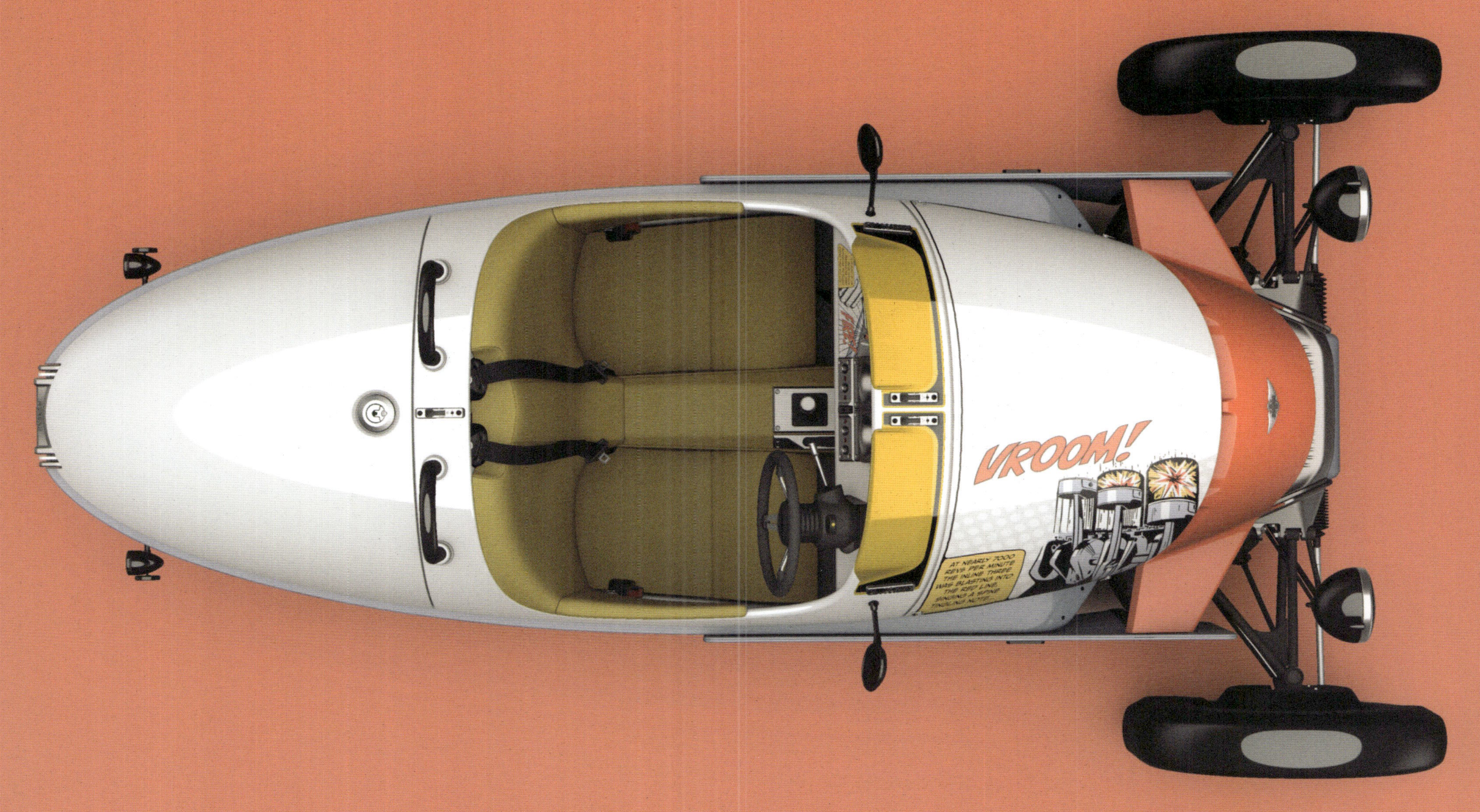
VROOM!
AT NEARLY 7000 REVS PER MINUTE THE INLINE THREE WAS BLASTING INTO THE RED LINE, MAKING A BONE TINGLING NOTE!

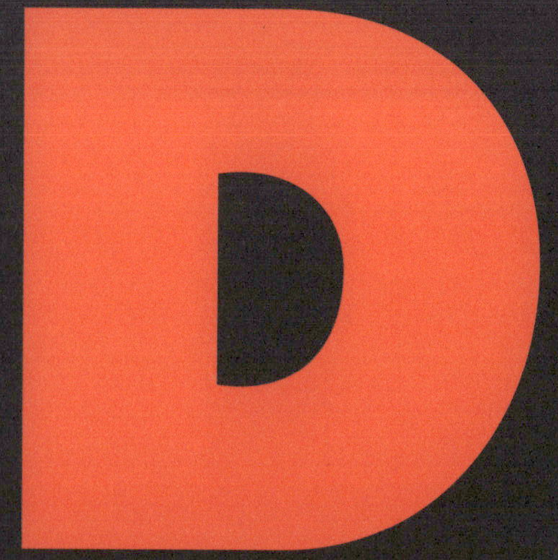

Kari Piippo (1945–2024): Simple, Strong, and Sharp

KARI PIIPPO KNEW HOW TO BE LOUD AND CLEAR
IN A QUIET WAY. HE WAS A POSTER ARTIST. KARI
PIIPPO VERSTAND ES AUF LEISE WEISE LAUT UND
DEUTLICH ZU SEIN. ER WAR EIN PLAKAT-KÜNSTLER.

Uwe Loesch, *Designer, Studio Uwe Loesch*

KARI PIIPPO'S WORK IS SIMPLY TIMELESS. WHY?
IT IS IDEA-DRIVEN, INTELLIGENT, AND TO THE POINT:
NO FRILLS, NO MAINSTREAM HYPOCRISY, ALWAYS
FRESH, AND ALWAYS GRATIFYINGLY UPLIFTING!

EACH OF KARI'S SOLUTIONS IS A JOY TO LOOK
AT AND TO "CONSUME." THEY SIMPLY EXUDE A
JOY FOR LIFE. BRAVO, KARI! WE WILL MISS YOU.

Fritz Gottschalk, *Designer & Co-founder, Gottschalk+Ash Int'l*

KARI PIIPPO CREATED POSTERS THAT CAPTURED
THE ESSENCE OF THEIR MESSAGE THROUGH
THEIR SIMPLICITY AND GRAPHIC PERFECTION.

HIS POSTERS WILL NOT LOSE THEIR RELEVANCE
IN THE FUTURE AS THEY UNIQUELY REFLECT
HIS DISTINCTIVE ARTISTIC SIGNATURE.

Melchior Imboden, *Freelance Artist, Graphic Designer, & Photographer*

KARI PIIPPO IS ONE OF FINLAND'S DESIGN TREASURES
WITH HIS POWERFUL, IMPACTFUL IMAGES.

B. Martin Pedersen, *Designer & Creative Director, Graphis, Inc.*

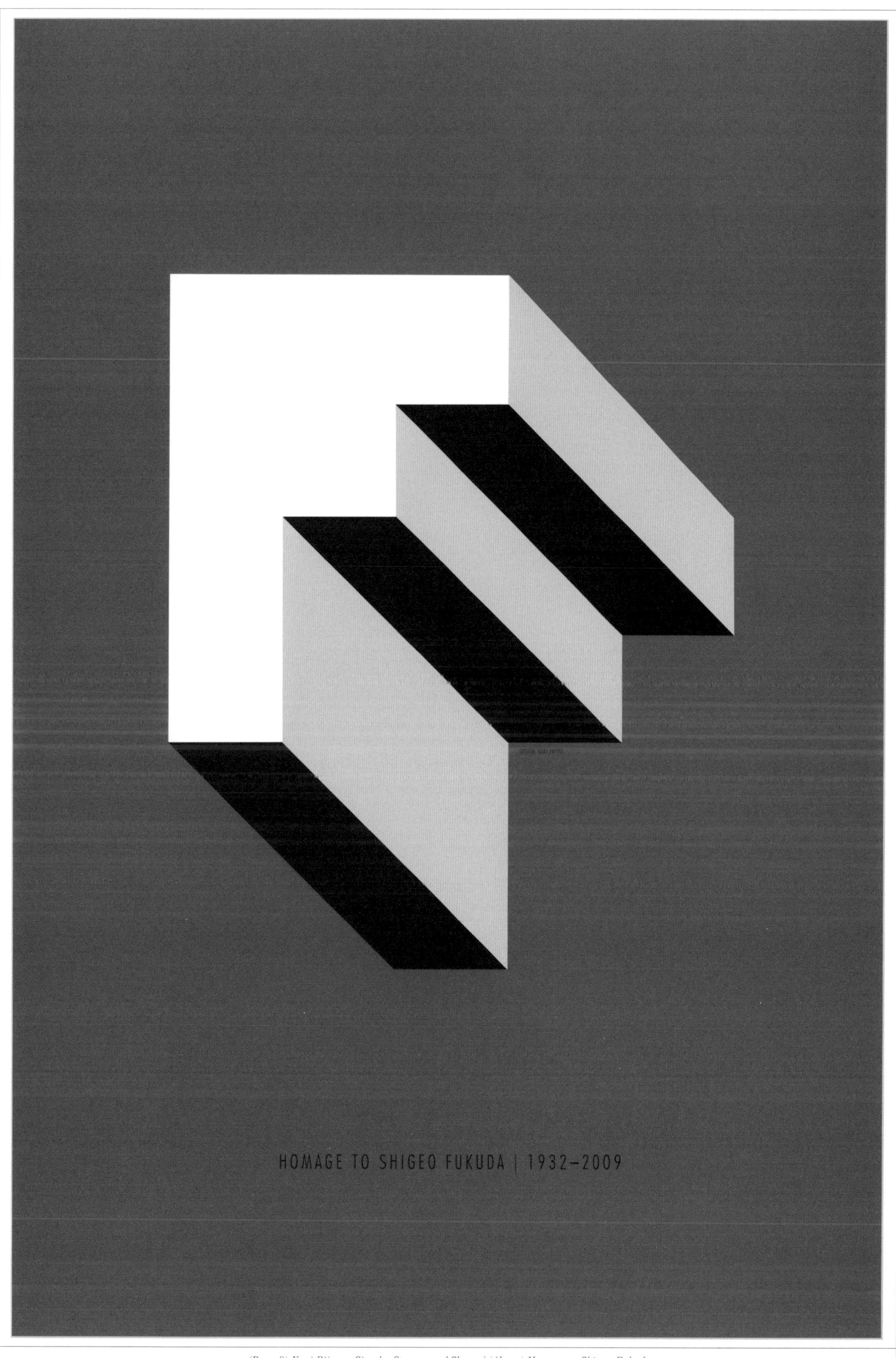

(Page 9) Kari Piippo: Simple, Strong, and Sharp / (Above) Homage to Shigeo Fukuda

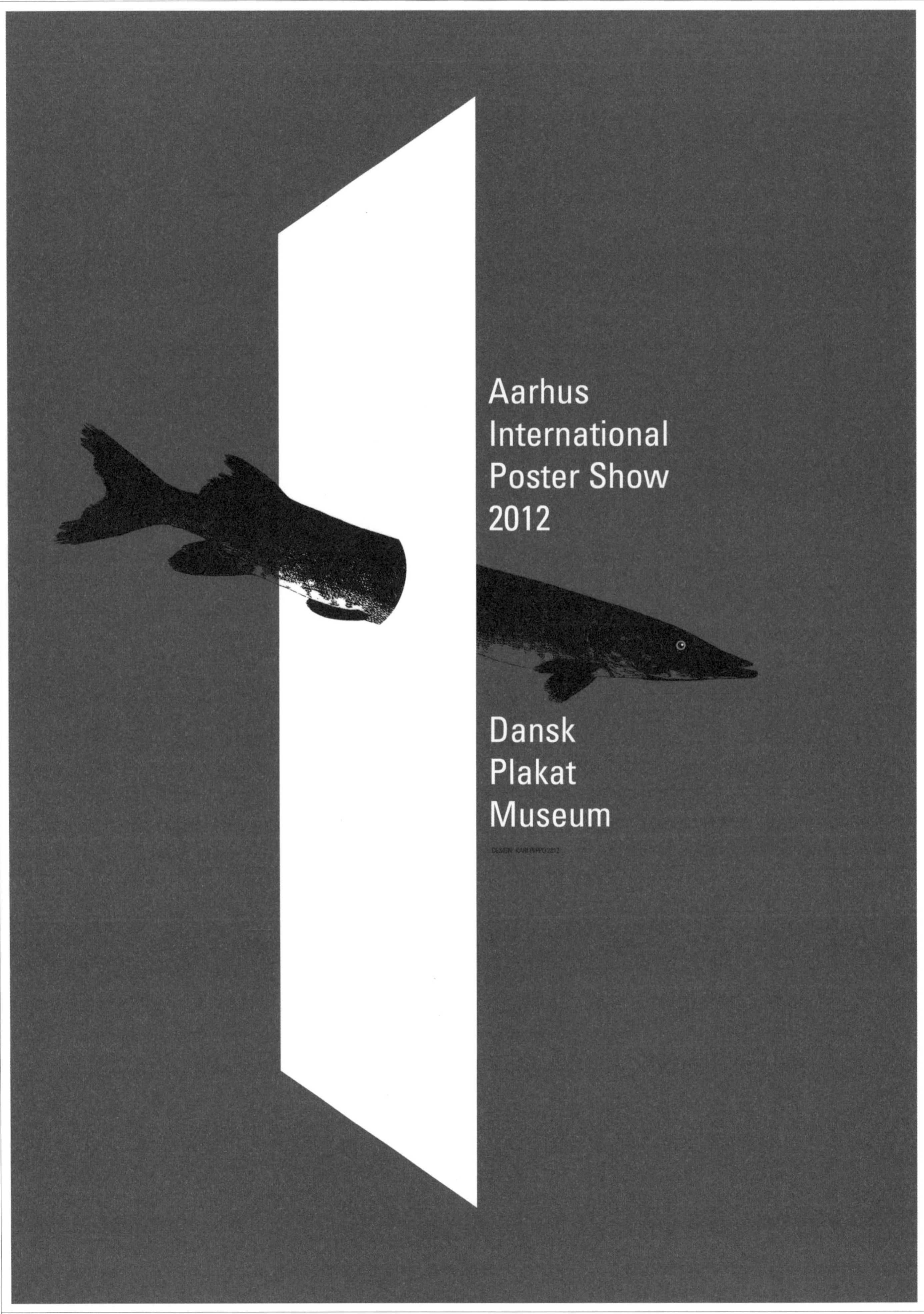

Aarhus
International
Poster Show
2012

Dansk
Plakat
Museum

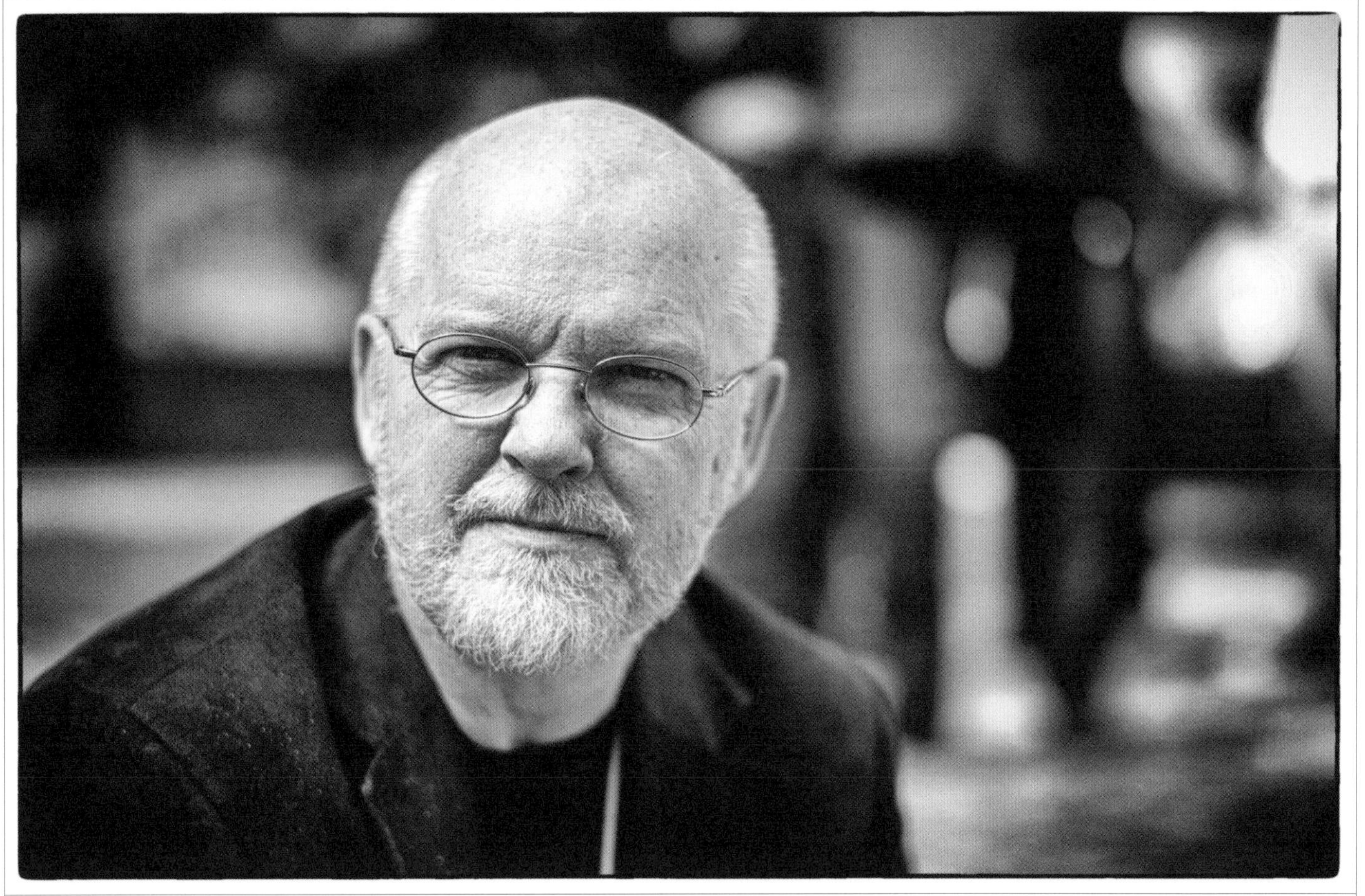

Kari Piippo Portrait. Photo by Finn Nygaard©

Dearest Kari, my clever and strong Finnish friend, A mutual friend of ours, graphic designer and AGI member Finn Sködt, wrote these words many years ago: "I work with colors, calligraphy, and climbing roses. In my next life, I will work with colors, calligraphy, and climbing roses." I hope that you can relate to these wise words and their whole essence from the place beyond, where you are now. Remembering our friendship, our many meetings and conversations—I know for sure you can. Your whole approach—to life, to love, to design and art, and to various upcoming challenges—indeed supports my assumption. "Simple, Strong, and Sharp"—another set of wise words that formed a fundamental basis for your long and unrelenting work as one of the world's greatest poster designers. "Simple, Strong, and Sharp" was your design philosophy—actually, your consistent philosophy. Nothing unnecessary was included, and nothing essential was left out. All bringing your mention, honor, and design awards all over the world. You will be remembered, Kari, for your great design... and for you: your kindness, cleverness, wit, and cunning smile. You and I met each other back in the '80s. We were frequent lecturers and guest teachers in design schools in Europe (mainly) and eastern countries, and we met each other at international poster biennials. We became members of AGI in the same year, 1997. We share a Nordic approach to being that is also reflected in our way of working with design and posters. We always looked forward to seeing each other. Between the meetings, we called each other frequently and discussed design, our daily activities, family, and the weather (an important and recurrent subject in our northern part of the world). I will miss you, Kari. So will many others. We will miss you, and we will miss you and Paula; the two of you together participated in almost all AGI meetings and biennials... You turned up in your nice clothes—leaving no one to doubt which country you came from. Best wishes from your friend, Finn Nygaard, Denmark.

Free elections =
Democracy

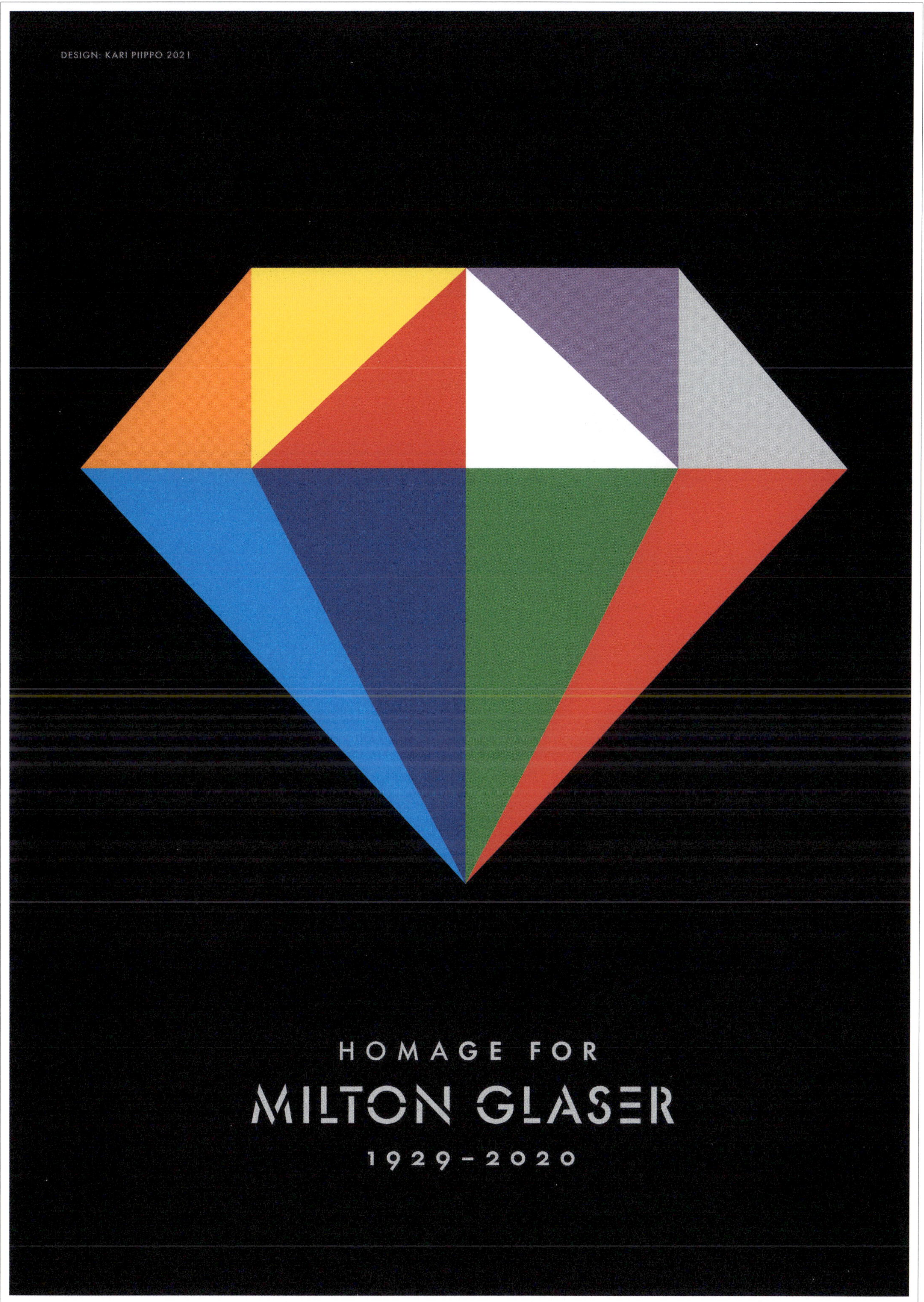

Homage for Milton Glaser 1929–2020

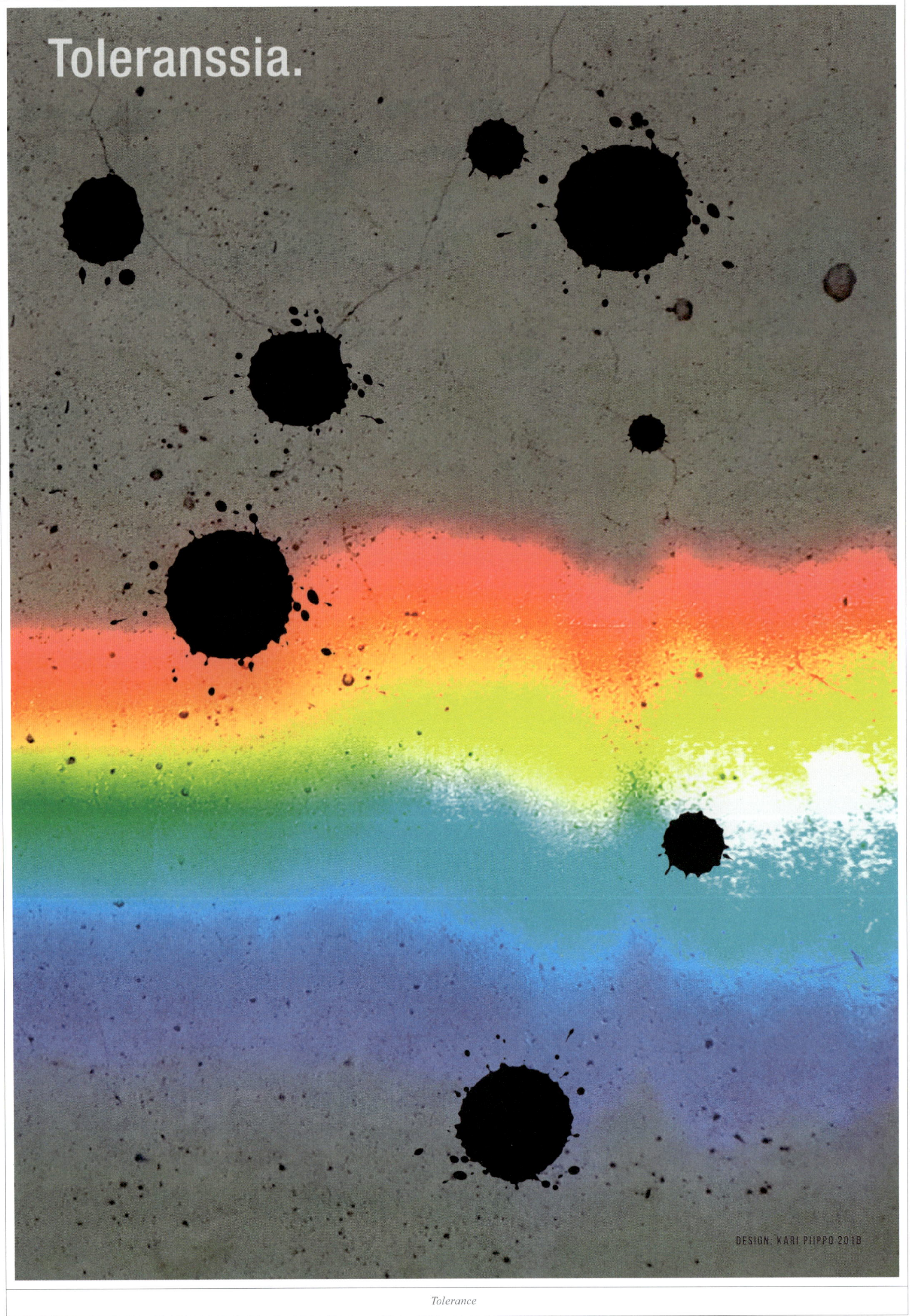

Tolerance

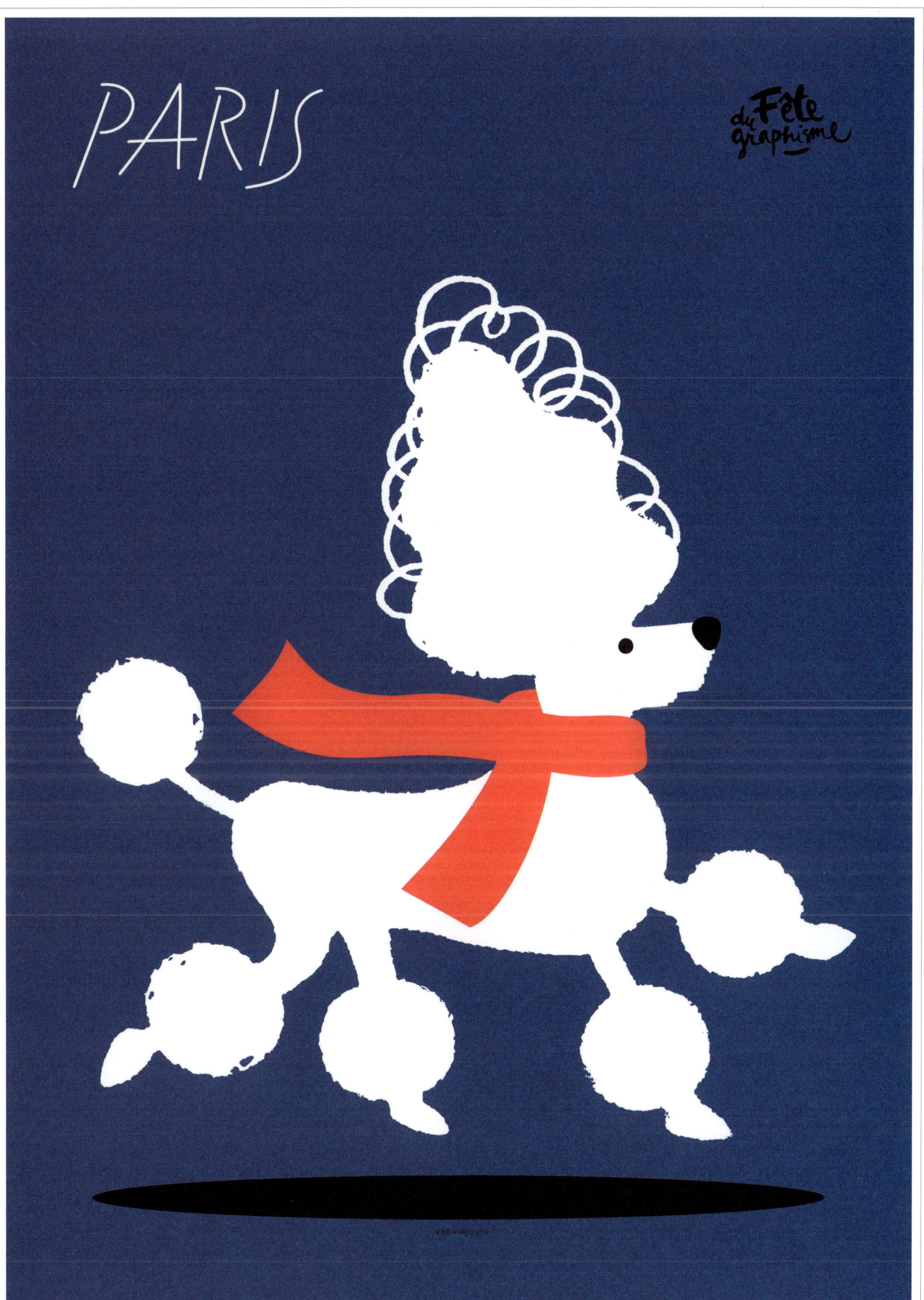

Paris

Kari Piippo | Finland
卡里·碧波 (芬兰)

Poster Workshop & Lecture 19–29.9.2011
海报设计训练营 & 讲座

Kari Piippo Workshop & Lecture

DESIGN: KARI PIIPPO 2011

Kari Piippo | Finland
卡里·碧波 (芬兰)

Art & Design Department Advertising School of CUC
International Students Creative Lab of CUC

中国传媒大学广告学院　艺术设计系
中国传媒大学国际大学生创意培养实验区

Kari Piippo Workshop & Lecture

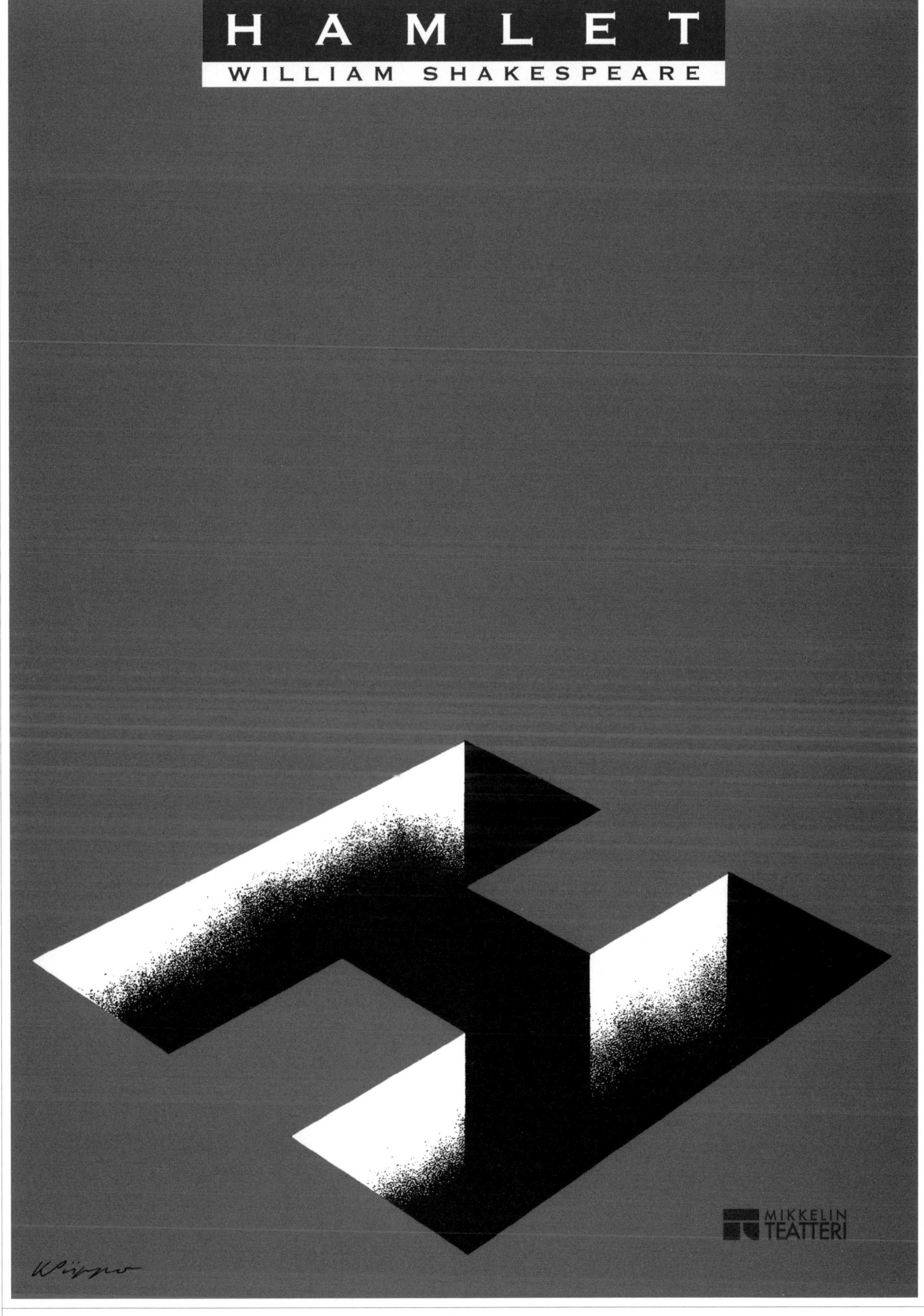

Hamlet

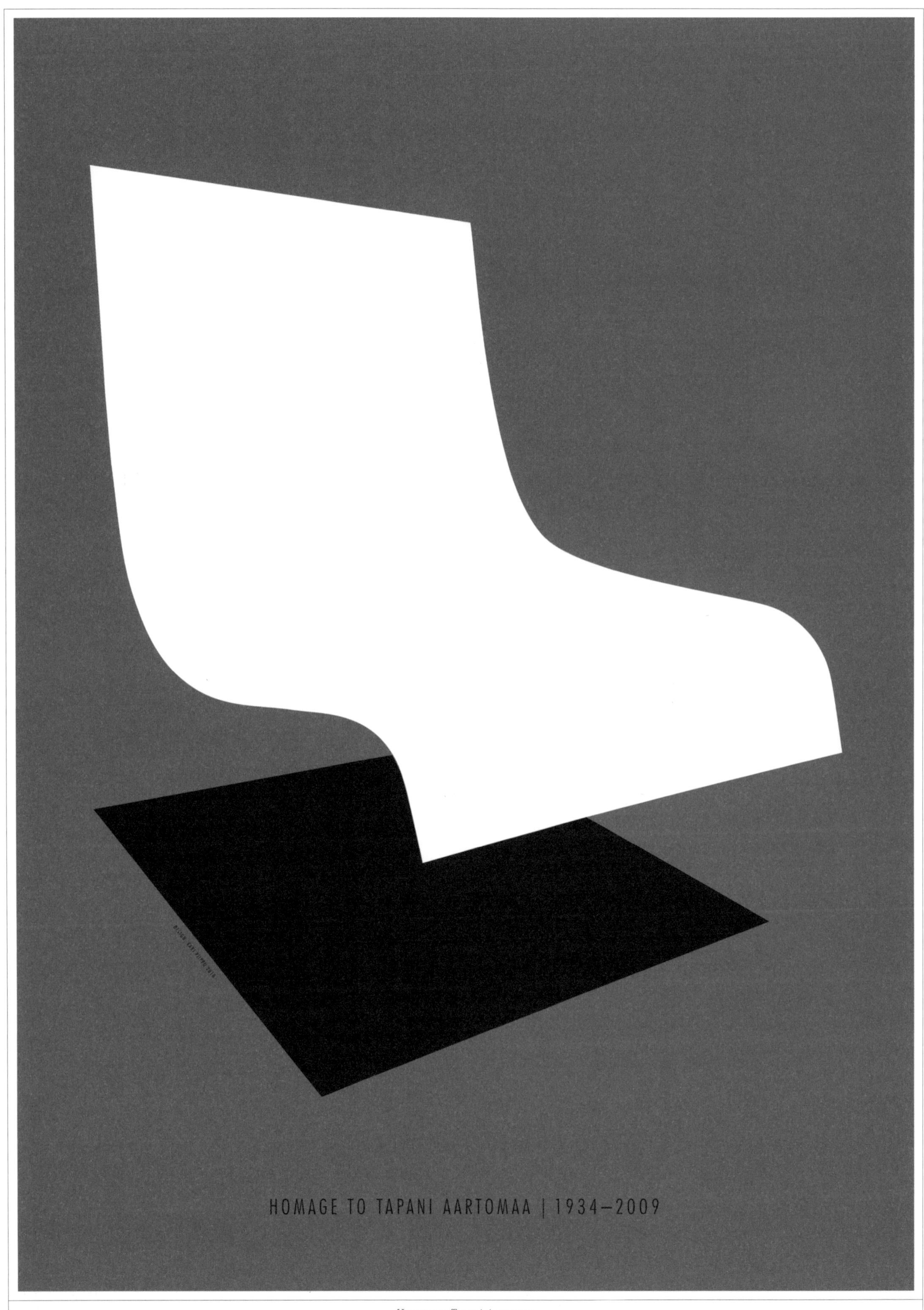

Homage to Tapani Aartomaa

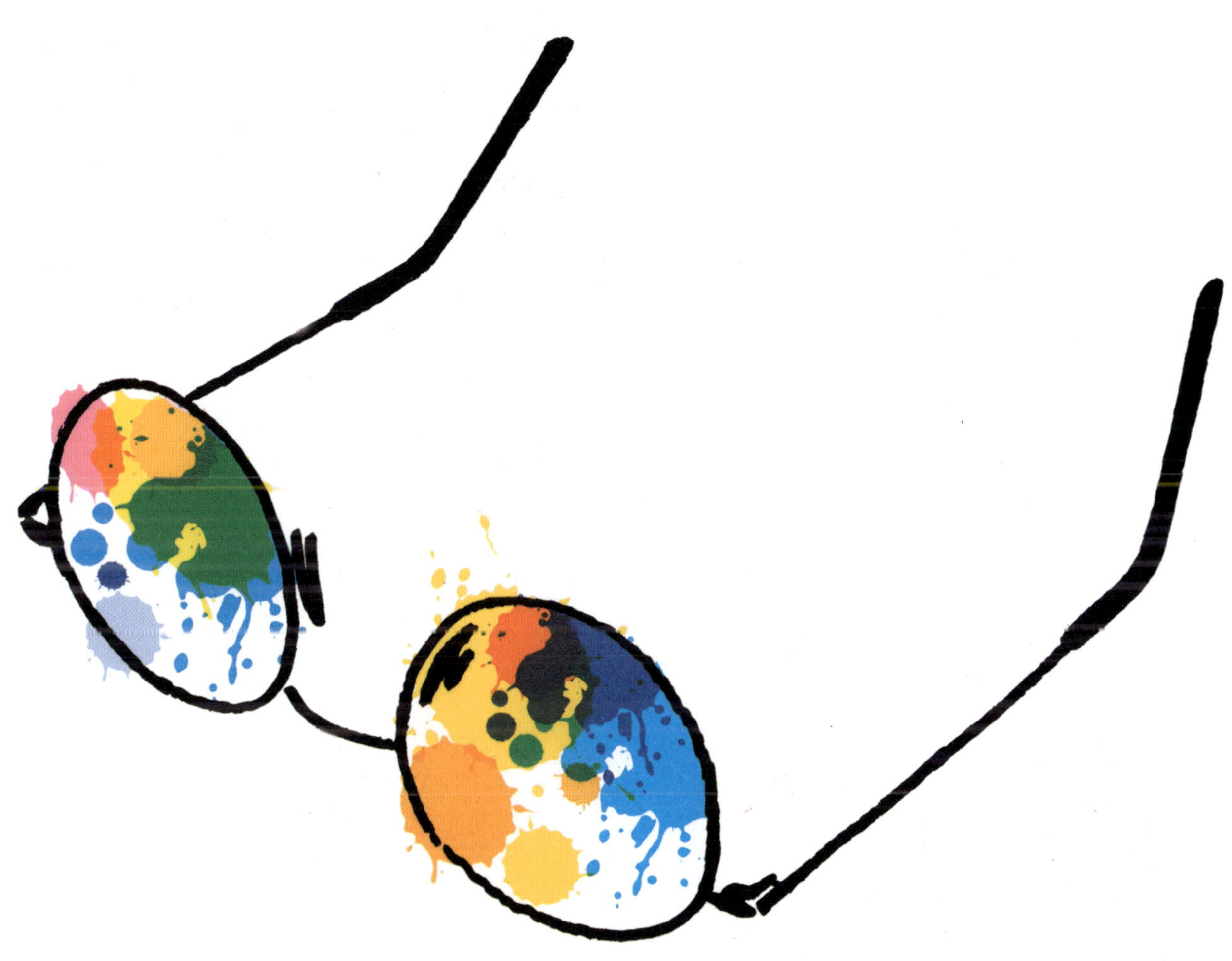

DESIGN: KARI PIIPPO 2014

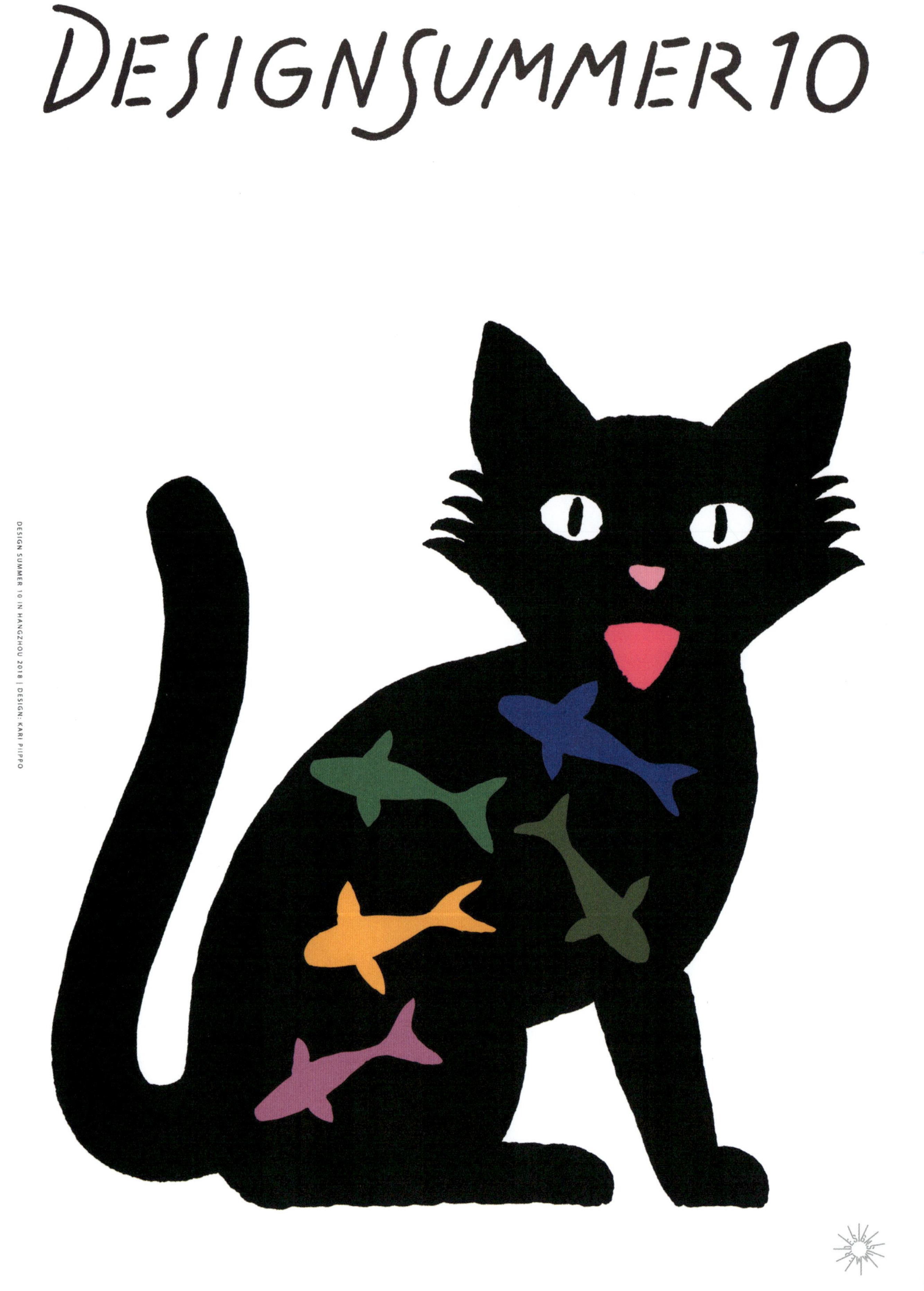

DESIGNSUMMER10

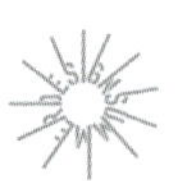

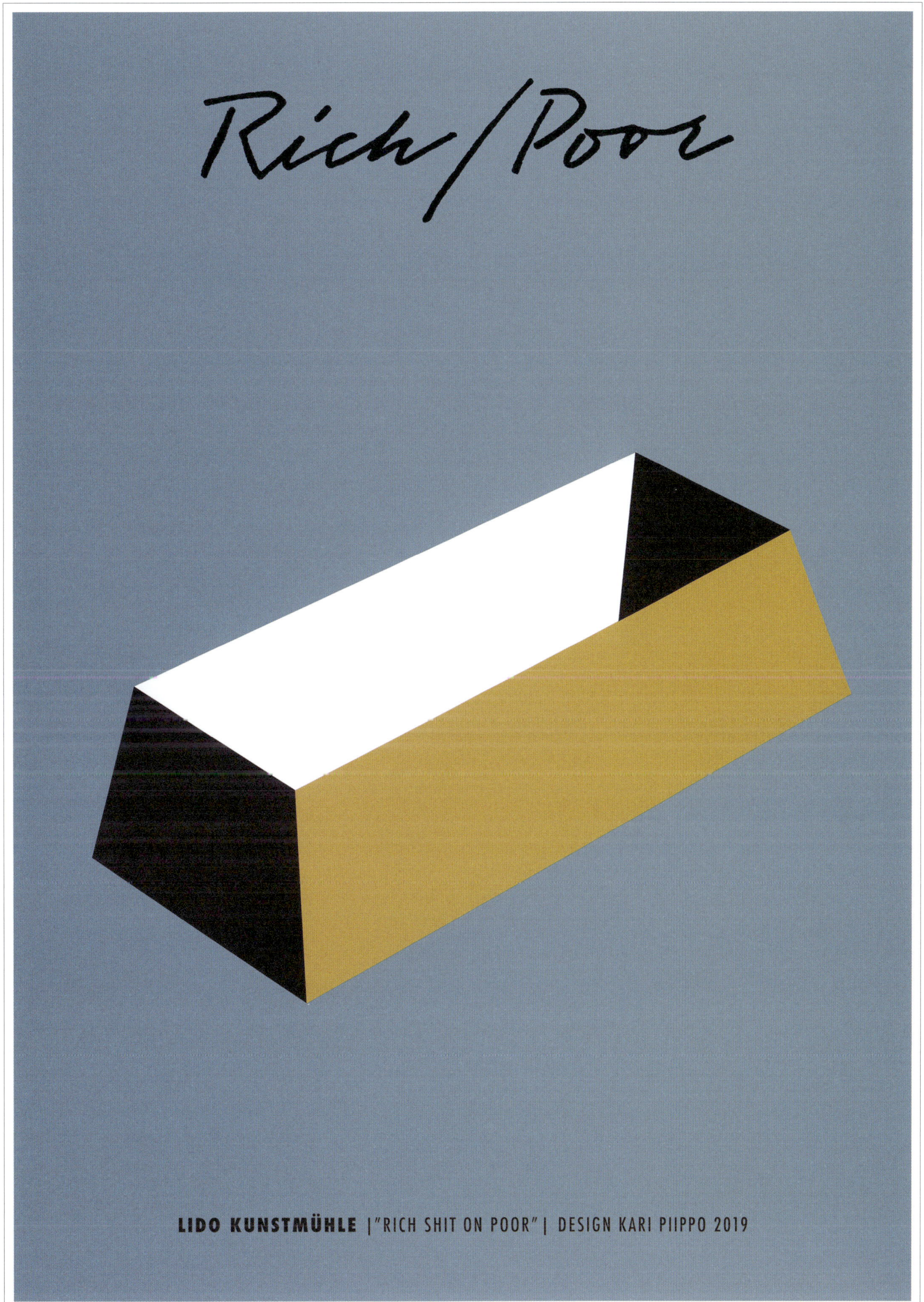
Rich/Poor
LIDO KUNSTMÜHLE |"RICH SHIT ON POOR"| DESIGN KARI PIIPPO 2019

Vishal Vora, Sol Benito: Balancing Creativity with Practicality

VISHAL'S DESIGN STYLE IS EXCEPTIONALLY REFINED. HE IS ADEPT AT USING PATTERNS AND ILLUSTRATIVE STORYTELLING TO CONVEY THE THEME OF HIS DESIGNS.

VISHAL EMPLOYS CONTRASTING MATERIALS TO CREATE A STRIKING VISUAL IMPACT, WITH TEXTURES LIKE GLASS, LEATHER, AND METAL ADDING RICH LAYERS TO THE OVERALL DESIGN.

Lu Chen, *Senior Design Director, Xiaomi*

WHAT I ADMIRE MOST ABOUT HIM IS HIS INCREDIBLE CREATIVITY—THE WAY HE ENVISIONS AND TRANSFORMS HIS DESIGNS IS TRULY UNMATCHED.

Jyoti Pithwa, *E-commerce Designer, Beauty Concepts Pvt. Ltd.*

VISHAL VORA'S EXCEPTIONAL DESIGN IN THE FRAGRANCE CATEGORY EXUDES LUXURY WITH FINESSE, OFTEN WITH AN UNEXPECTED SENSE OF WHIMSY AND AN ABSOLUTE MASTERY OF FORM AND MATERIALS.

Steve Sandstrom, *Designer & Founder, Sandstrom Partners*

VISHAL VORA IS A RENOWNED DESIGNER AND A COLLEAGUE WITH WHOM I HAVE ENJOYED SHARING THE STAGE. I TRULY ENJOY HIS WORK AND GREATLY APPRECIATE HIS ATTENTION TO DETAIL.

Diogo Gama Rocha, *Director General, Omdesign*

VISHAL VORA IS A DESIGN PRO WHO HAS A MIX OF A METICULOUS MIND AND A HEDONISTIC HEART THAT CONVERTS INTO BRILLIANT DESIGN LANGUAGE IN EACH OF HIS PROJECTS.

Ajit Jani, *Creative Director, BetterHalf Communications*

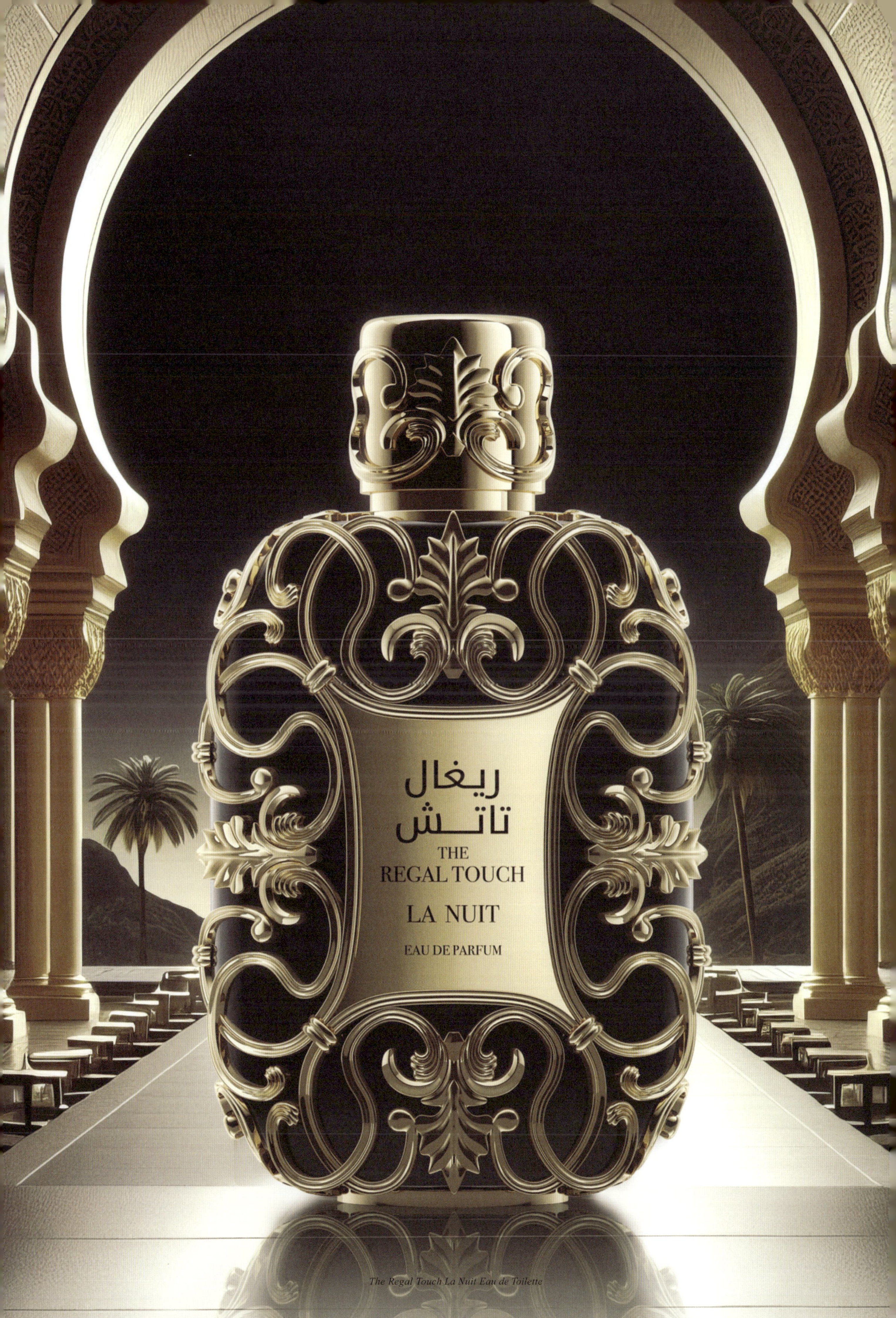

The Regal Touch La Nuit Eau de Toilette

In this *Graphis Journal* Q&A, award-winning Indian designer Vishal Vora, the designer and founder of Sol Benito, reflects on a journey marked by childhood inspirations and mythological artistry that transformed a simple fascination with matchbox graphics into a refined design philosophy. Embracing both aesthetic appeal and practical innovation, Vishal's method—a seamless blend of art, idea, and execution—evolved through formal studies at the I.S. College of Fine Arts and the invaluable lessons imparted by esteemed mentors and the steady guidance of time. He views design as a universal language that not only solves problems but also inspires meaningful change, making each project a testament to his lifelong passion for crafting visuals that resonate deeply and function effectively.

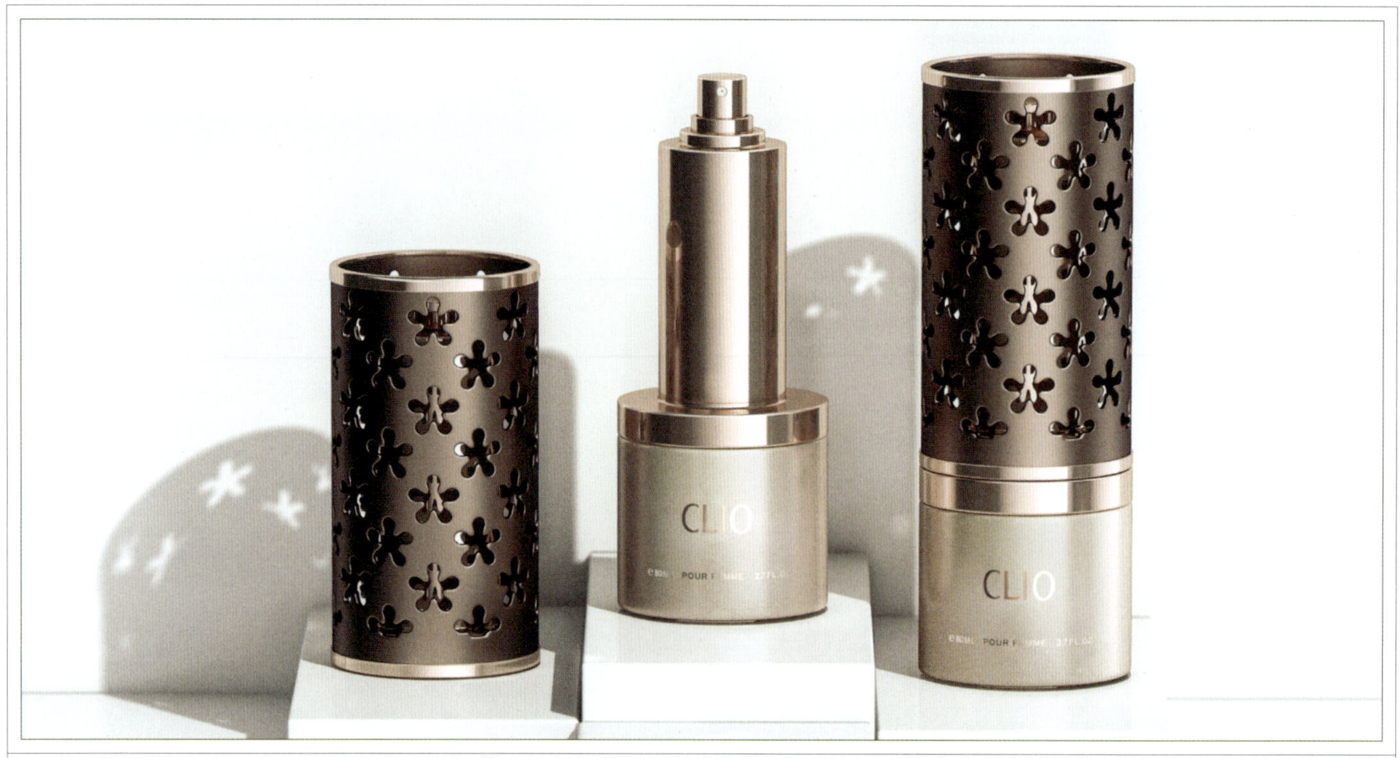

(Above) Clio Eau de Parfum / (Opposite page) Bonita Eau de Parfum / (Page 29) Casabella Twilight Eau de Parfum

Q&A: Vishal Vora, Designer & Founder, Sol Benito

What inspired or motivated you to have a career in design?
My inclination toward design comes naturally. Each of us is born with some natural flair; for me, art is one of them. Since childhood, I've been drawing mythological characters such as Indian gods and goddesses—each symbolizing something profound. We've all grown up listening to stories, and these stories shape us. We love stories instinctively, and art and design are powerful mediums to express our emotions, just like dance, music, literature, or performing arts.

I vividly remember collecting empty matchboxes as a kid, drawn to their intriguing graphics. At the time, I didn't realize that these designs were the work of skilled professionals. My collection grew over the years, and it wasn't until one of my school teachers suggested that I pursue an art career that I considered formal design education. That advice led me to prepare for and eventually study applied art at the I.S. College of Fine Arts.

What is your work philosophy?
Whether we call it a philosophy or a method, I always adhere to this approach when working on any project: We focus on three key elements—art, idea, and execution. I believe that design is a fusion of these three components.

When I refer to art, I mean the aesthetic and visual presence of the design. Any design is first perceived by our eyes, which is why understanding the science of visual appeal is crucial in any design process. Idea involves addressing the problem at hand, whether it's functional, emotional, environmental, or user-centric. It's essential to meet the objective and solve the problem according to the specific requirements. Execution is what ultimately determines the success of a design. There's a term in design called "lost in translation," where the art and idea are strong, but the final product doesn't align with the original vision, rendering the entire effort ineffective.

Therefore, these three elements—art, idea, and execution—must be harmonious to achieve the desired outcome. This is how we collectively create good design, in my view.

Who is or was your greatest mentor?
This might sound a bit philosophical, but I believe my greatest mentor is time. It has imparted invaluable lessons through experiences, challenges, and successes. Time has taught me the importance of patience, resilience, and growth, shaping my perspective and guiding my journey in design and life.

What is it about design that you are most passionate about?
The process of turning ideas into tangible, impactful visuals is endlessly fascinating to me.

Design is a universal language that transcends words and can tell a story, solve a problem, or inspire change. I love how design can distill a complex idea into something visually com-

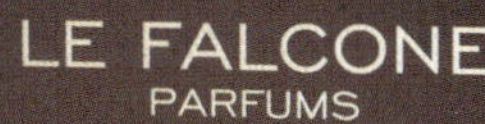

LE FALCONÉ
PARFUMS

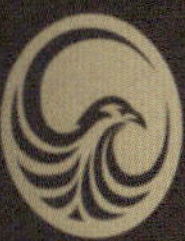

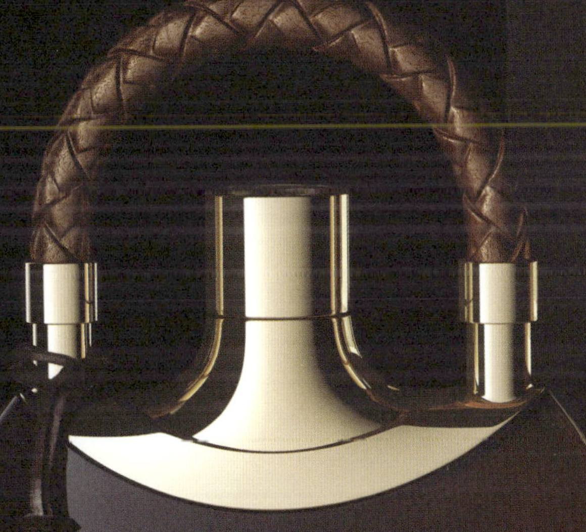

BONITA
POUR FEMME

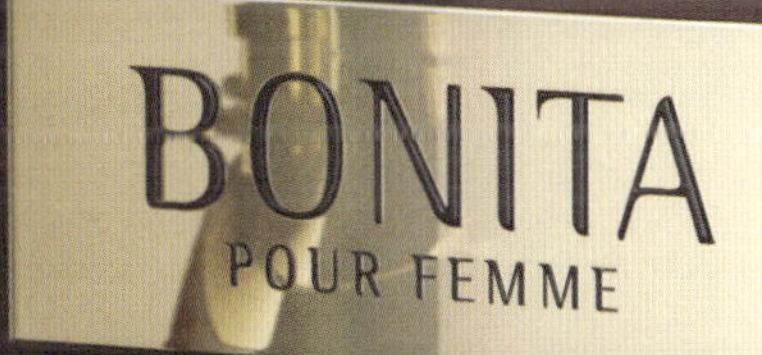

BONITA
POUR FEMME

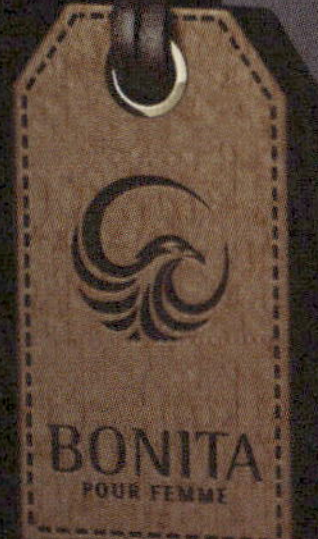

BONITA
POUR FEMME

100 ML VAPORISATEUR NATURAL SPRAY 3.4FL.OZ

pelling and accessible. The blend of creativity and functionality, where aesthetics meet purpose, is what truly excites me.

What is the most difficult challenge you've overcome to reach your current position?
Balancing creative vision with practical constraints while building a strong and impactful portfolio.

Who have been some of your greatest past influences?
Some of my greatest past influences have been my design mentors, Mr. Abhay Shah and Mrs. Jyoti Bedi Shah, whose guidance and wisdom have profoundly shaped my journey as a designer. I am deeply grateful for the impact they've had on my life. Additionally, the challenges I've faced and the lessons learned from both successes and failures have played a crucial role in shaping my perspective and approach to design. These influences have collectively guided me toward growth, innovation, and a deeper understanding of my craft.

Who among your contemporaries today do you most admire?
I admire everyone because each person puts in their best effort, and there is so much to learn from everyone.

What's the origin story for Sol Benito? How did it get its name?
Sol Benito was born from my desire to fully realize my potential as a designer and entrepreneur, free from the constraints of a traditional work environment. To embrace change and growth, I embarked on this journey. The name "Sol Benito" was suggested by a writer friend, and I was immediately drawn to its sound and resonance. "Sol" means "sun," symbolizing energy and life, while "Benito" means "benediction," reflecting a sense of blessing and positivity. Together, the name embodies the spirit of light, growth, and inspiration I aim to bring into my work.

What are some awards Sol Benito has won, and which one are you most proud of?
We are proud winners of prestigious global awards from the Graphis Design Awards, the Pentawards, the iF Design Awards, the A' Design Awards, the World Brand Design Society Awards, Topawards Asia, India's Best Design Awards, and the MUSE Design Awards.

Our work has also been published in various global design forums like Packaging of the World, World Brand Design Society, and *Lürzer's Archive*.

What would be your dream assignment?
My dream assignment would be to create a perfume bottle design that becomes immortal—something that transcends time and is continuously admired and cherished for its beauty, symbolism, and impact on the world of fragrance.

What are the top things you need from a client to do successful work for them?
To do successful design work for a client, we need the following key elements: clear objectives and goals, target audience insights, open communication, feedback, and budget and resources.

What do you consider your greatest professional achievement so far?
Seeing the tangible impact of my work on the client's business and the positive response from their consumers is incredibly rewarding and reinforces my passion for the power of design.

What about your work gives you the greatest satisfaction?
The greatest satisfaction is seeing a project go from concept to completion and then witnessing it in the marketplace. There's a unique fulfillment in knowing your design is making a tangible impact, whether it's enhancing a brand's presence, engaging customers, or solving a problem. The journey from idea to execution, and then seeing the final product being used and appreciated by others, is what makes all the effort worthwhile.

What part of your work do you find the most demanding?
The most demanding part of design work is often balancing creativity with practicality. It involves finding the right equilibrium between pushing creative boundaries and meeting the client's needs, budget, and timeline. Translating a bold, innovative idea into a design that looks great and functions effectively in the real world can be challenging. Additionally, ensuring that the design resonates with the target audience while staying true to the brand's identity requires careful thought and attention to detail—the process of refining and iterating on a design.

What professional goals do you still have for yourself?
I still have several professional goals in the design field I want to achieve. I aspire to work on projects that push the boundaries of creativity and innovation, particularly in sustainable design.

What advice would you give to students starting out today?
Live what you love.

What do you value most in life?
Continuously learning, evolving, and embracing new experiences are essential to me. I also deeply value meaningful connections with others and the time and opportunities that allow me to pursue my passions and contribute positively to the world.

What would you change if you had to do it all over again?
I believe there's always room for growth and improvement. If you're completely satisfied with what you did yesterday, it means you haven't evolved. I embrace the idea that nothing is ever perfect and everything can be refined or changed for the better. Every experience offers a chance to learn and improve, so I wouldn't want just to repeat the past—I'd want to build on it, adapt, and make it even better.

Where do you find inspiration?
I find inspiration in many places—nature, art, everyday life, and even the challenges I encounter. The natural world, with its intricate patterns and colors, often sparks creative ideas. Art, whether classical or contemporary, fuels my imagination and pushes me to think beyond conventional boundaries. I also draw inspiration from observing people and their interactions, as well as from travel, which exposes me to diverse cultures and perspectives. Ultimately, inspiration comes from staying curious and open to the world around me, constantly seeking out new experiences and ideas.

How do you define success?
I define success as achieving meaningful growth and making a positive impact while staying true to my values and passions.

In what ways do you see your field changing over the years?
I see the design field increasingly embracing technology, sustainability, and user-centered approaches. There will be a stronger focus on integrating AI, virtual reality, and data-driven insights into design processes.

Sol Benito

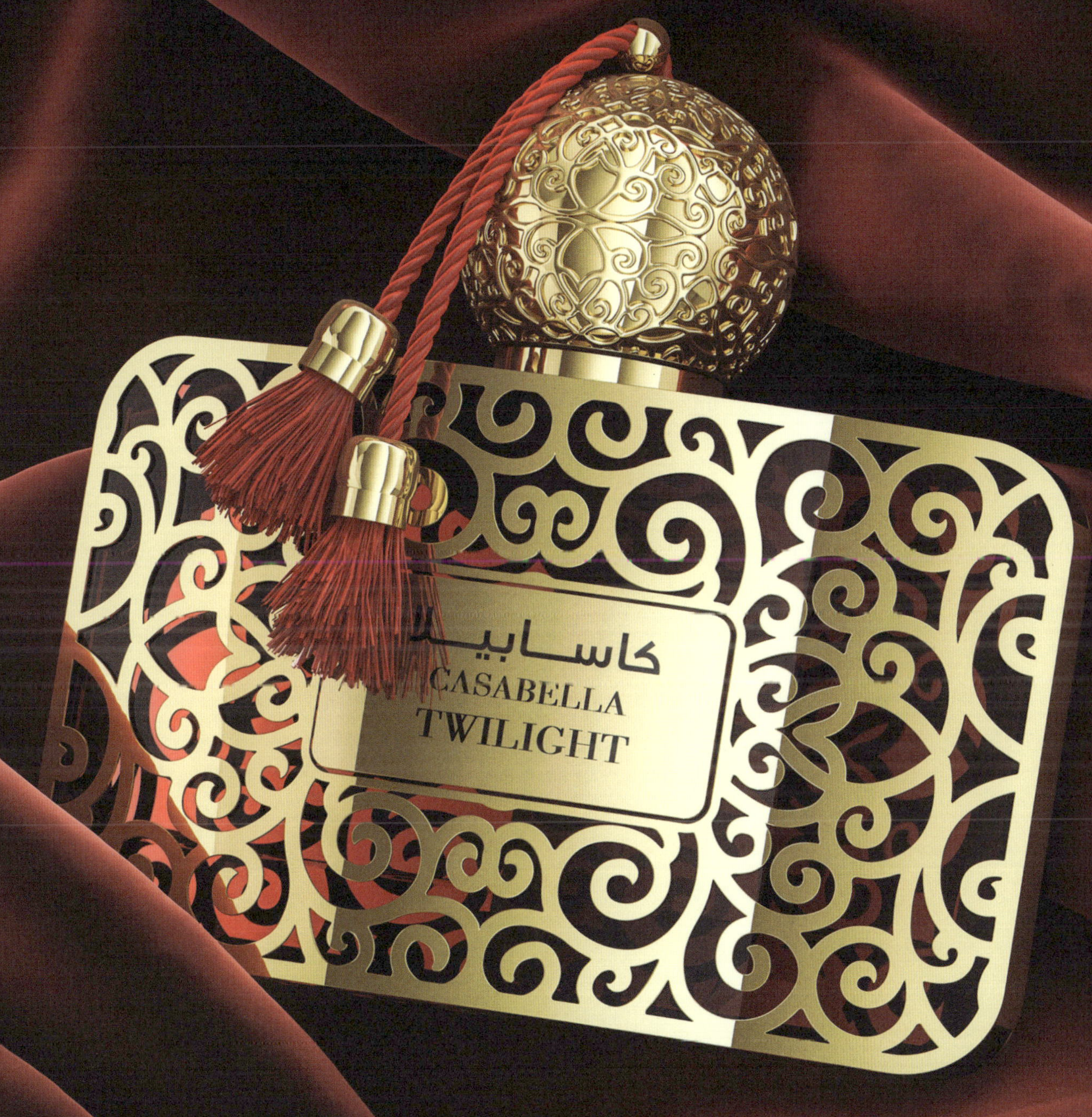

كاسابيلا
CASABELLA
TWILIGHT

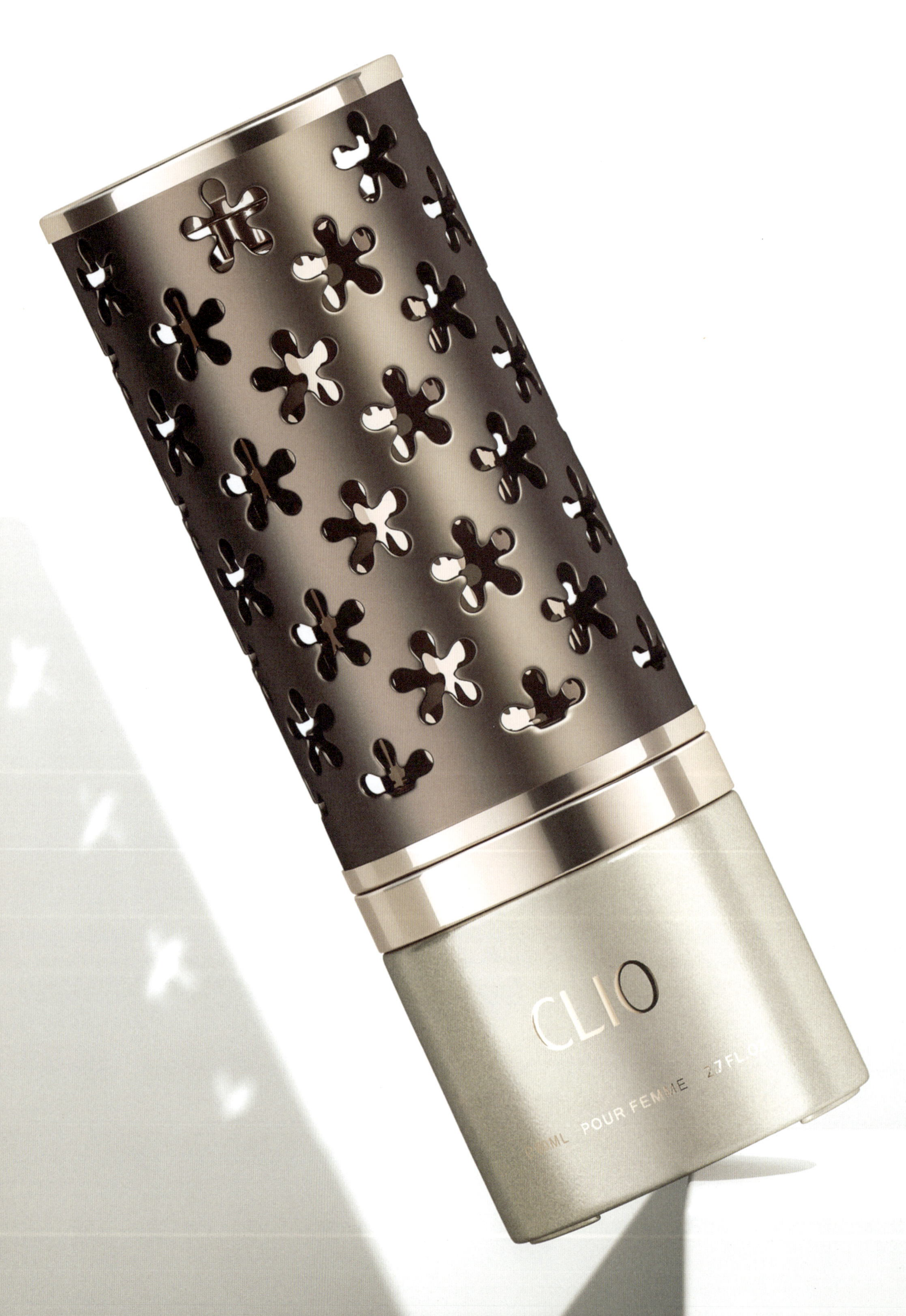

CLIO
ML POUR FEMME 2.7 FL O

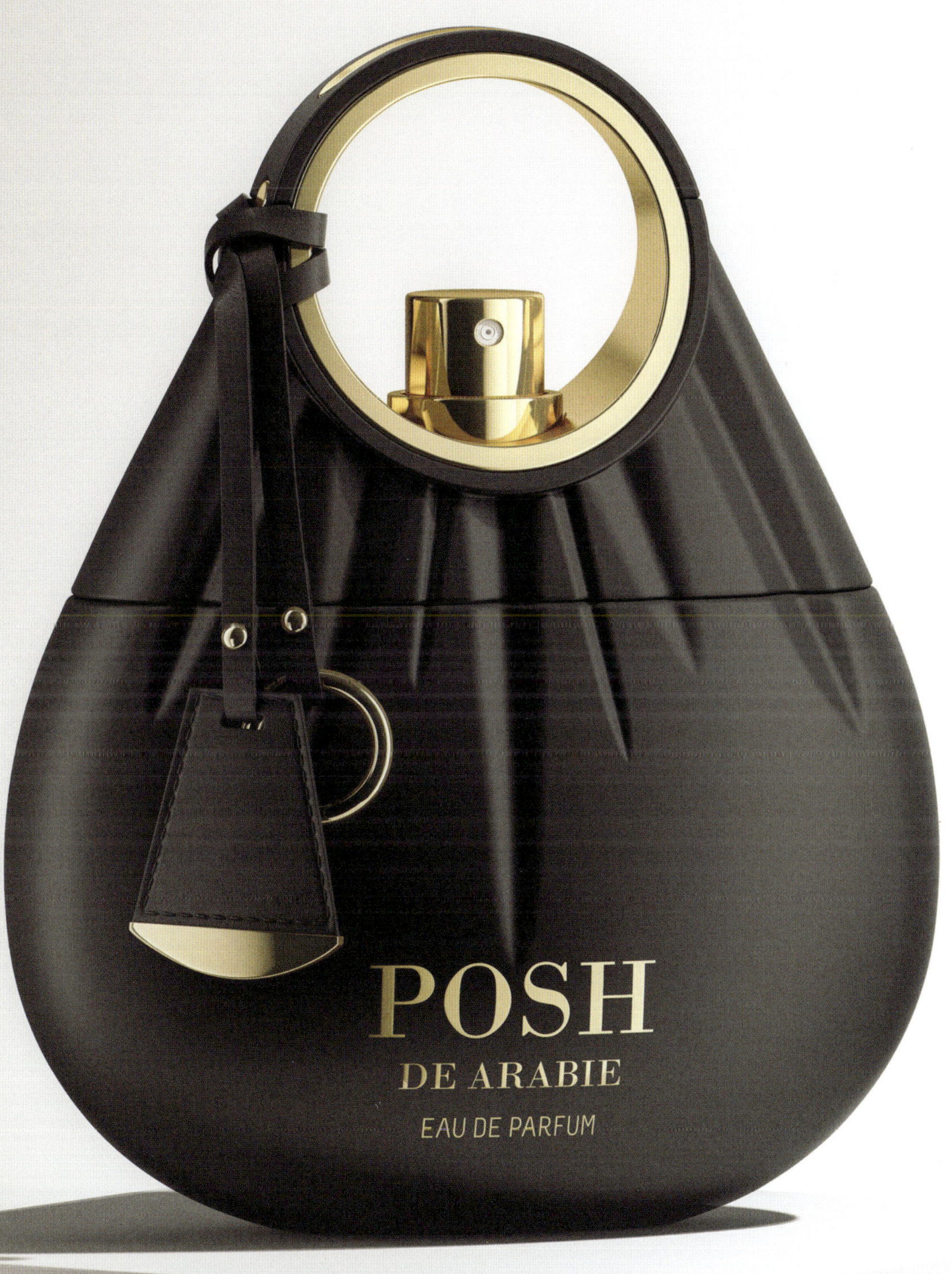

(Opposite page) Clio Eau de Parfum / (Above) Posh Eau de Parfum

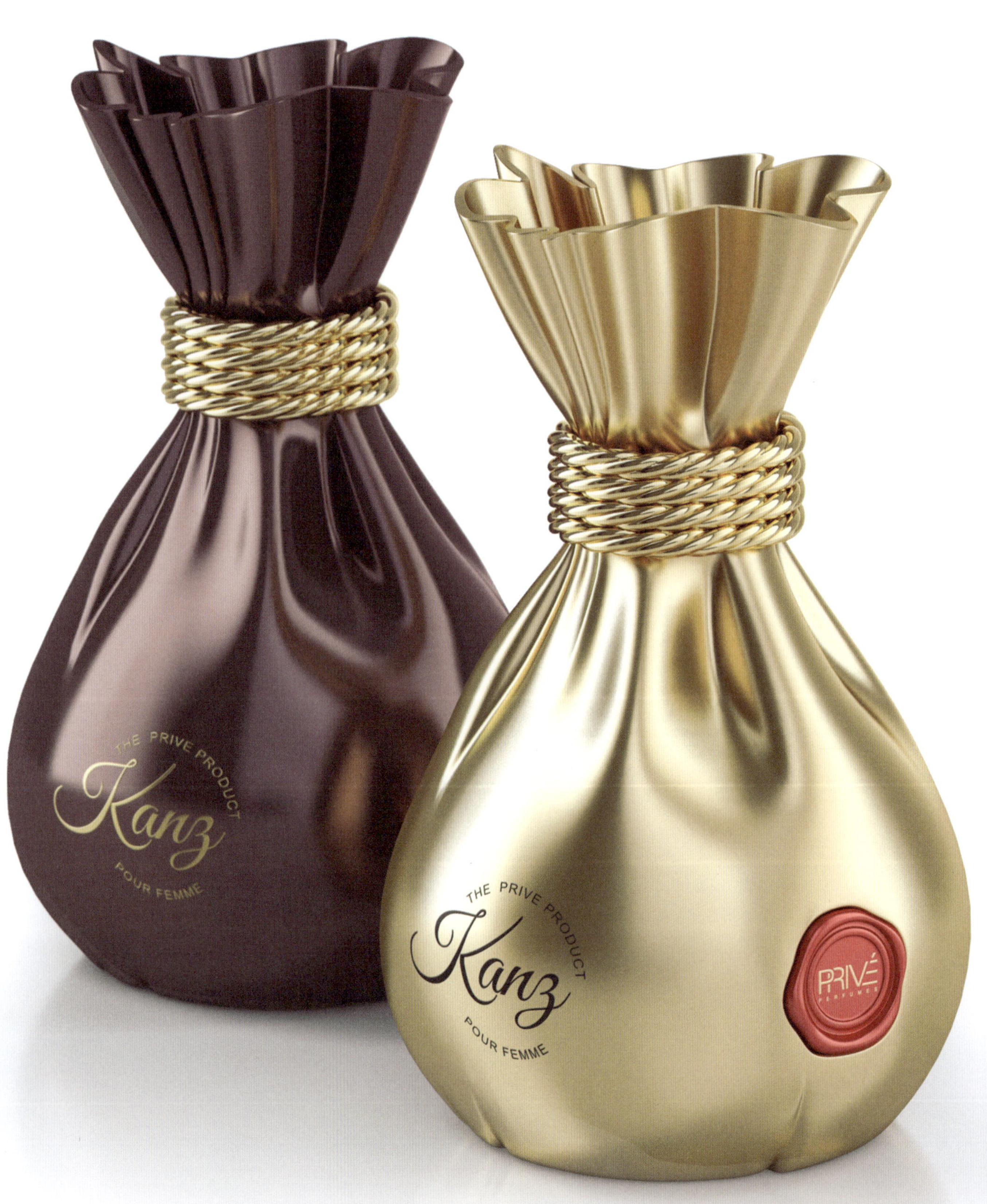

THE PRIVE PRODUCT
Kanz
POUR FEMME
THE PRIVE PRODUCT
Kanz
POUR FEMME
PRIVÉ
PERFUMES

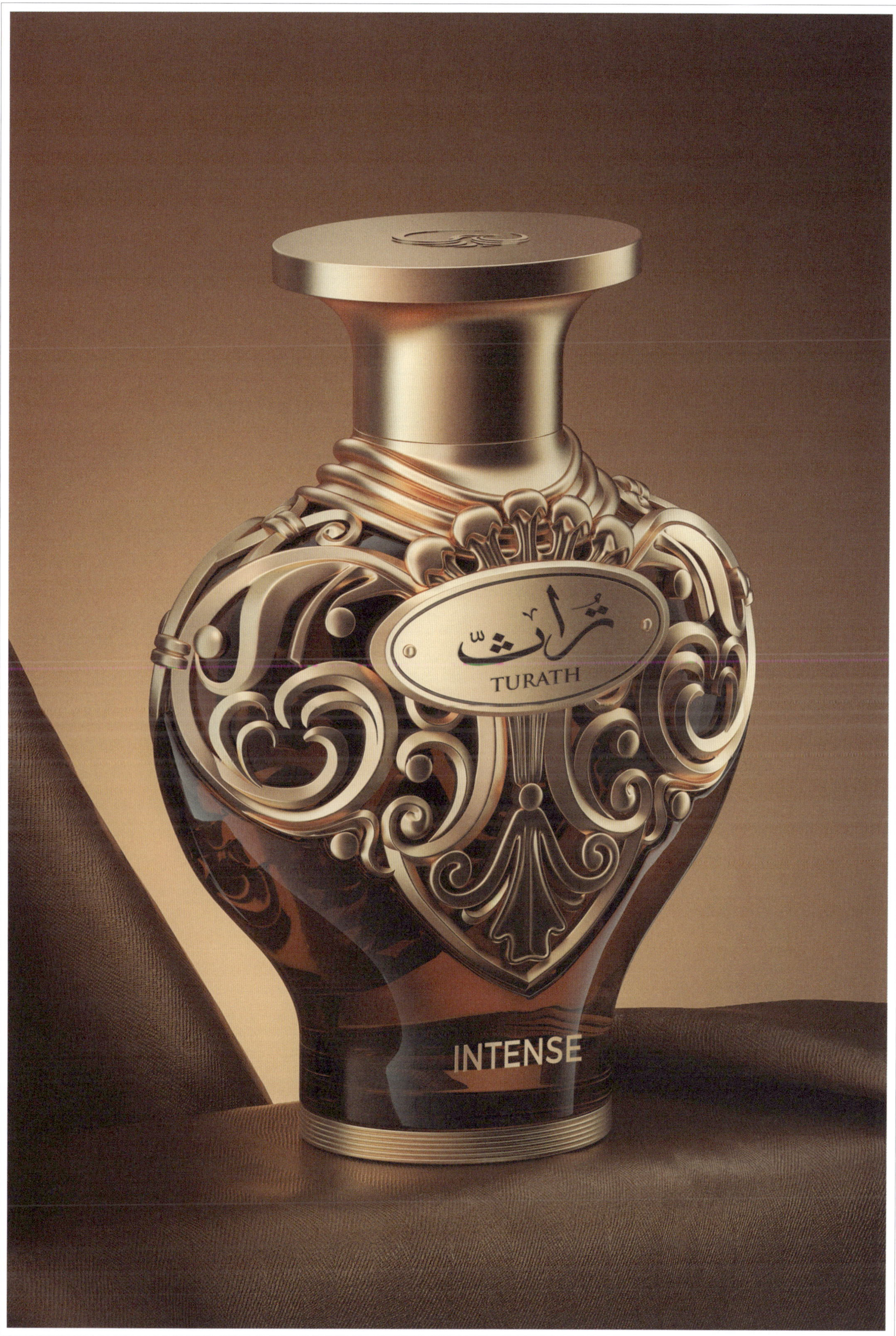

(Opposite page) Kanz Eau de Parfum / (Above) Turath Eau de Parfum

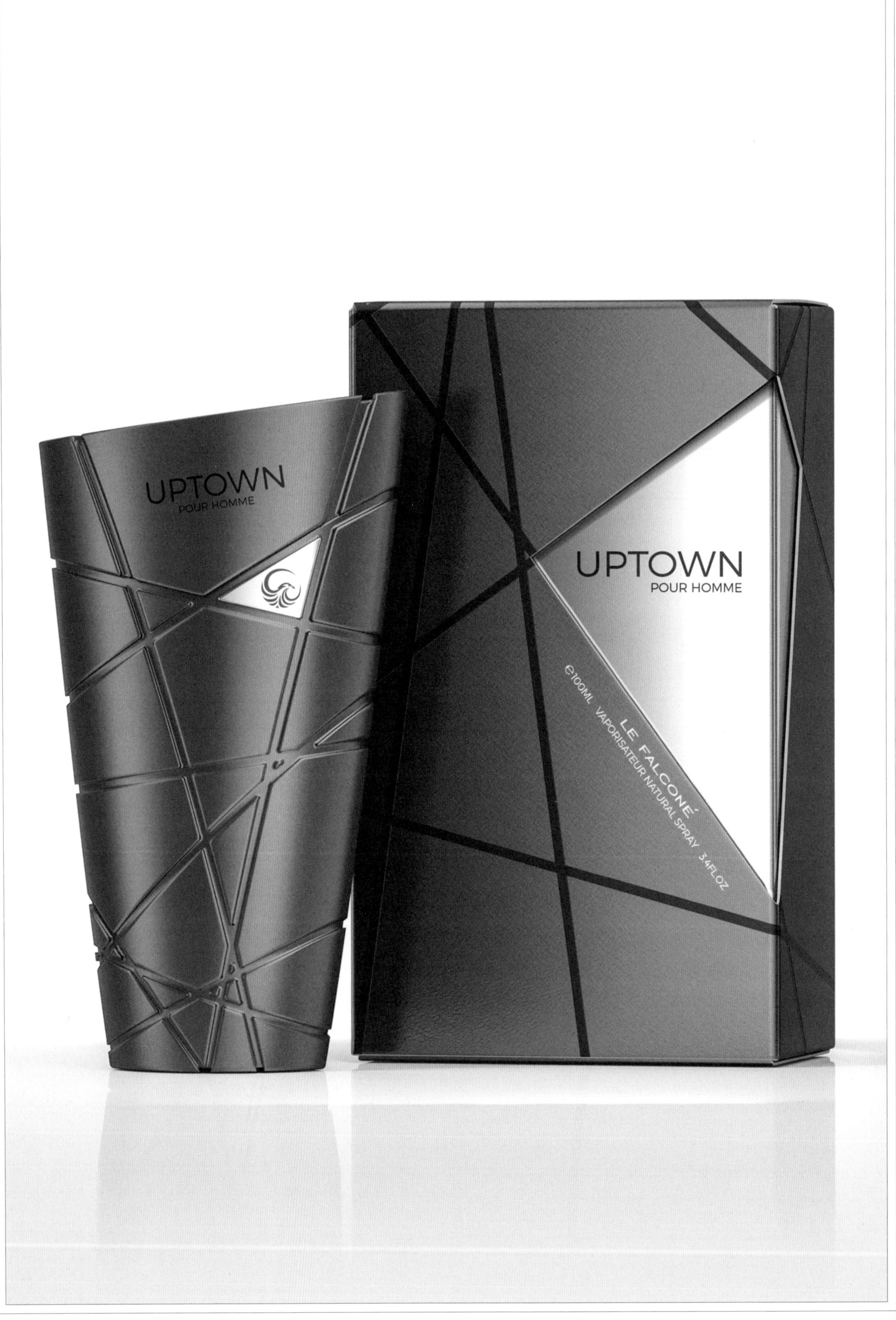

(Above) Uptown Eau de Parfum / (Opposite page) Al Majd Eau de Toilette

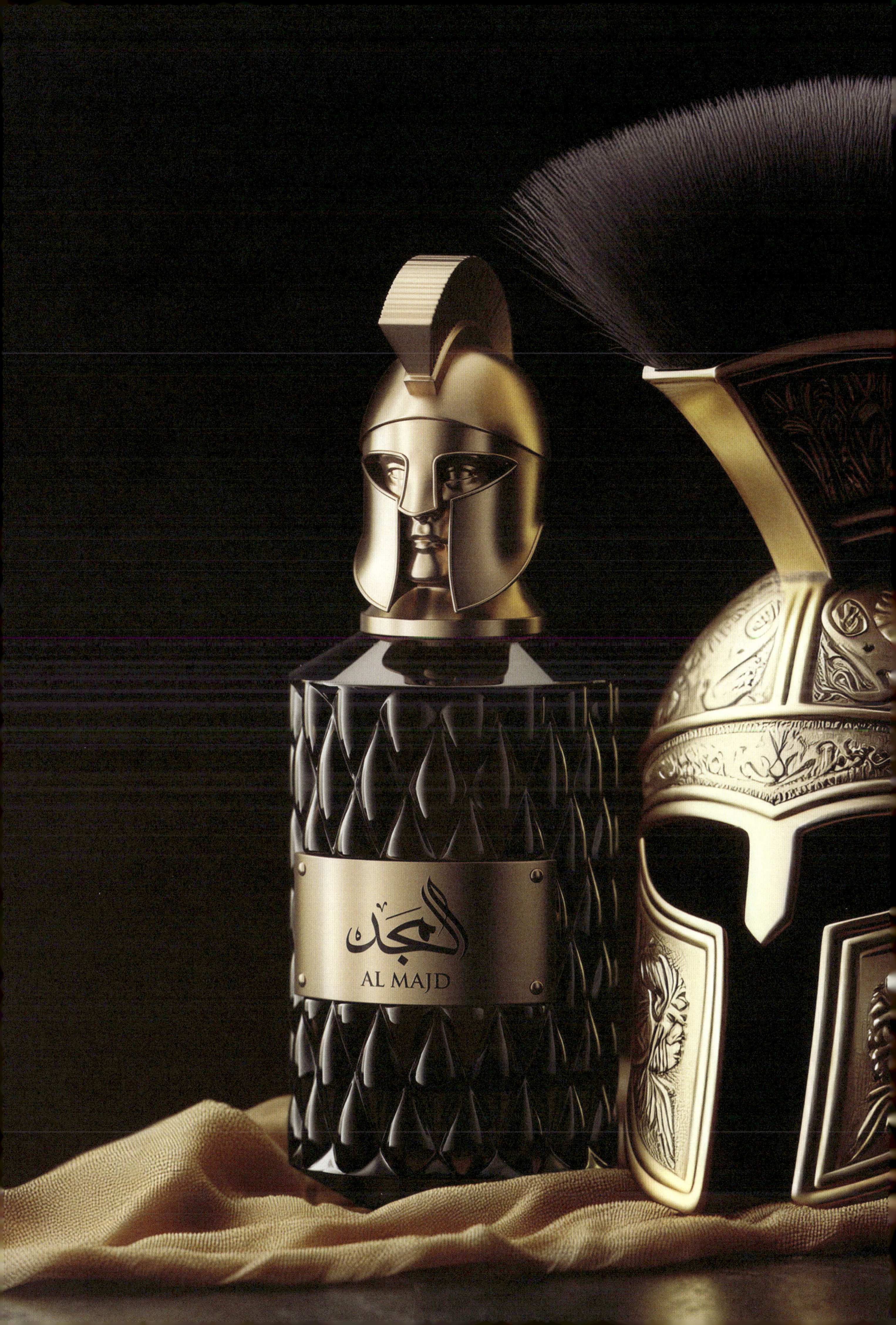

الـمجد
AL MAJD

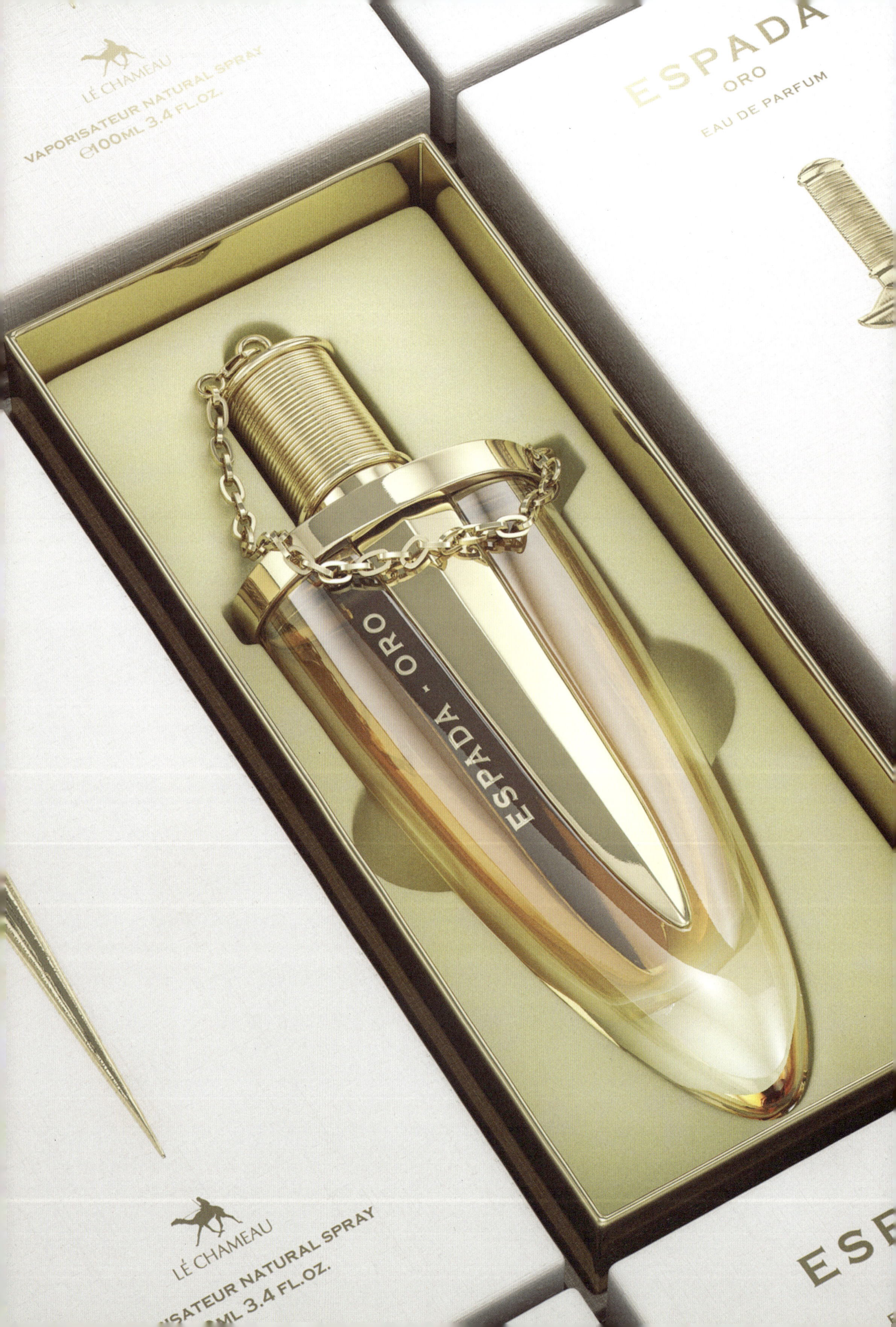

LÉ CHAMEAU
VAPORISATEUR NATURAL SPRAY
℮100ML 3.4 FL.OZ.
ESPADA
ORO
EAU DE PARFUM
ESPADA · ORO
LÉ CHAMEAU
LÉ CHAMEAU
VAPORISATEUR NATURAL SPRAY
ML 3.4 FL.OZ.
ESPA

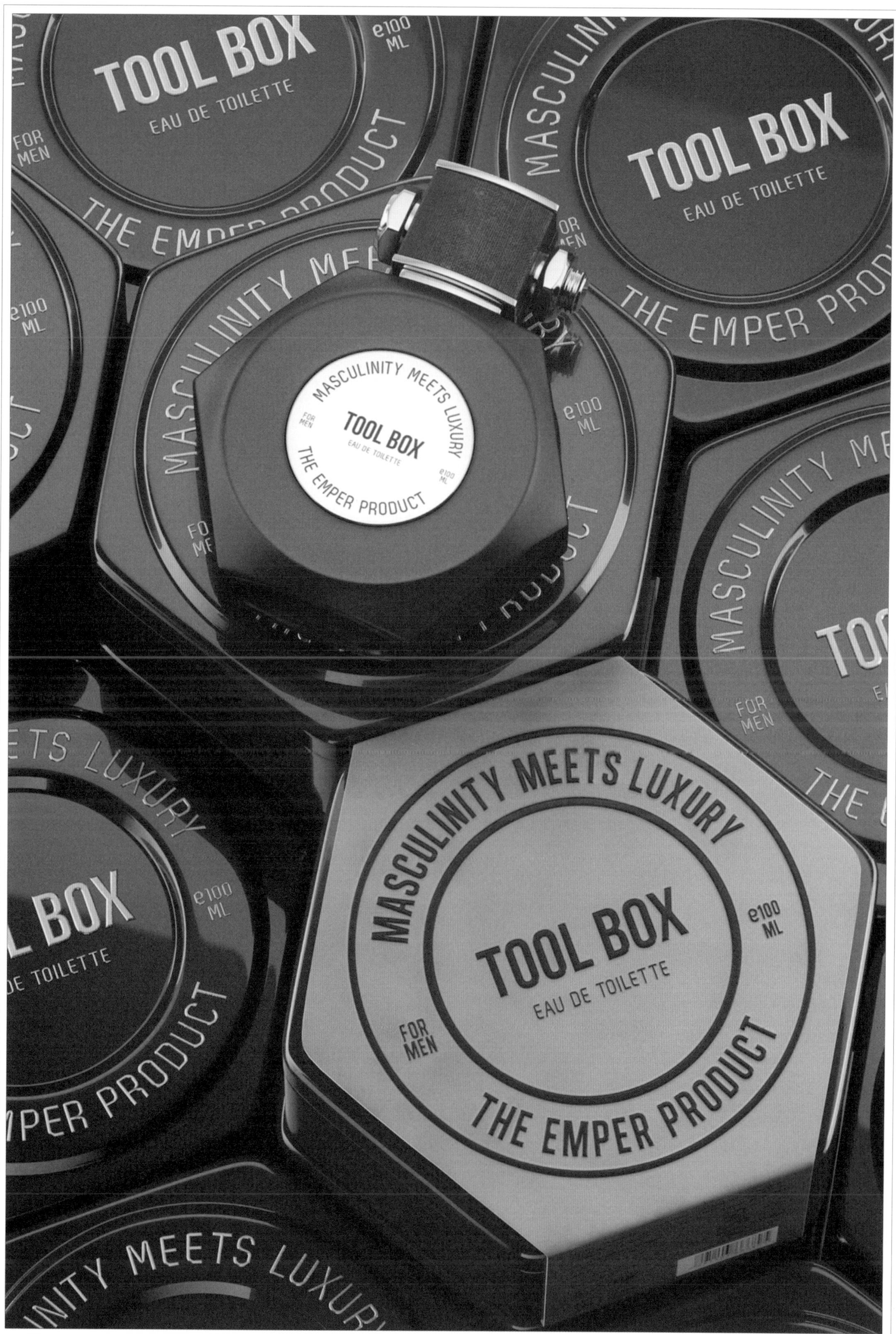

(Opposite page) Espada Eau de Parfum / (Above) Tool Box Eau de Toilette

Brad Hochberg, The Refinery:
Pursuing the Same Elevated Passion

BRAD WAS MY FIRST BOSS OUT OF COLLEGE.
THE TEAM AT THE REFINERY WAS ENERGETIC,
AND EVERYONE WAS WARM AND WILLING TO HELP.
BRAD LED THAT CULTURE, AND I AM THANKFUL
FOR THAT INTRODUCTION TO THE WORKFORCE.

Shawna Navaro, *Co-founder, Innerspace*

BRAD HOCHBERG IS AN ICONIC VISIONARY
LEADER—PAIRING CREATIVE EXCELLENCE WITH
GENEROSITY, INTEGRITY, AND A RARE ABILITY
TO CHAMPION INDIVIDUAL EXPRESSION.

Nate Lake, *Freelance Creative Director, NateLake.com*

FEW CREATIVES POSSESS THE RARE BLEND
OF ARTISTRY, INTELLECT, AND COLLABORATION
THAT BRAD BRINGS TO EVERY PROJECT.

Whitney Abeel, *SVP of Originals & Digital Marketing, Starz*

IT WAS A PRIVILEGE AND A GREAT EXPERIENCE
WORKING WITH BRAD AT THE REFINERY AS A
FREELANCE ART DIRECTOR. HE CHALLENGED US
AS DESIGNERS TO BE QUICK WITH OUR CONCEPTS
AND ALWAYS PUSHED FOR EXCELLENCE.

Lilian Wong, *Associate Creative Director, LEROY & ROSE*

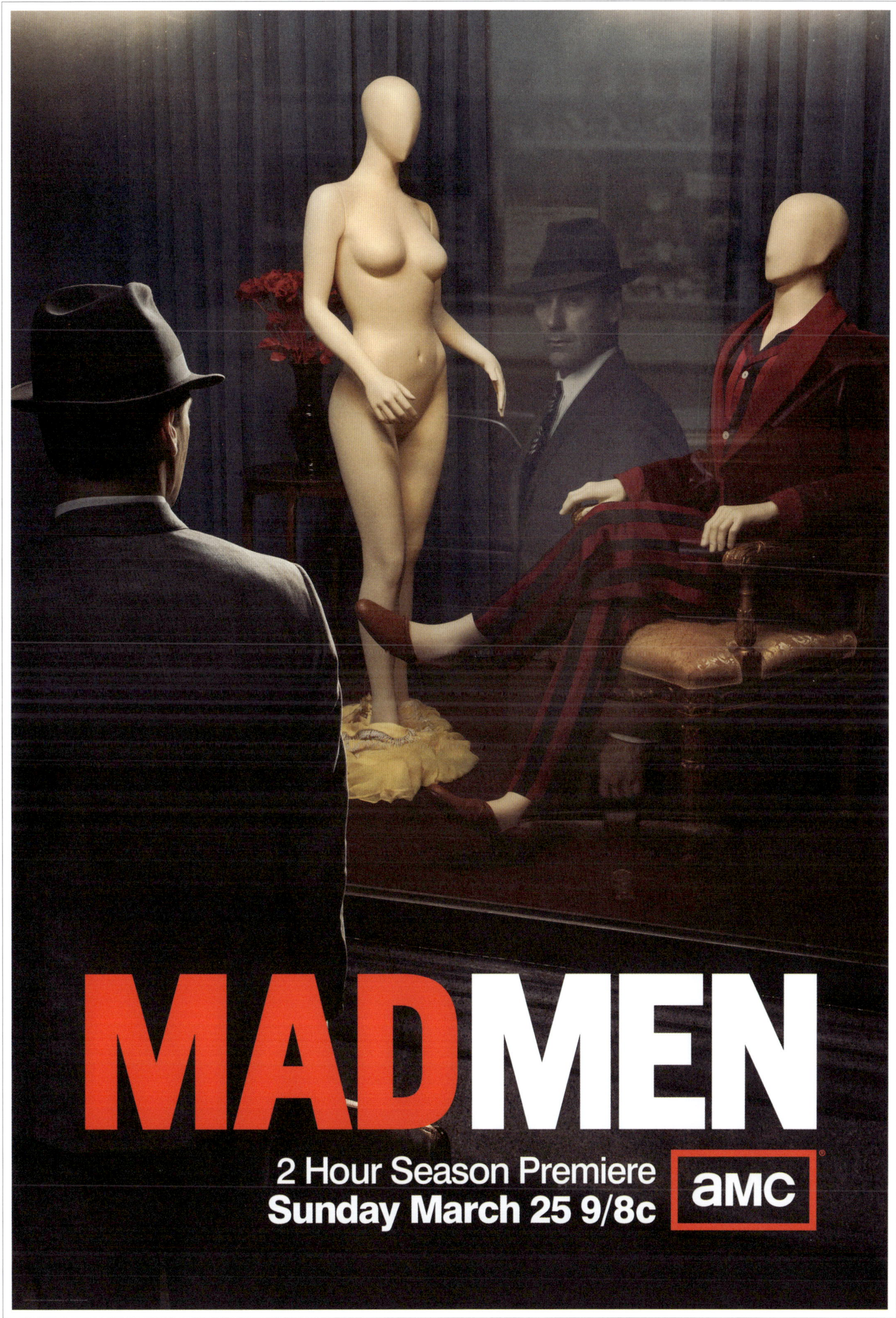

Mad Men Window. Clients: Linda Schupack, Alison Hoffman, AMC Network. Photographer: Frank Ockenfels III.
Creative Director: Brad Hochberg. Account Executive: Janelle Cipriano. Art Director: Michael Valle.

Introduction by **Jim Pascoe** *Partner & Creative Director, RAVE Collective*

Inspiration comes from many places—some distant, some remarkably close. Having worked alongside Brad Hochberg for nearly two decades, I've witnessed firsthand his passion, his drive, his kindness, his meticulous attention to detail, and his boundless creativity. Brad's distinctive vision shines clearly, like an illuminated signature, through every facet of his work: the posters he designs, the team he leads, the company he built, the family he raised, and the intimate photographs he captures. His artistry has been a fount of inspiration for me—one that never runs dry. I'm fortunate to know him, and for those encountering Brad's work now, consider yourselves equally lucky.

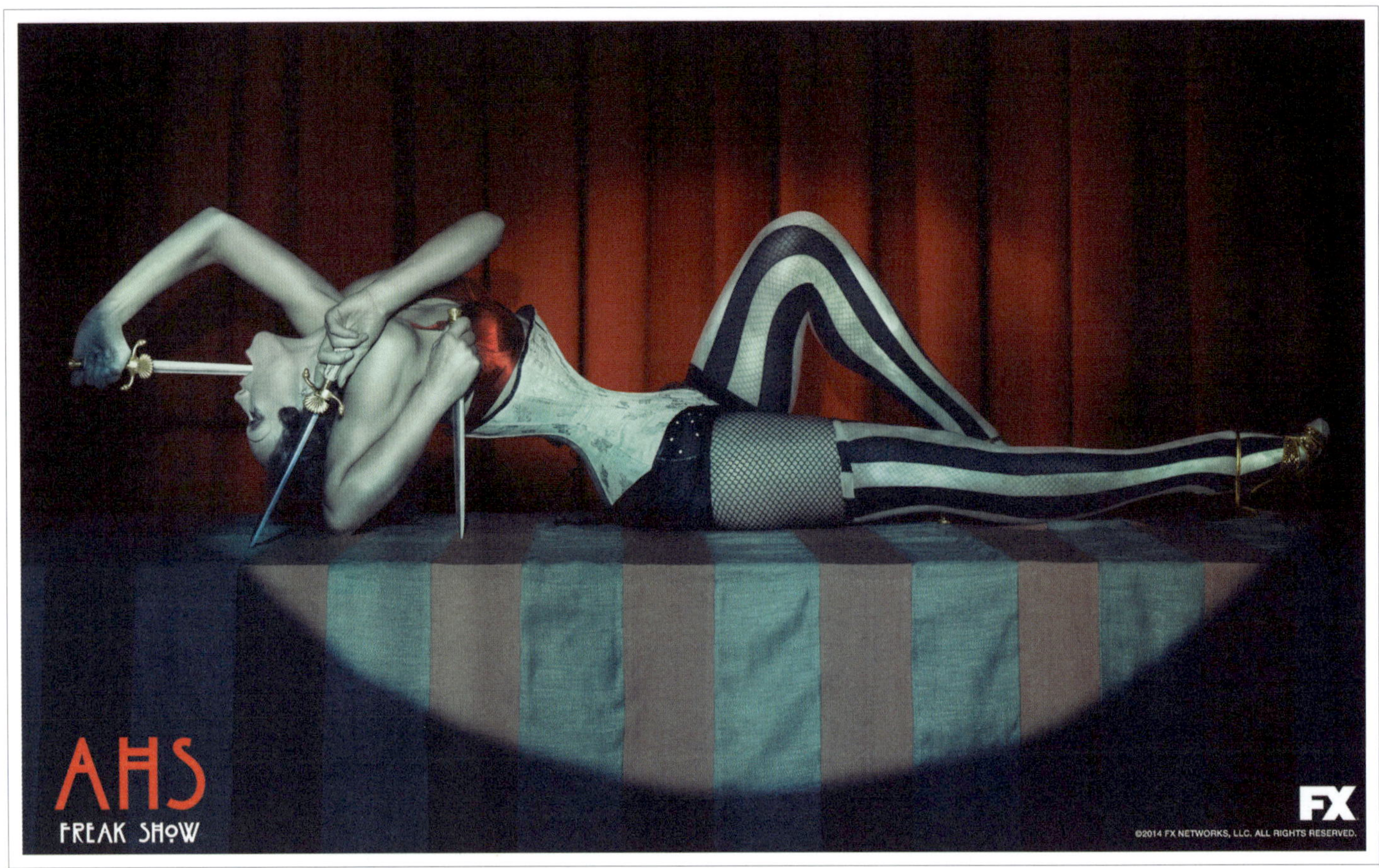

AHS Knives. Clients: Stephanie Gibbons, Todd Heughens, FX Network. Photographer: Matthias Clamer.
Creative Director: Brad Hochberg. Account Executive: Jenny Jamin. Art Director: Sean Dunkerley.

I'VE ALWAYS HAD THIS ADMIRATION AND
RESPECT FOR THE VISUAL, TYPE, AND MESSAGE.
TO UNITE THOSE ELEMENTS IN A PERFECT
SYMPHONY IS A TRIUMPH, AND WHEN YOU SEE
IT DONE WELL, IT LEAVES YOU IN AWE.

Brad Hochberg, *Founding Partner & Creative Director, The Refinery*

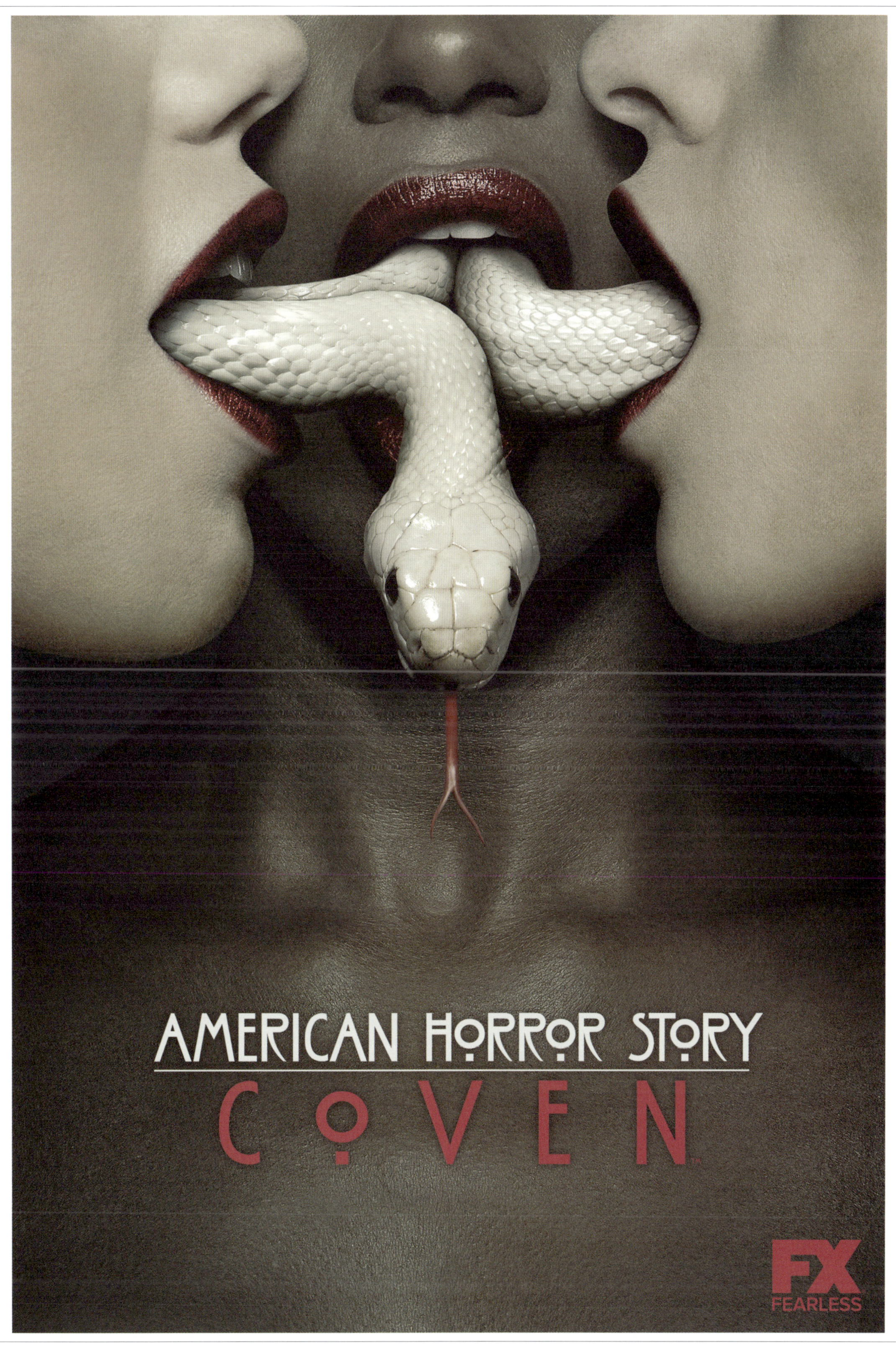

AHS Snakes. Clients: Stephanie Gibbons, Todd Heughens, FX Network. Photographer: Frank Ockenfels III.
Creative Director: Brad Hochberg. Account Executive: Jenny Jamin. Art Directors: Michael Valle, Gabe Flores.

What inspired or motivated you to have a career in design?
Design, art, and photography really spoke to me. Everything else felt confusing and loud, but design was a place of peace and understanding.

Who is or was your greatest mentor?
For me, it has always been a partnership between everyone who collaborates on a project. Outside our agency, that would include clients, photographers, stylists, producers—all the partners needed to accomplish great work. Inside our agency, I learn from everyone all the time and count on them to help me grow as a creative and agency leader.

What is it about design that you are most passionate about?
I've always had this admiration and respect for the visual, type, and message. To unite those elements in a perfect symphony is a triumph, and when you see it done well, it leaves you in awe. Our industry, as a collective, often leaves me in wonderment as I look at the work being produced.

The Refinery focuses on providing print, AV, and digital work for the entertainment industry. What has that been like for you? What do you like most about working in entertainment?
It's a thrill to be part of a series or film's journey to success—to see audiences discover it and to have played a role in that is always a wonderful feeling. It's also been a joy to see the work being shared around the globe, either directly through a media buy or organically by audiences that fall in love with it.

Who have been some of your favorite people or clients you have worked with?
We have been incredibly fortunate to collaborate with the very best clients, filmmakers, and partners over the years. So many of them pursue the same elevated passion for creativity that we do. There are truly too many to name, but I'm really thankful for their support and trust over the years. It's been a remarkable experience.

Who are some of your greatest past influences?
It's a great cross-section of artists, designers, typographers, and photographers from day one of art school. Having a solid foundation of the past helps you grow through time as a visual storyteller.

In no particular order, folks like Paul Rand, Saul Bass, Herb Lubalin, Alexey Brodovitch, Hermann Zapf, Jackson Pollock, Mark Rothko, Robert Motherwell, Alberto Giacometti, Richard Avedon, Irving Penn, Walker Evans, Garry Winogrand, and William Eggleston, to name a few.

What is your greatest professional achievement?
Being a part of so many great organizations over the years and folding all those experiences into The Refinery has been the top of the mountain. Taking the risk to try this with my business partner, Adam Waldman, in 2016 has been a transformative experience and one I will always cherish and count as my greatest professional achievement.

What advice would you give to students starting out today?
Challenge yourself to learn the history of the visual arts world and build that base. Strive to diversify your skill set: learn to paint, love typography, make pictures, and get your hands dirty. You never know when you will tap into this skill set. Beyond that, don't be afraid to connect with people whose work inspires you or draws you to it; you'd be surprised how receptive artists are to helping another artist grow.

What interests do you have outside of work?
I have been working on a body of personal photographic work. I find it gives me the outlet to explore concepts and solutions outside the daily collaborative environment. This exploration has fed back into my Refinery work in a positive way. I'd encourage all artists to pursue work that isn't their primary focus as a way of self-expression.

The Refinery www.therefinerycreative.com

STRIVE TO DIVERSIFY YOUR SKILLSET: LEARN TO PAINT, LOVE TYPOGRAPHY, MAKE PICTURES, AND GET YOUR HANDS DIRTY. YOU NEVER KNOW WHEN YOU WILL TAP INTO THIS SKILL SET.

Brad Hochberg, *Founding Partner & Creative Director, The Refinery*

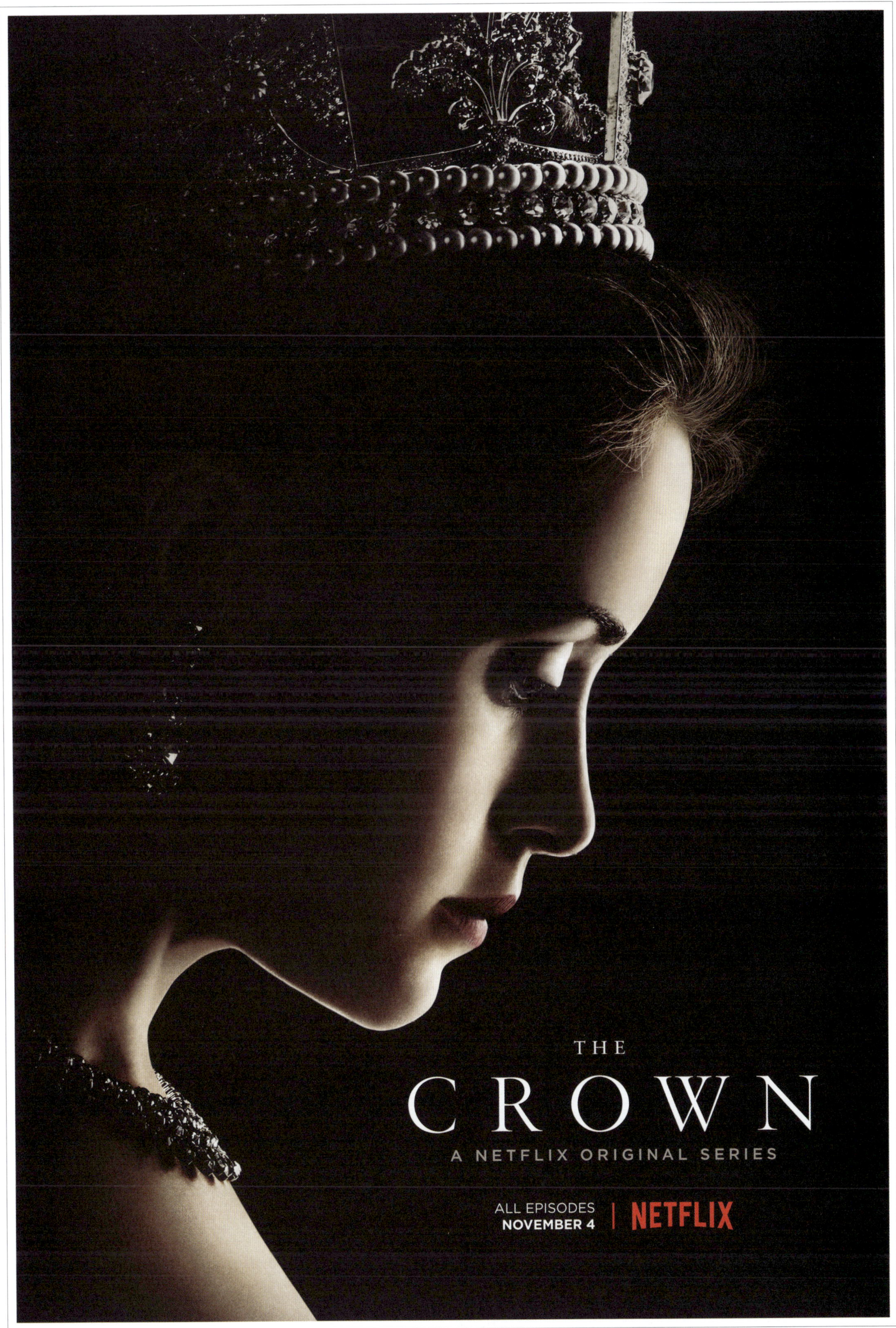

The Crown. Clients: Ashleigh Lew, Netflix. Photographer: Jason Bell. Creative Director: Brad Hochberg. Account Executive: Michelle Mellinger. Art Director: Nike Chapman.

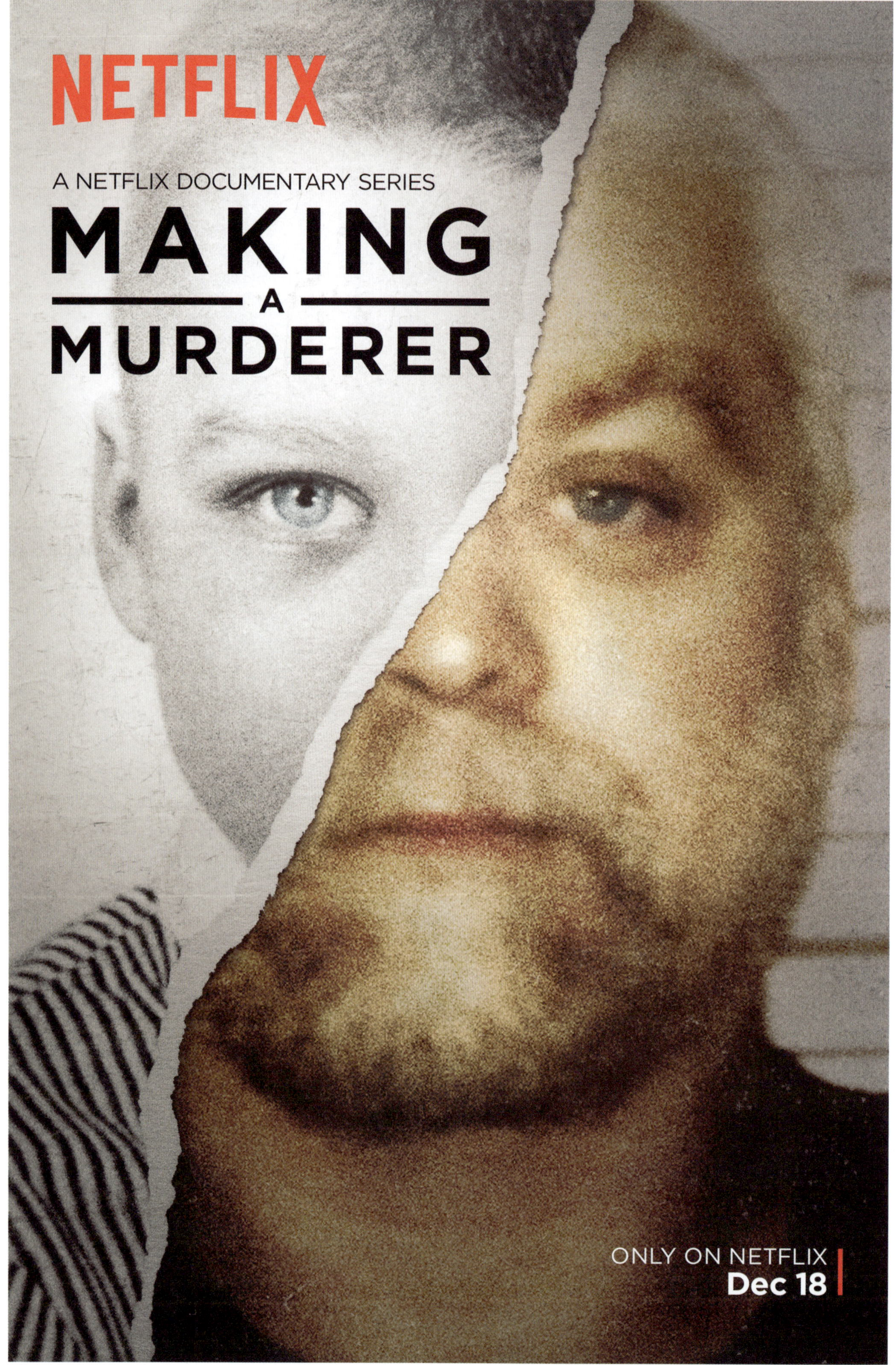

Making a Murderer. Clients: Peter Stone, Netflix. Creative Director: Brad Hochberg. Account Executive: Michelle Mellinger. Art Director: Emma Claffy.

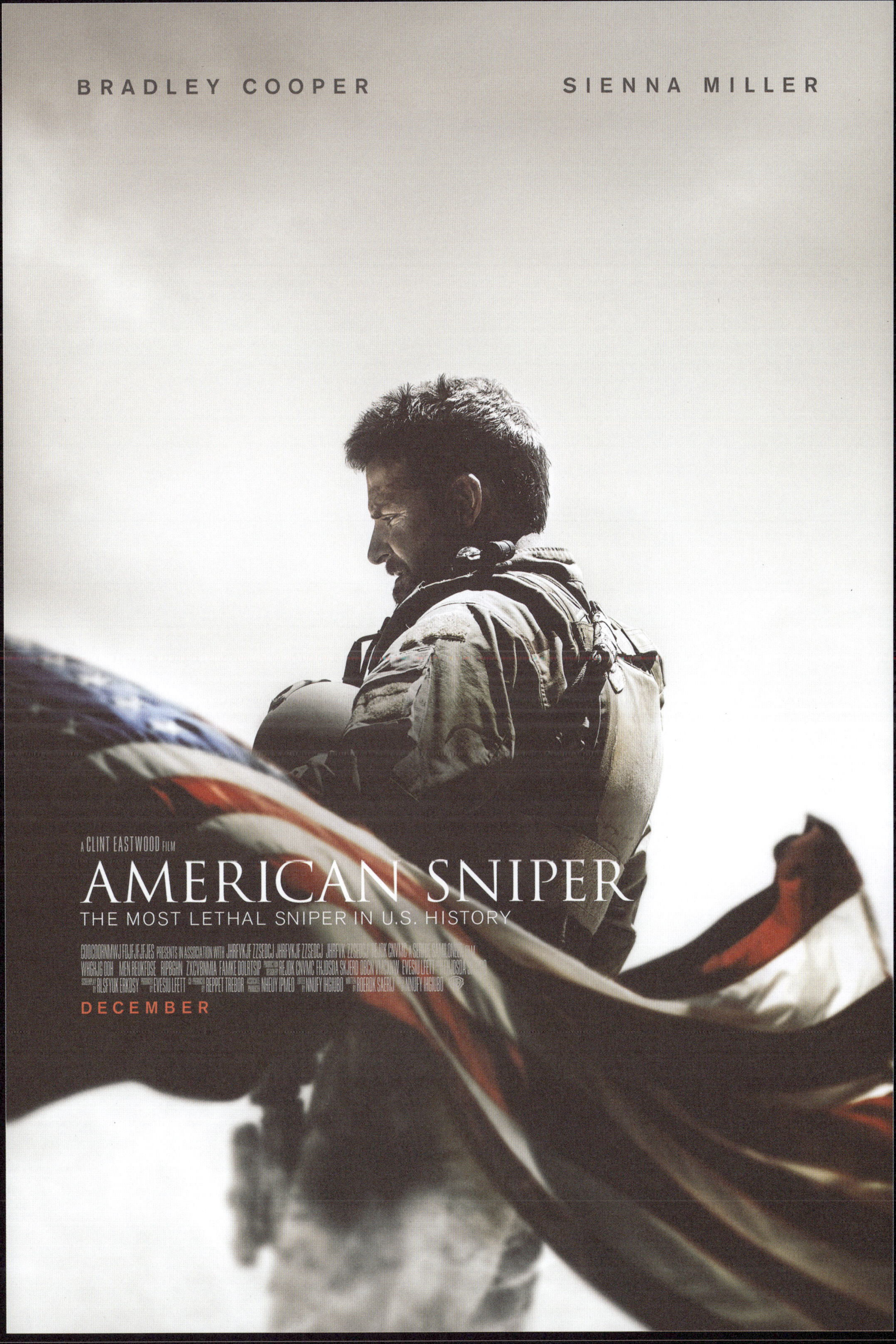

BRADLEY COOPER
SIENNA MILLER
A CLINT EASTWOOD FILM
AMERICAN SNIPER
THE MOST LETHAL SNIPER IN U.S. HISTORY
DECEMBER

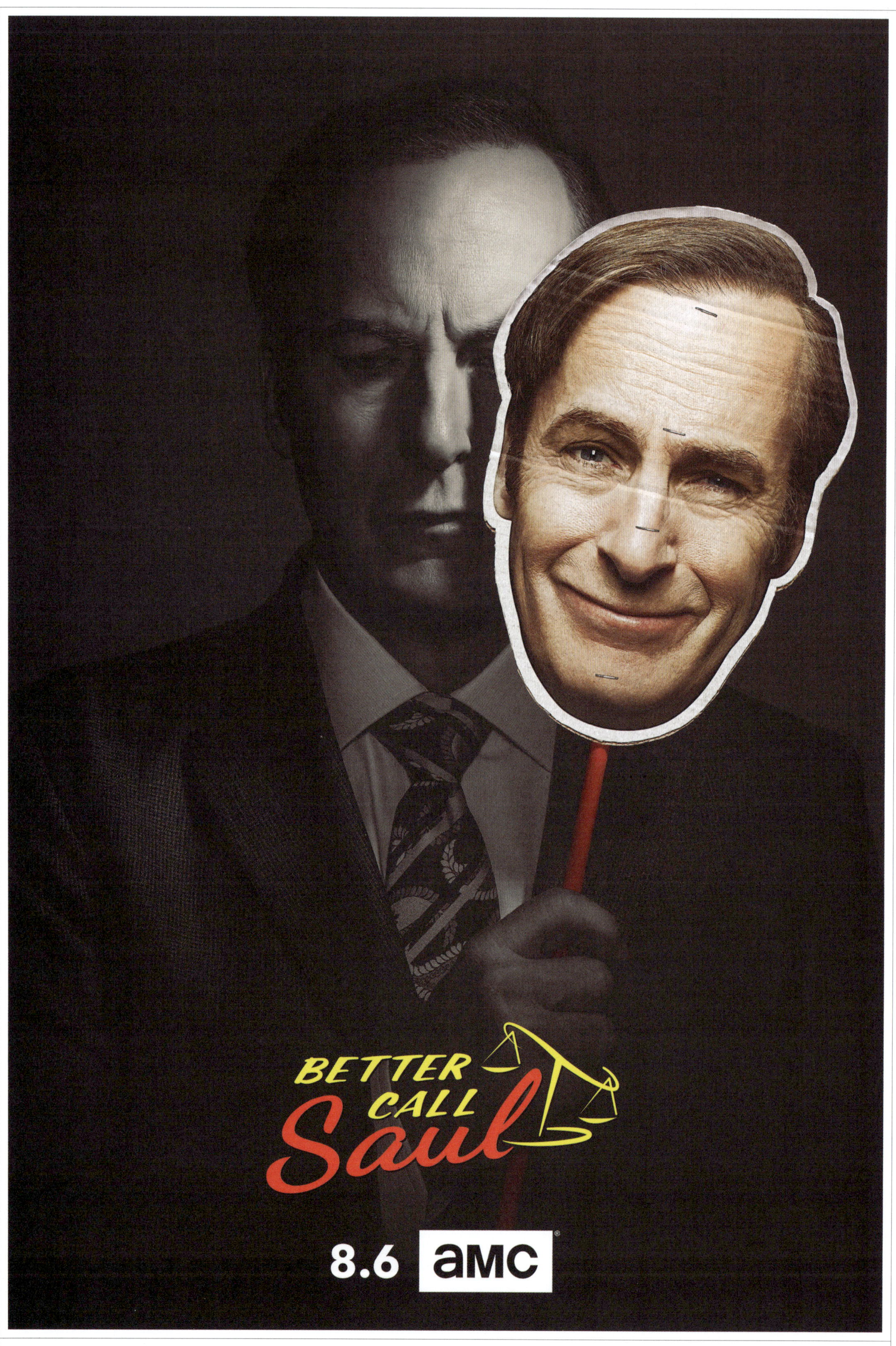

Better Call Saul Mask. Clients: JC Cancedda, AMC. Photographer: Matthias Clamer. Creative Director: Brad Hochberg. Account Executive: Lindsay Artof. Art Director: Emma Claffy.

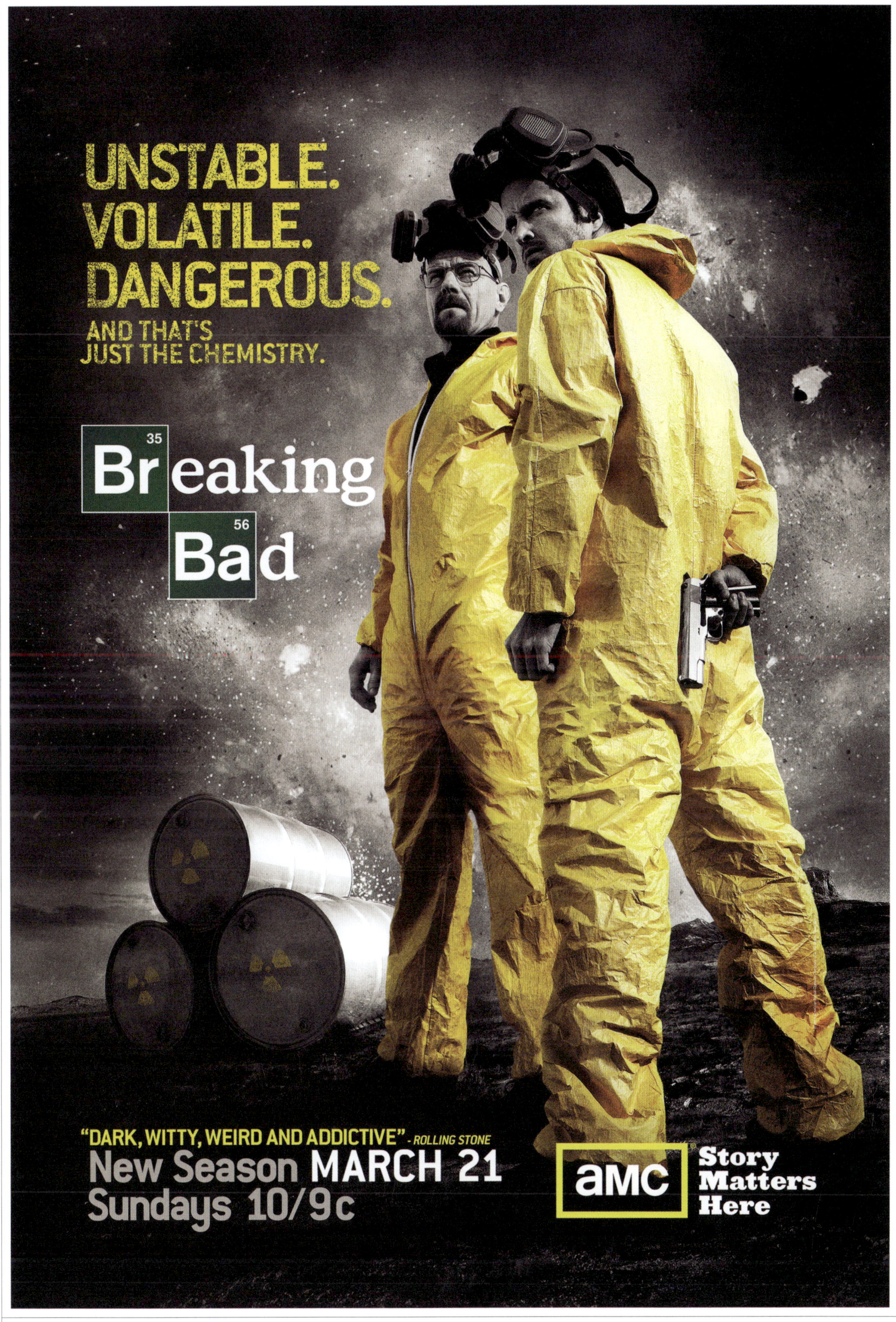

Breaking Bad Yellow. Clients: Linda Schupack, Alison Hoffman, AMC Network. Photographer: Ben Leuner.
Creative Director: Brad Hochberg. Account Executive: Jenny Jamin. Art Director: Sean Dunkerley.

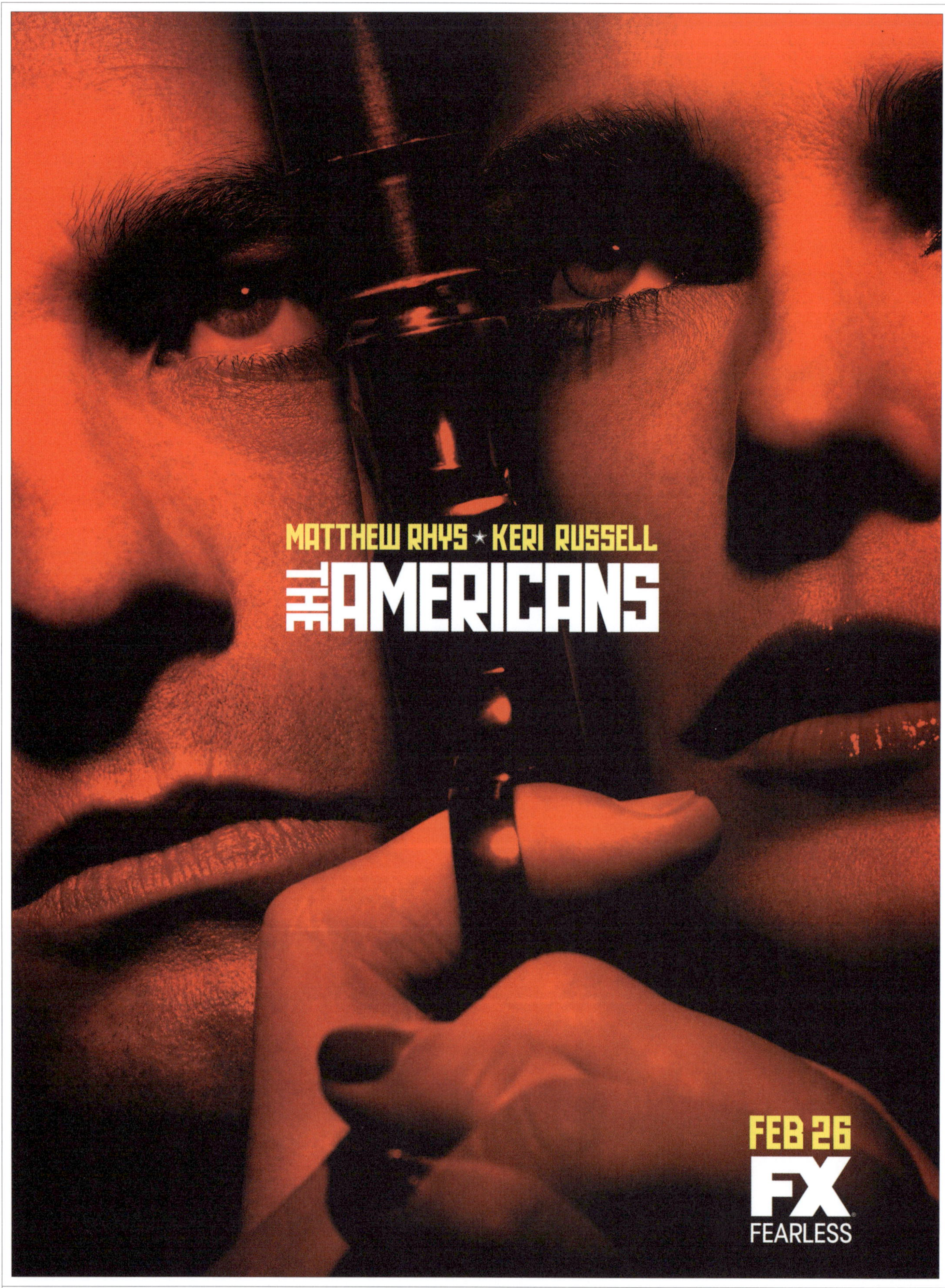

The Americans. Clients: Stephanie Gibbons, Todd Heughens, FX Network. Photographer: James Minchin III. Creative Director: Brad Hochberg. Account Executive: Jenny Jamin. Art Director: Sean Dunkerley.

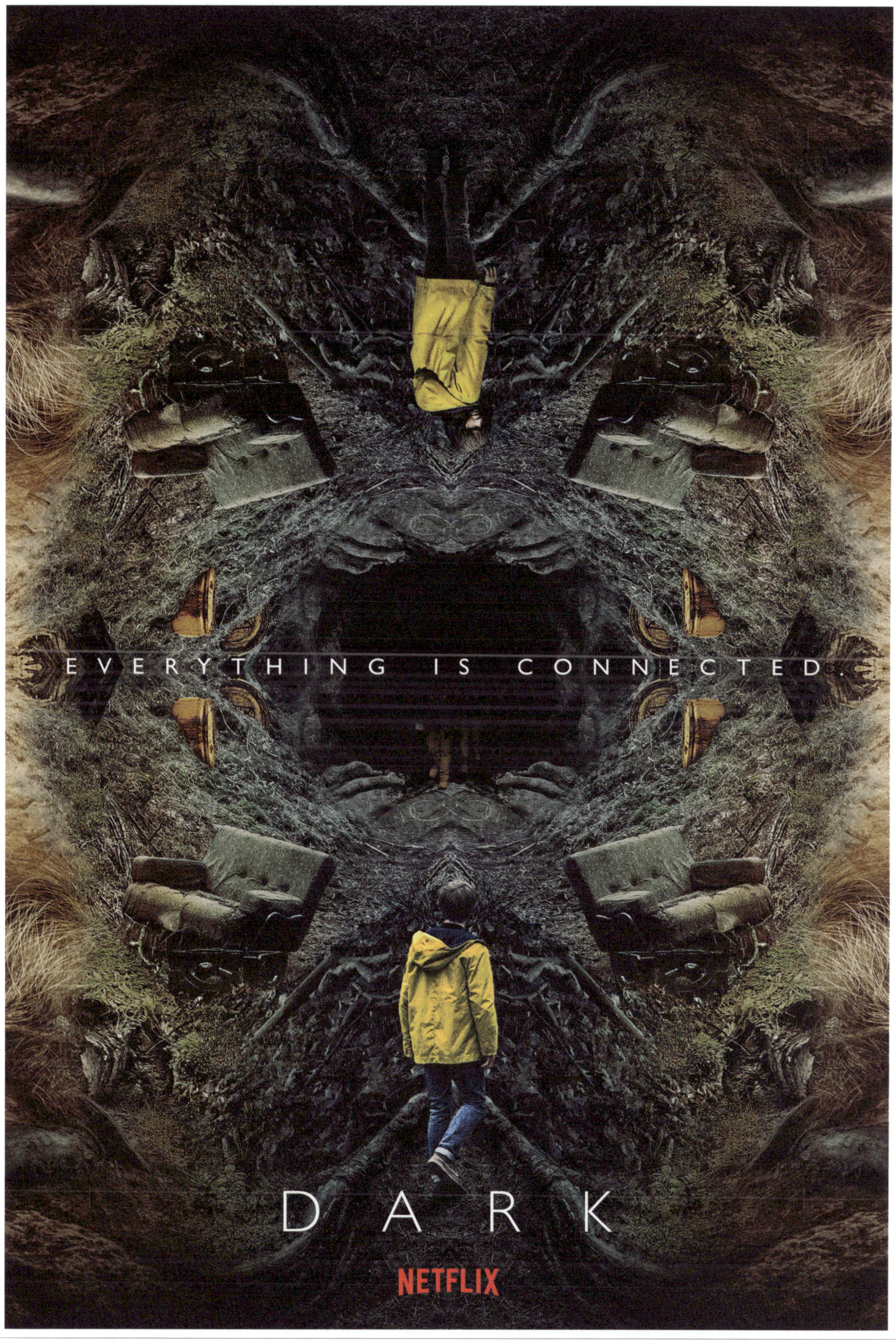

Dark. Clients: Eli Hoy, Daniel Tobin, Netflix. Creative Director: Brad Hochberg. Account Executive: Michelle Mellinger. Art Director: Tatsu Miyoshi.

JOHNNY DEPP

ONE PART OUTRAGE.

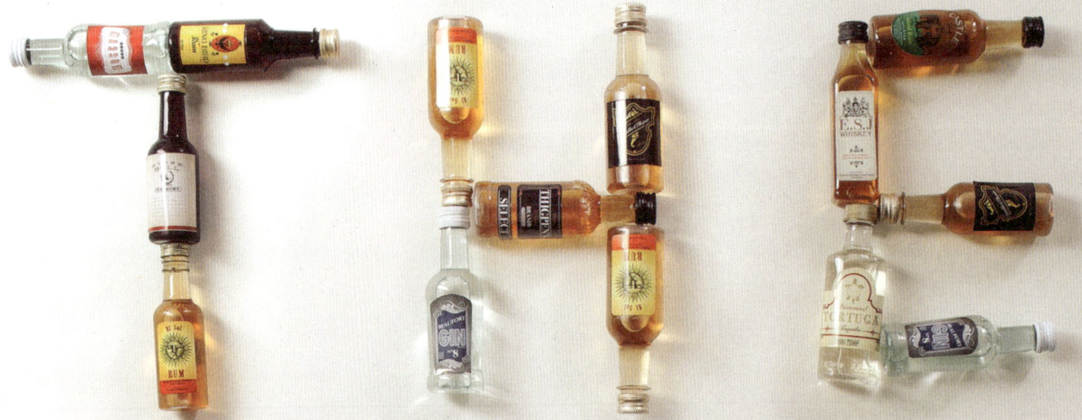

ONE PART JUSTICE.

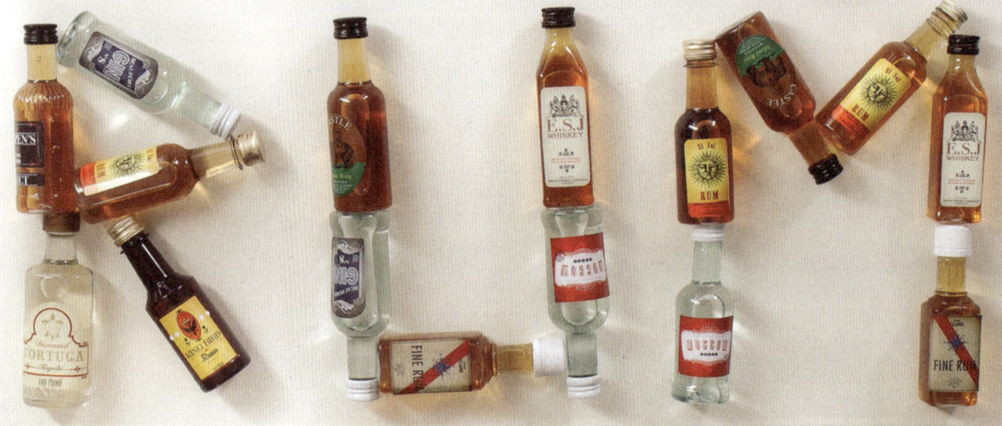

THREE PARTS RUM.

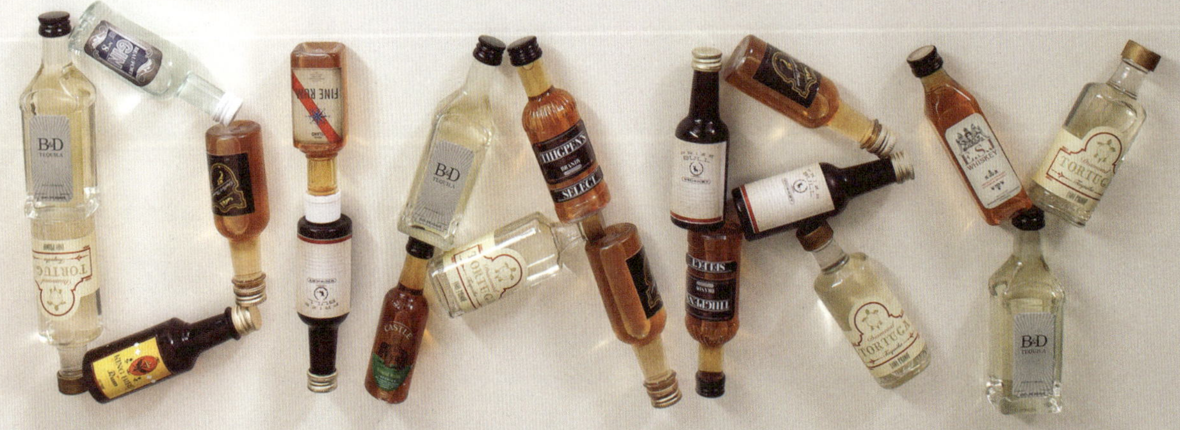

MIX WELL.

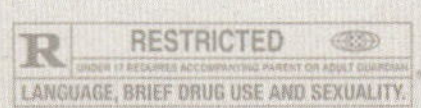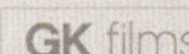

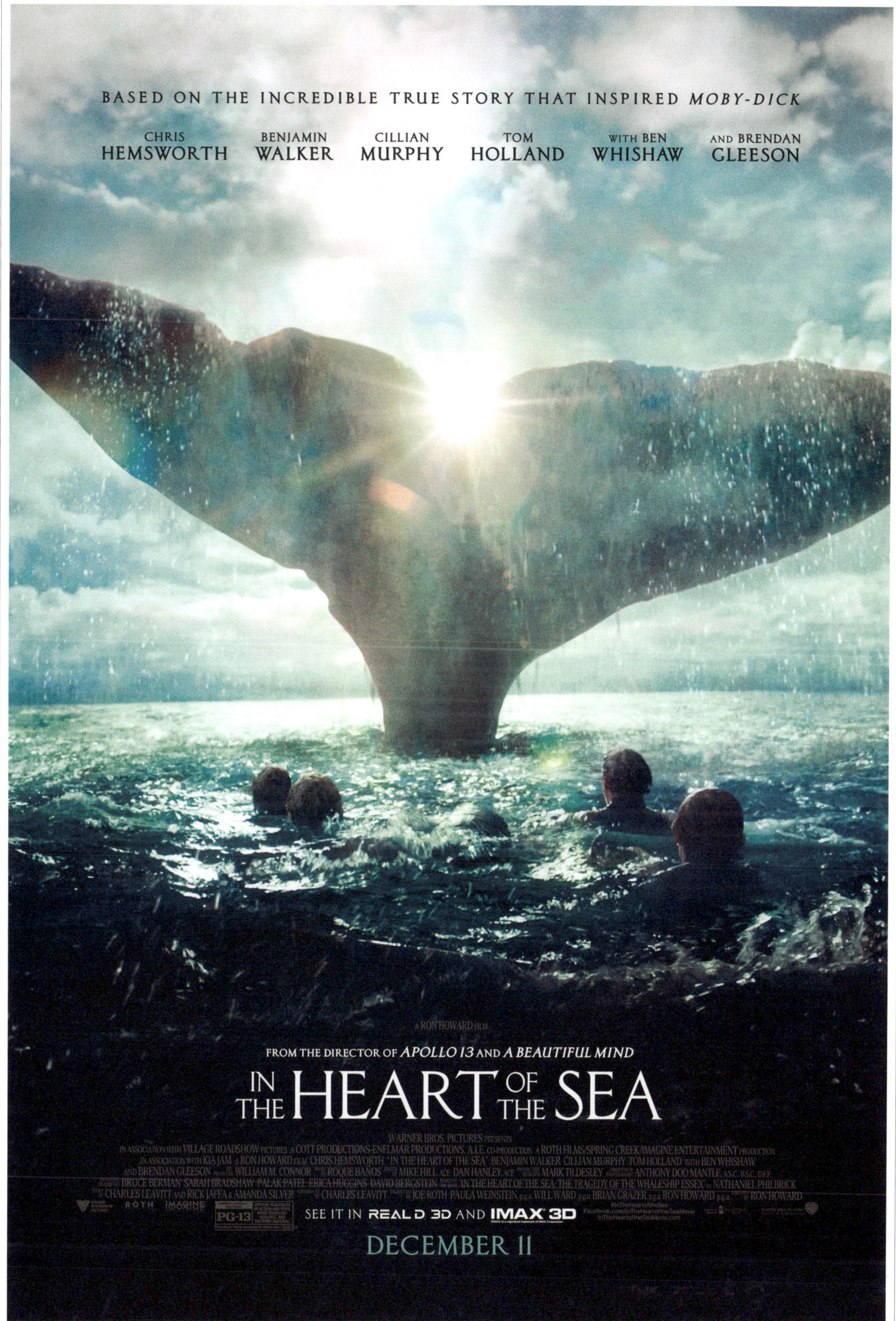

In the Heart of the Sea. Clients: John Stanford, Ari Chucholowski, Warner Bros. Creative Director: Brad Hochberg. Account Executive: Michelle Mellinger. Art Director: Sean Dunkerley.

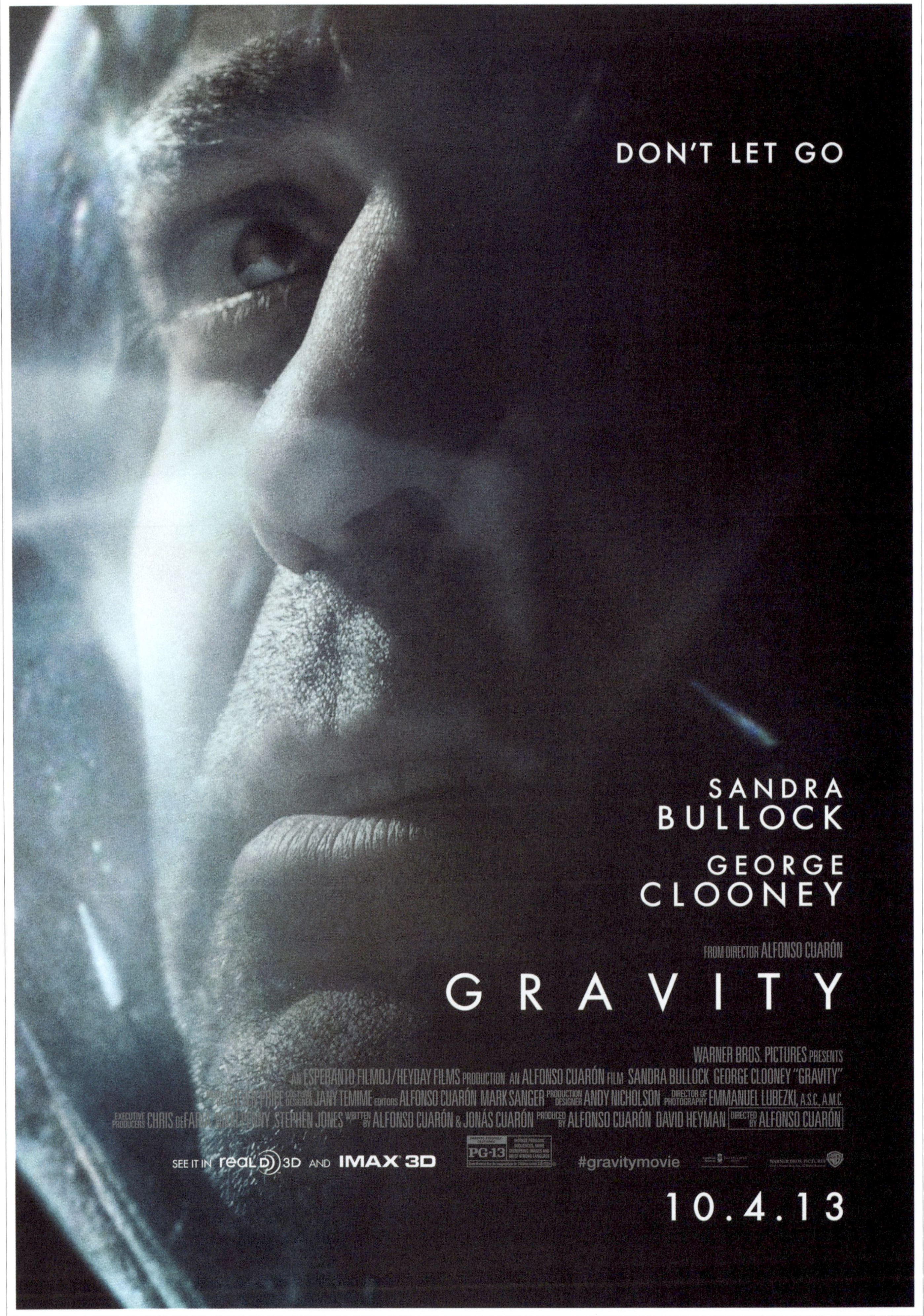

Gravity. Clients: John Stanford, Ari Chucholowski, Warner Bros. Creative Director: Brad Hochberg. Account Executive: Janelle Cipriano. Art Director: Sean Dunkerley.

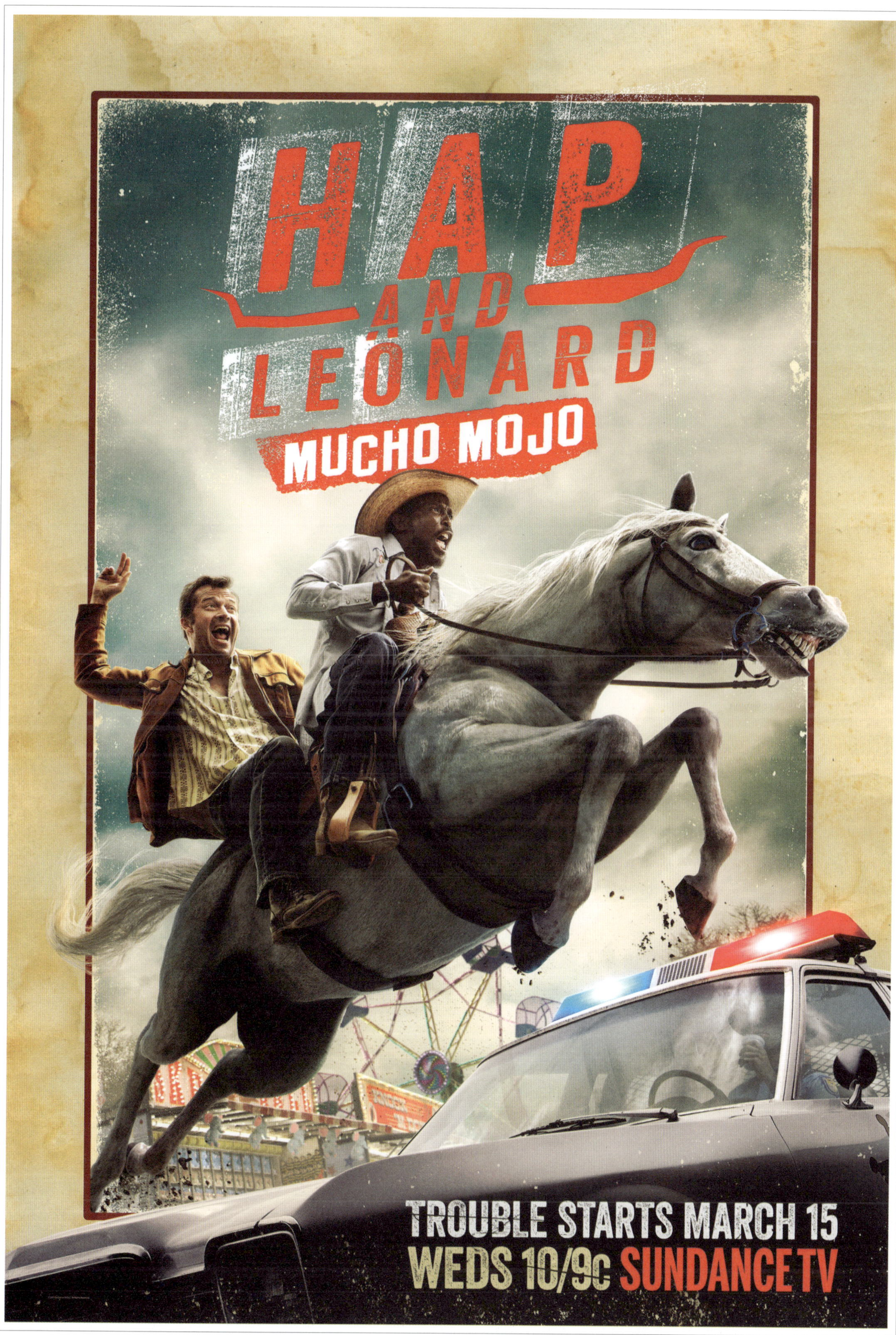

Hap and Leonard. Clients: JC Cancedda, Sundance. Director of Photography: Christine Ramage. Photographer: James Minchin III. Creative Director: Brad Hochberg. Account Executive: Lindsay Artof. Art Director: Sean Dunkerley.

A

ADVERTISING

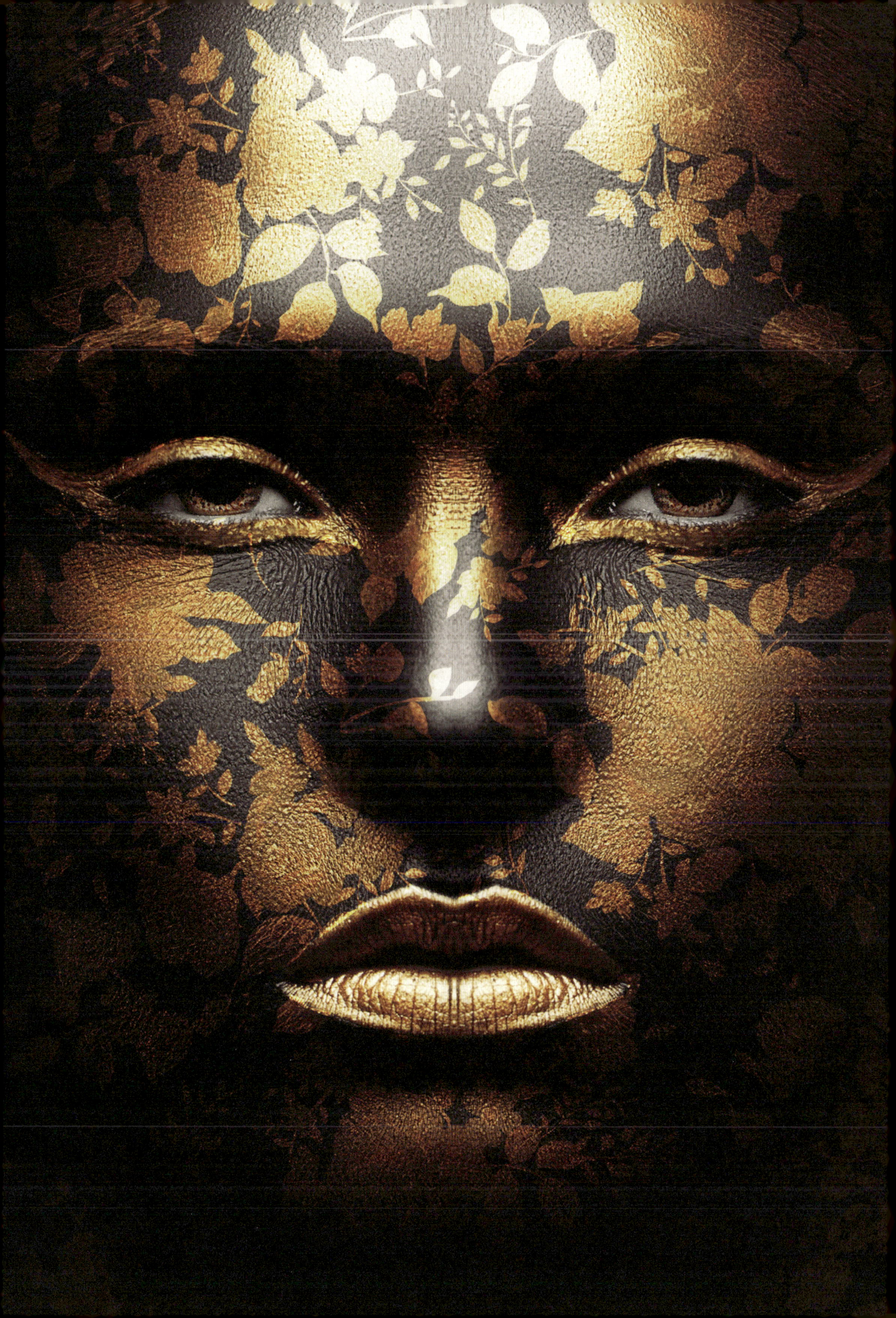

PETROL HAS CEMENTED ITSELF AS ONE OF THE MOST POWERFUL FORCES IN THE ADVERTISING INDUSTRY. THE QUALITY OF THEIR WORK AND COUNTLESS ACHIEVEMENTS ARE BEYOND COMPARE.

Dan Jaugey, *Head of Growth, Compass*

MY TIME AT PETROL OPENED MY EYES TO PURE CREATIVE BRILLIANCE. OUR VISIONARY CAMPAIGNS TRANSFORMED BRANDS INTO ARTISTIC MASTERPIECES.

Bobby Besabe, *Vice President of Creative, UFC*

PETROL HAS BEEN AN INCREDIBLE PARTNER. WE GEEKED OUT OVER IDEAS TOGETHER AND ALWAYS FELT LIKE WE COULD RELY ON THEM, ESPECIALLY WHEN THINGS WERE MOVING A MILLION MILES A MINUTE. THEY'RE A SUPER CREATIVE, TALENTED CREW.

Emanuel Palalic, *CEO, EmptyVessel*

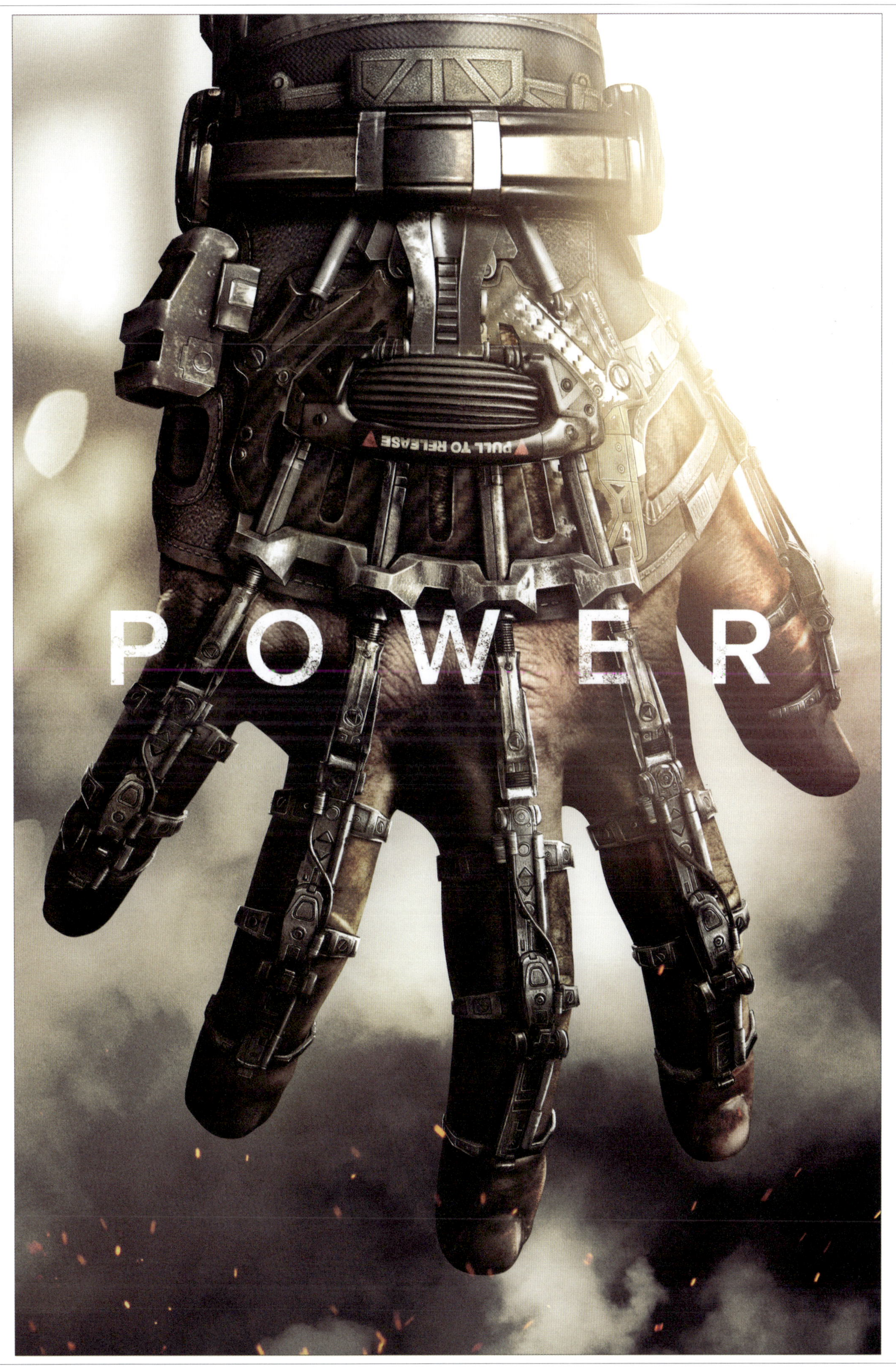

(Page 55) Western Digital. Credits: Western Digital, PETROL Advertising. / (Above) Call of Duty: Advanced Warfare. Credits: Activision, Sledgehammer Games, PETROL Advertising.

I worked at PETROL from its very beginning in 2003 and for over a decade. In that time, I've been a part of what eventually became a fully integrated, 360° marketing creative force that has always been driven to deliver results to its clients and to do so by developing solid, top-tier campaigns. What Alan and Ben pioneered in video game marketing with PETROL and what it evolved into is nothing short of astonishing, as proven by the multiple awards and recognition within the industry. I'm proud of what we accomplished together and in awe of the unequaled work PETROL continues to produce.

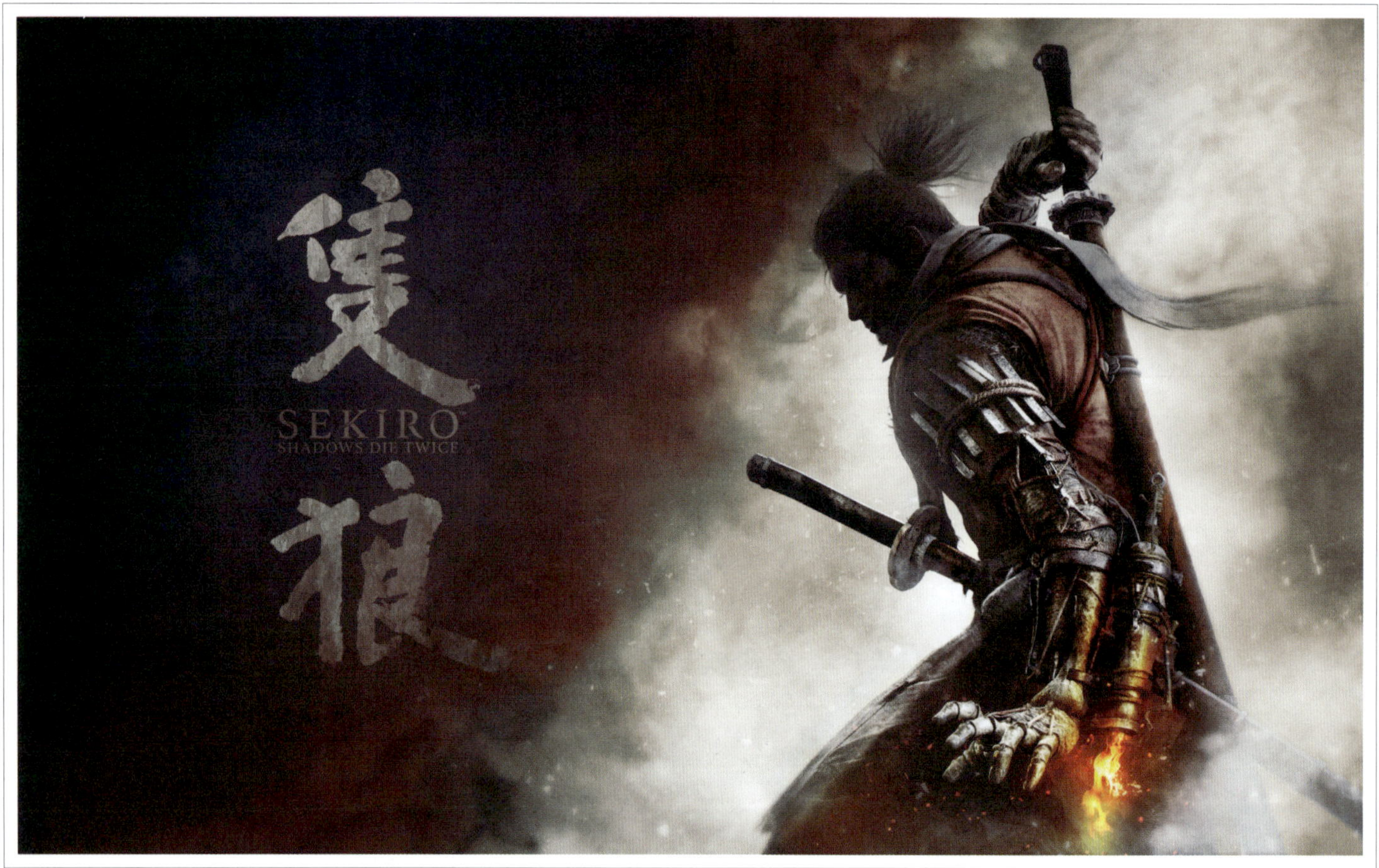

Sekiro: Shadows Die Twice. Credits: Activision, FromSoftware, PETROL Advertising.

Q&A: PETROL Advertising

What's the story behind PETROL? How was it founded?
Alan Hunter, President & Chief Creative Officer: We founded PETROL in 2003. There were seven of us, including two partners, and we all left very high-paying entertainment marketing jobs because we wanted to pursue both games and movies. A $500,000 line of credit on my house and my $100,000 life savings were gone in six months, and when we were down to just a few thousand dollars in the bank, our first check from Sony came in. Ever since then, we have never looked back!

Soon, we were at 30 people, then 50, and, eventually, our sweet spot of around 75, with support teams of 25 globally. We have been fortunate enough to have launched over 2,500 video game titles and a few hundred movies. Most importantly, we were able to create a business where we can grow from within: The average length of stay at PETROL is over seven years.

I can't underestimate the value of loving what you do, which is a gift, and that is at the core of what our success has been based on. We were acquired by a global development group in 2019 and continue to grow our company into our twenty-second year.

PETROL focuses on entertainment advertising for video games. Why that specific focus?
A.H.: In the late 1990s and early 2000s, we knew that interactive entertainment was going to grow beyond traditional theatrical entertainment. We all love movies, but there is a different strategic challenge to get someone to spend $10 on a ticket that will occupy two hours of their life compared to $50-$100 on something that they're going to spend potentially hundreds of hours on. It's campaign building that gets people to invest in the lifestyle of the game and what it represents, and that is an incredible creative opportunity for us at PETROL.

That audience knowledge has brought clients who wanted PETROL to help them reach gamers for their brands and consumer products. Companies like Western Digital, Seagate, NVIDIA, JBL, and even the UFC have partnered with PETROL.

We also feel very strongly that games are the international entertainment language that unites people around the world inside a platform of fun and not negativity… even with the most mature content.

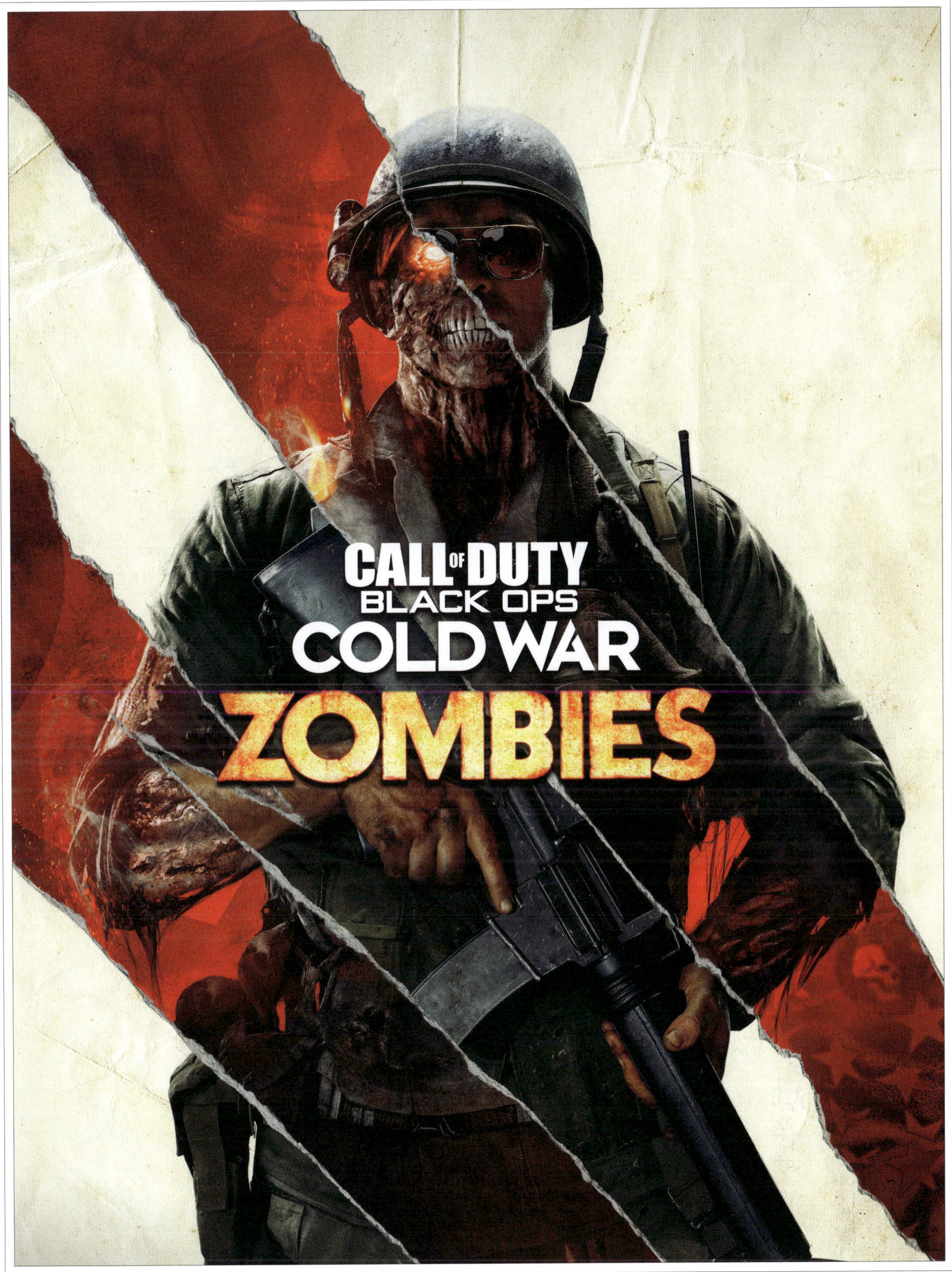

Call of Duty: Black Ops Cold War. Credits: Activision, Treyarch, PETROL Advertising.

When compared to other advertising firms, what makes PETROL unique?

A.H.: Being specialists at speaking with, marketing to, and converting a massive audience like gamers as both marketers and consumers makes us very unique. PETROL was created to service the video game industry with design, and our staff reflects that. We do all of our 3D, Unreal Engine, and game capture in-house and are able to work in the game developers' engines. That allows us to be intimately connected to the product we are branding and marketing, and we have built an incredible knowledge base throughout the agency.

Our agency philosophy is to train and promote from within and develop talent that has an inherent love of the product so our Petrolians feel less like they're working and more like they're creating iconic moments in and for an industry they love.

Who is or was your greatest mentor?

Ben Nessan, Account Executive: Professionally, my greatest mentor has been Sam Clarke, the VP of strategic partnerships and development here at PETROL. I originally joined Sam's "account team" in 2016, and we've been working closely together ever since. Sam is a great leader, and the traits I love most about him are his focus on family and relationships, his leadership and ability/desire to teach other young professionals, and his ability to talk to and relate to anyone from any walk of life or part of the world.

What has inspired or motivated you in your career?

Gilbert Moran, Director of Strategy: I was initially inspired to take my first steps into advertising via a *Mad Men* ad circa 2007. The vibe of that whole show was incredibly motivating because it showed me—at a pivotal time in my life—that there is power in advertising to convince people of a story and to take an action that they might not have realized they needed to take.

Once I was on the path, inspiration came from all directions: colleagues, competitors in our vertical, advertising across the industry, discussions with fans, unexpected activations, and stunts. Advertising and marketing are such living, breathing entities that you can find inspiration just by bringing up your socials for the day, seeing something a coworker puts in Slack, or going on YouTube and seeing a new recommendation.

What is it about advertising that you are most passionate about?

A.H.: We are very passionate about the content we create, which reaches tens of millions of people and brings them happiness in countless ways. When a movie or a game director is interviewed to promote their release, they usually sit in front of our posters, and we see that as such a unique privilege. That work represents thousands of people's craft, and we don't take that for granted.

We also love that great creativity transcends all things like language, borders, and cultural backgrounds… We love that the content we create may sit on a kid's shelf for years as a shining light of happiness, and we hope that the work we do helps unite people inside of an experience… It's an amazing feeling when it works and when you see it happen.

What makes someone a Petrolian?

Neel Kar, VP of Innovation: Over the past decade, I've had the privilege of working alongside many incredibly talented Petrolians. One observation has stood out in every interaction: Everyone here is solution-first. In an industry that thrives on tight deadlines and high expectations, this shared approach turns even the toughest challenges into opportunities for growth and innovation. It's not just a skill—it's a way of life that creates an environment of mutual trust, collaboration, and unwavering solidarity.

This shared ethos defines PETROL as a creative tribe where even a small team can dream big. Our president, Alan Hunter, exemplifies this spirit with initiative, versatility, a relentless pursuit of business intelligence, and an unwavering compassion for teamwork. These core values fuel the multi-talented Petrolians.

Every member contributes not only their expertise but also their support, creating a culture where no challenge feels insurmountable and no success is achieved alone. This collective mentality is what allows PETROL to transform ambitious dreams into reality, project after project. As individuals, Petrolians excel; as a team, they achieve the extraordinary.

What's your favorite brand you have worked with?

A.H.: I think we'd have to say that we've been fortunate enough to do 17 *Call of Duty* branding campaign launches and all of the *Soulsborne* games, as well as over 2,500 game launches…

However, one of our favorite brands that we have been lucky enough to work with for 21 years is the UFC! They are an incredibly smart and ambitious client, and they love pushing boundaries and promoting their events. It has enabled us to travel all over the world, meet all different kinds of fighters, and go to well over a hundred live events. They have experienced such iconic milestones, and we've been on that journey with them, from their beginnings as a small pay-per-view event getting 20,000 views to a billion-dollar organization that is a global phenomenon. Our favorite thing about it is the storytelling of competition and martial arts, which is built around the backstories of the fighters and the platform that UFC creates for them to change their lives. It's incredibly rewarding to have had Graphis recognize some of that work in previous years!

Who among your contemporaries today do you most admire?

N.K.: Jama Jurabaev, as a contemporary conceptual storyteller, has been a beacon of inspiration throughout my career! I started following his journey as a conceptual artist, and since then, he has transcended into a flourishing entrepreneur with a startup that provides the art community with incredibly refined 3D assets that empower storytelling.

At PETROL, we've had the privilege of collaborating with Jama on several fortunate occasions. Each time, we were struck by his humility, collaborative spirit, and unparalleled ability to innovate visual storytelling with unexpected tools like VR.

I have personally been deeply influenced by his art and, even more so, by his relentless appetite to keep evolving in the creative space by embracing technology.

What would be your dream assignment?

Andrea Voskanian, Creative Director: I truly love the type of work I do now, but if I were to mix it up, it would probably be a rebranding project for a high-profile fashion or lifestyle company. The idea of refreshing a brand's image while staying true to its heritage and style excites me. It would be incredibly rewarding to create something that resonates with today's audience in a fresh way and leaves a lasting impact.

Who have been some of your favorite colleagues or clients?

B.N.: PETROL houses such a unique collection of talent and team members across departments—it's fun to come to work each day and work toward a common goal. As an account team member, some of my favorite colleagues are the creative team (art directors, illustrators, 3D, audio/visual), as they are so integral to what PETROL does and so different from what I do that I appreciate their skills/expertise and creativity.

We're fortunate to have so many great clients/partners, so it is hard to narrow down the list. However, some of my favorite clients include those who truly value partnership/collaboration and view PETROL as an extension of their team. We've had the pleasure of building continued partnerships over the years

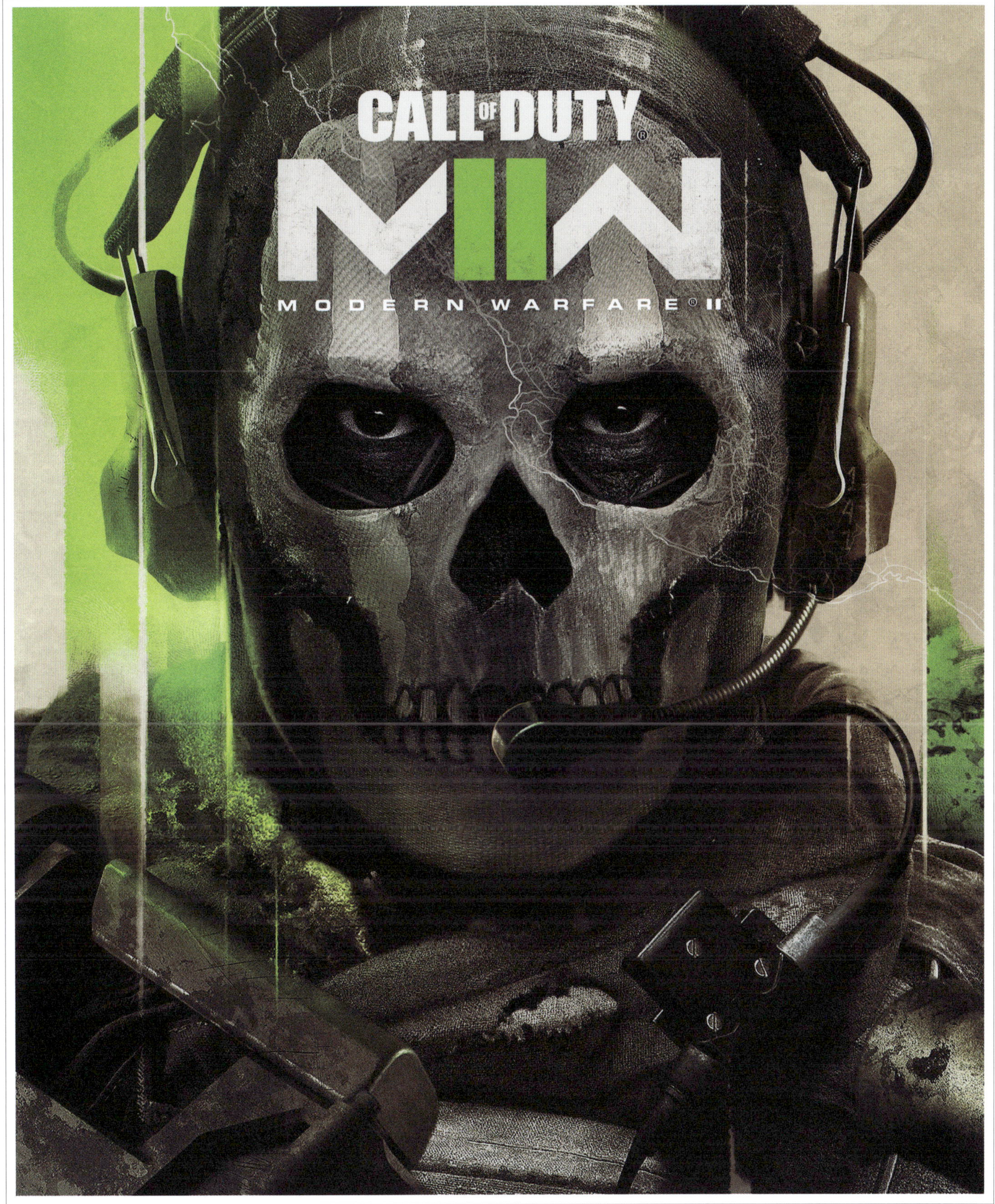

Call of Duty: Modern Warfare II. Credits: Activision, Infinity Ward, PETROL Advertising.

of work and supporting many games or events with Ubisoft, UFC, and the EmptyVessel team—all are great partners, and we're very proud of the work we've done together!

What do you consider your greatest achievement so far?
A.H.: This is an easy question for me and a lot of our leaders to answer. Our greatest personal achievements are helping our creatives (who may not have the best education or financial support) become incredibly successful in our business and in the advertising world.

It has always been in my and our company's DNA to share every piece of knowledge you have because it only makes you stronger, and the person you're helping will never forget that they got help along the way. When it really comes full circle is when you see them doing it with new young creatives, and that knowledge and passion get passed on.

While the entertainment business is based a lot on personal success and ambitions, nothing is more rewarding than helping others succeed.

What about your work gives you the greatest satisfaction?
B.N.: The greatest satisfaction in my work is participating in day-to-day conversations/meetings/calls, running into challenges, and then working with the team to find solutions—adding value and ultimately being helpful to the greater team/collective is what motivates me and gives me the most satisfaction in my work.

We have the privilege that our work is seen/consumed by the world, so seeing our work go live to the public and be well-received is the cherry on top. However, the greater satisfaction comes from the journey to get to the end result.

What part of your work do you find the most demanding?
G.M.: Advertising and marketing in gaming is a particularly difficult beast to manage because it moves so fast. For example, sneakers change, sure, but they are essentially the same product with tweaks. Video gaming in 2025 is wildly different from video gaming in 2015 or 2005. Hardware updates, shifts in genre popularity, shifts in monetization, the emergence of the creator economy, changes in social usage for gaming, and new entrants from emerging markets all meaningfully affect how we are able to approach any particular campaign.

The most demanding thing is staying on top of the latest within the industry while also staying abreast of trends affecting the broader sector. Thankfully, that's not something I have to tackle alone. I'm fortunate to have allies at PETROL who continually push themselves to learn and adapt just like I do, and it makes tackling any particular challenge that much more manageable when I know I have talented people to lean on.

What professional goals do you still have for yourself?
G.M.: I want to continue to be a key part of building teams that give people the same opportunities that I have had in my career. I was fortunate to find an environment that allowed me to succeed, fail, learn, and see what potential ambitions I could have in my career while at PETROL, and I want to keep that a key part of the DNA for any department I'm fortunate enough to lead.

It's especially important for me as someone who has always prided themselves on leveling up despite their circumstances. As much as I may credit my own ability or skill, I know that so much of the career I have today is due to people more senior than me giving me a shot. I want to give that opportunity to future generations of people who enter this business.

What advice would you give to students starting out today?
B.N.: Students today have many opportunities ahead of them, and speaking from my experience, it was a challenge to enter the workforce with various passions or things I wanted to pursue that sounded interesting.

When you enter the workforce, and you're early in your career:

Try to identify what you're passionate about or good at and pursue related opportunities. However, I found that part is best learned and experienced while actually working. Being patient and flexible and gaining experience throughout the journey will help you realize what you ultimately want to pursue and where you can add value. Don't expect to have it all figured out at the beginning. From my experience, the type of role and industry you work in, from just starting to where you find yourself in five to ten years, will likely be different.

Find and work with good people—the people you work with and the relationships you have are equally as important as the work you do.

Be a team player and easy to work with—this will get you further than you know!

What interests do you have outside of work?
A.V.: I really enjoy baking and cooking, especially experimenting with new recipes. It's a creative outlet for me—playing with different flavors, trying out new techniques, and sometimes even inventing my own dishes. It's rewarding to see how ingredients come together to create something delicious, and I love sharing the results with friends and family.

What do you value most in life?
A.V.: Growth—both personally and professionally. I'm always looking to learn new things and challenge myself, which keeps me adaptable and motivated. I also love being part of an environment where everyone can grow together.

What would you change if you had to do it all over again?
G.M.: I might have started on the path to the ad world earlier, specialized in skills and classes in college that would ultimately be the foundation for my work, taken more internships, and been more conscious of how I spent my time.

But with that said, I think the rollercoaster ride that many of us go through to get where we are today is part of the growing process. I wouldn't be the thinker, leader, or man I am today without the things I went through and the ways I went through them. We're all the summation of the things we've done, and who's to say I would be a better version of myself if I did it differently?

Where do you find inspiration?
A.H.: For me, my team, and my students, it's about what's around you when you are the happiest.

There's so much incredible creativity and art on every digital outlet you can imagine, and that's very valuable. However, being retrospective and looking at what's around you where and when you're the happiest, whether it's the clothing you're wearing, the product you're interacting with, or the experience you're having—for us, that's the biggest inspiration. If you can partake in creating work like that—work that makes people happy and helps change their day-to-day lives—you're doing something great with your talents.

How do you define success?
A.H.: HELPING OTHERS WHILE DOING WHAT YOU LOVE. So few people get to say that they actually do that in their day-to-day lives, and we have been lucky enough to be in an industry where we get paid to do what we love. Building off of that and helping others by training and providing opportunities is really the way that success is defined for me and what I have tried to teach my team. It's great to be successful, and making money is awesome (especially after not having any in the beginning), but it really comes down to success being about the way you feel about what you're doing… That is priceless.

Where do you see yourself in the future?
A.H.: Creating, helping, teaching, and believing that great creativity is the thing that keeps you vital. When you stop expressing it, you really stop existing as a creative force, whether it's in your sketchbook or on a billboard. As long as I'm building PETROL and providing opportunities to young creative people to be on this journey to have the future I've had, the future is limitless!

How do you balance work with your personal life if there is a distinction between the two for you?
G.M.: You absolutely have to find time to enrich yourself by investing in your personal life. For me, that comes primarily in making the best use of our extended breaks (Thanksgiving and Christmas) and also actually taking meaningful vacations where I'm signed off. Both of those scenarios help me recharge my battery.

Beyond that, it's about maintaining those "I'm definitely available and working" hours and "I'm not technically working now, but I can answer questions or be helpful" hours, even at 11 at night or on the weekend. Rare is the time past our normal business hours that I'm completely off the clock, but I also recognize that expectation is something I must hold for myself and not necessarily expect of my coworkers or direct reports.

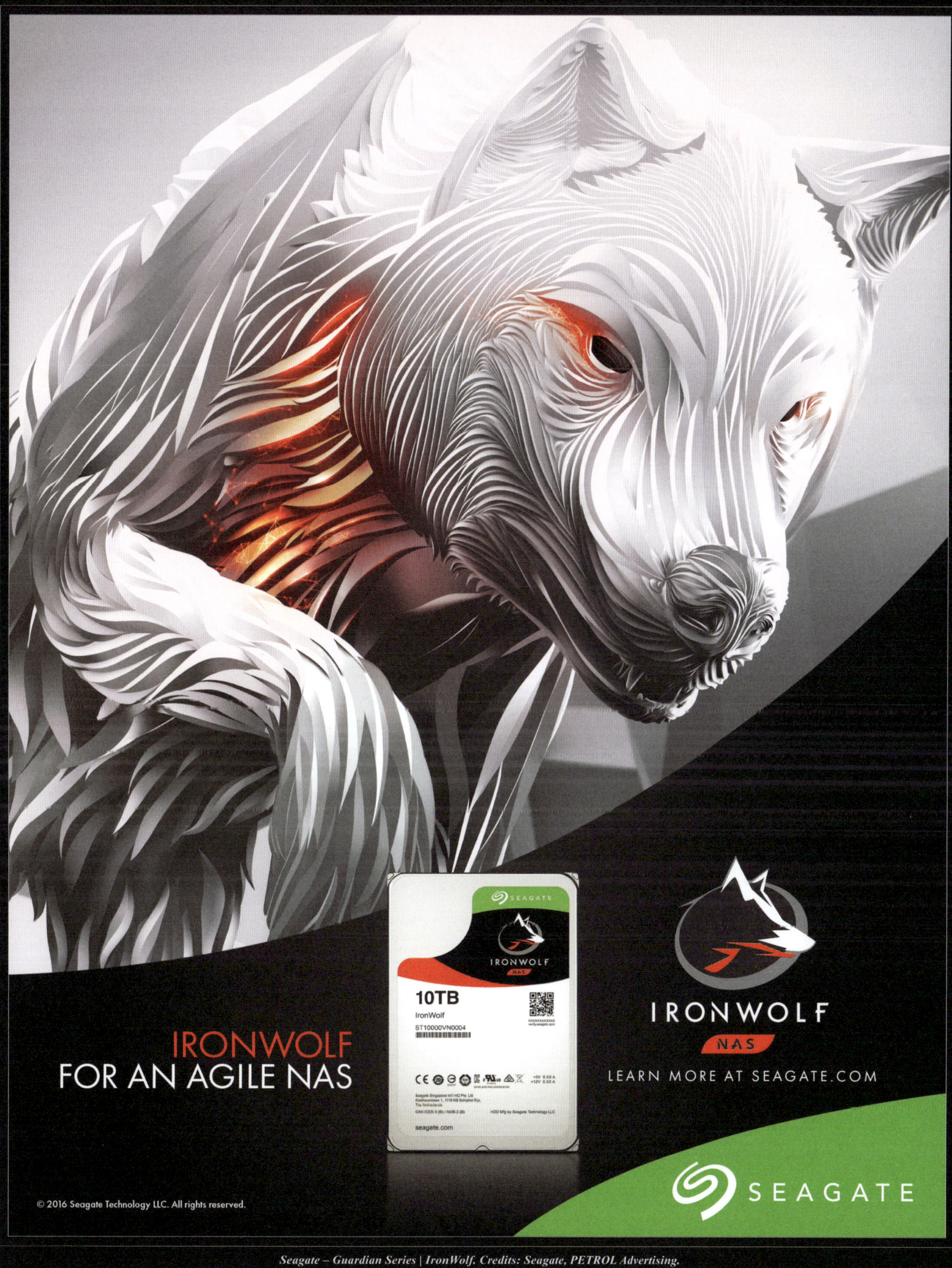

Seagate – Guardian Series | IronWolf. Credits: Seagate, PETROL Advertising.

In what ways do you see your field changing over the years?
N.K.: We are on the cusp of a quantum leap, where artificial intelligence and technological leaps are reshaping the creative world. Change is inevitable, but creativity remains profoundly human.

Ben Affleck recently articulated this beautifully: "Craftsman is knowing how to work. Art is knowing when to stop. And I think knowing when to stop is going to be a very difficult thing for AI to learn because [of its] taste." It's that intangible sense of taste—our ability to discern, refine, and create with soul—that will define the next generation of creative storytellers.

At PETROL, we champion human ingenuity over machine efficiency. The future belongs to those who blend innovation with human intuition.

PETROL Advertising www.petrolad.com

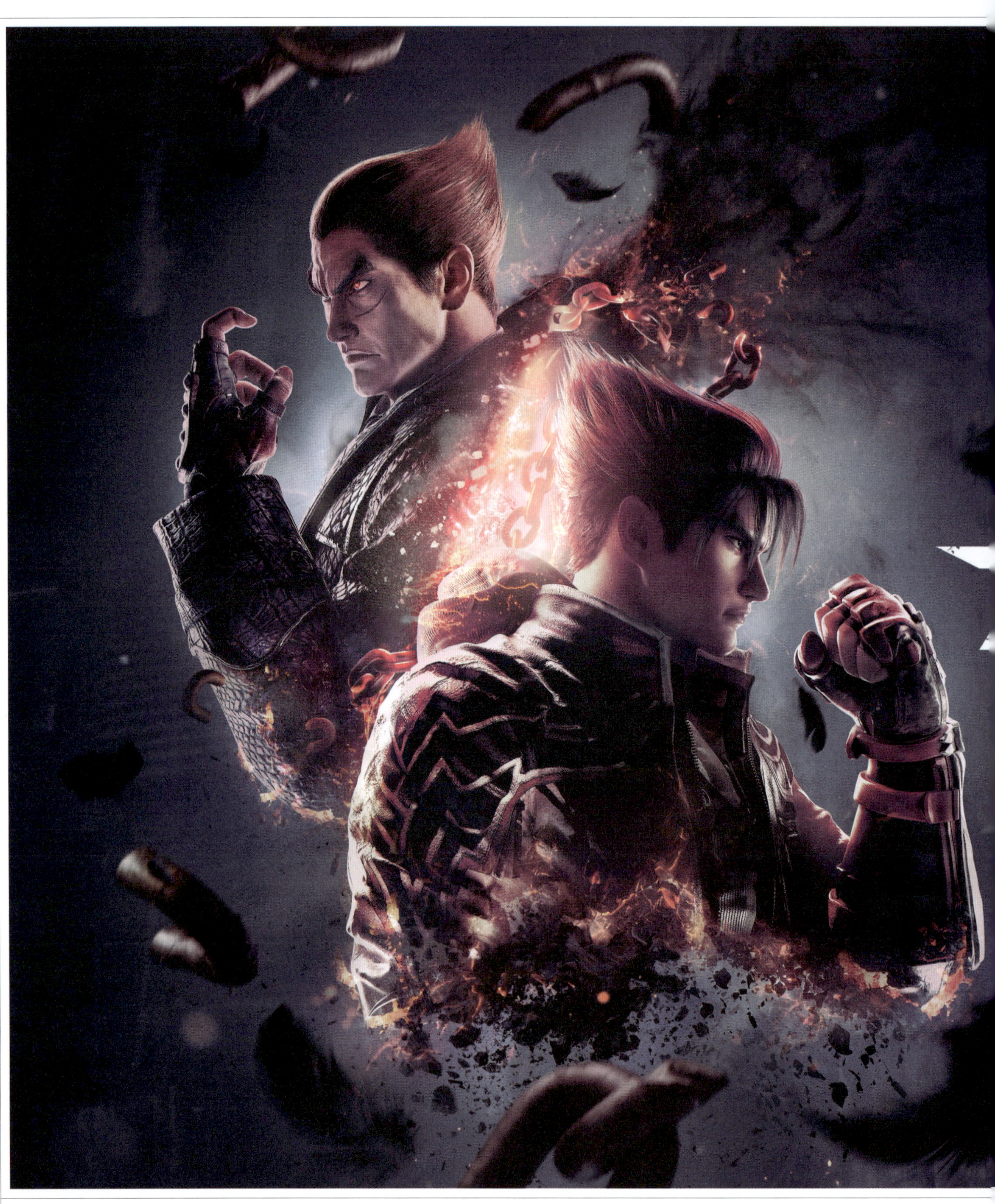

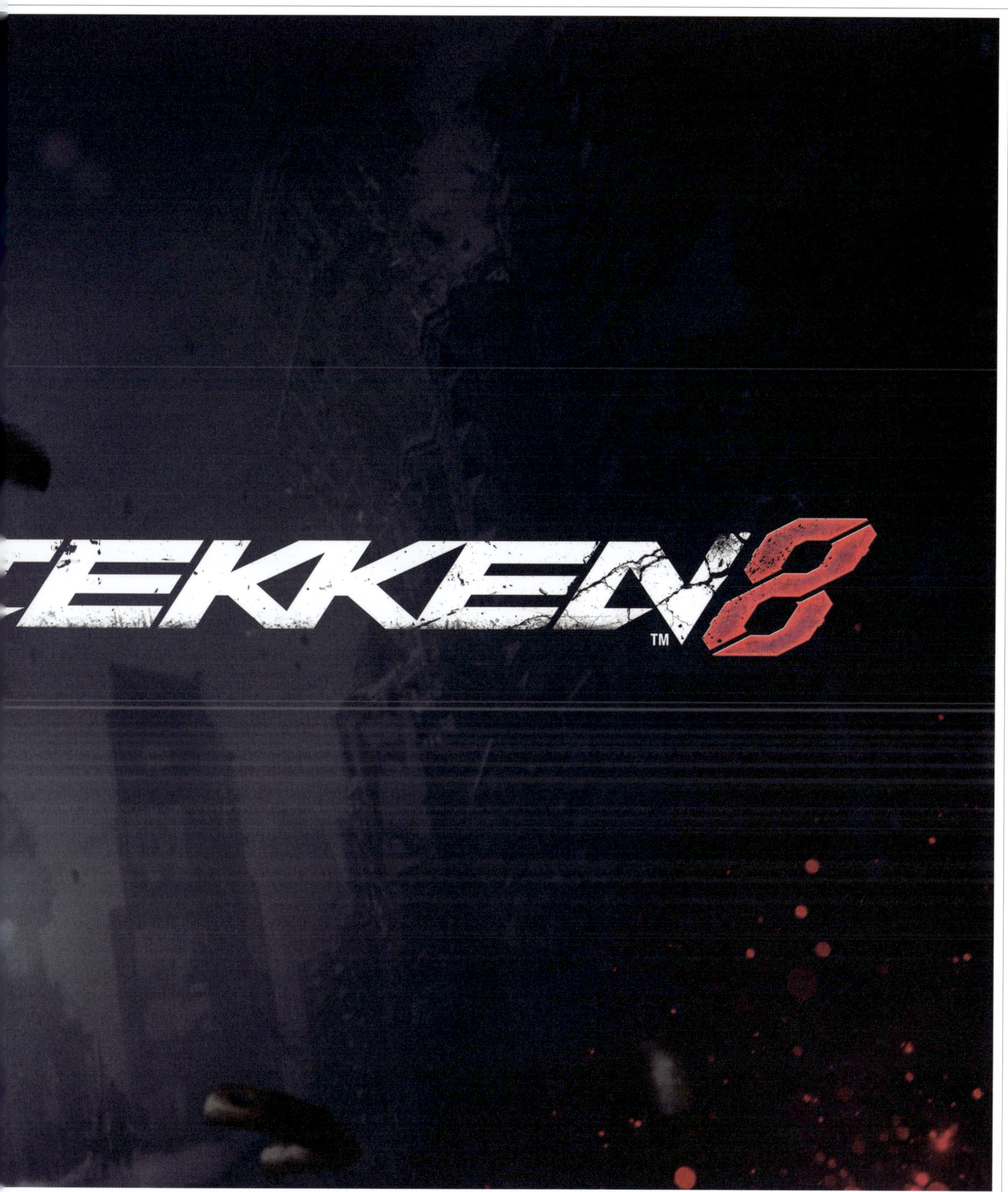

Tekken 8. Credits: Bandai Namco, PETROL Advertising.

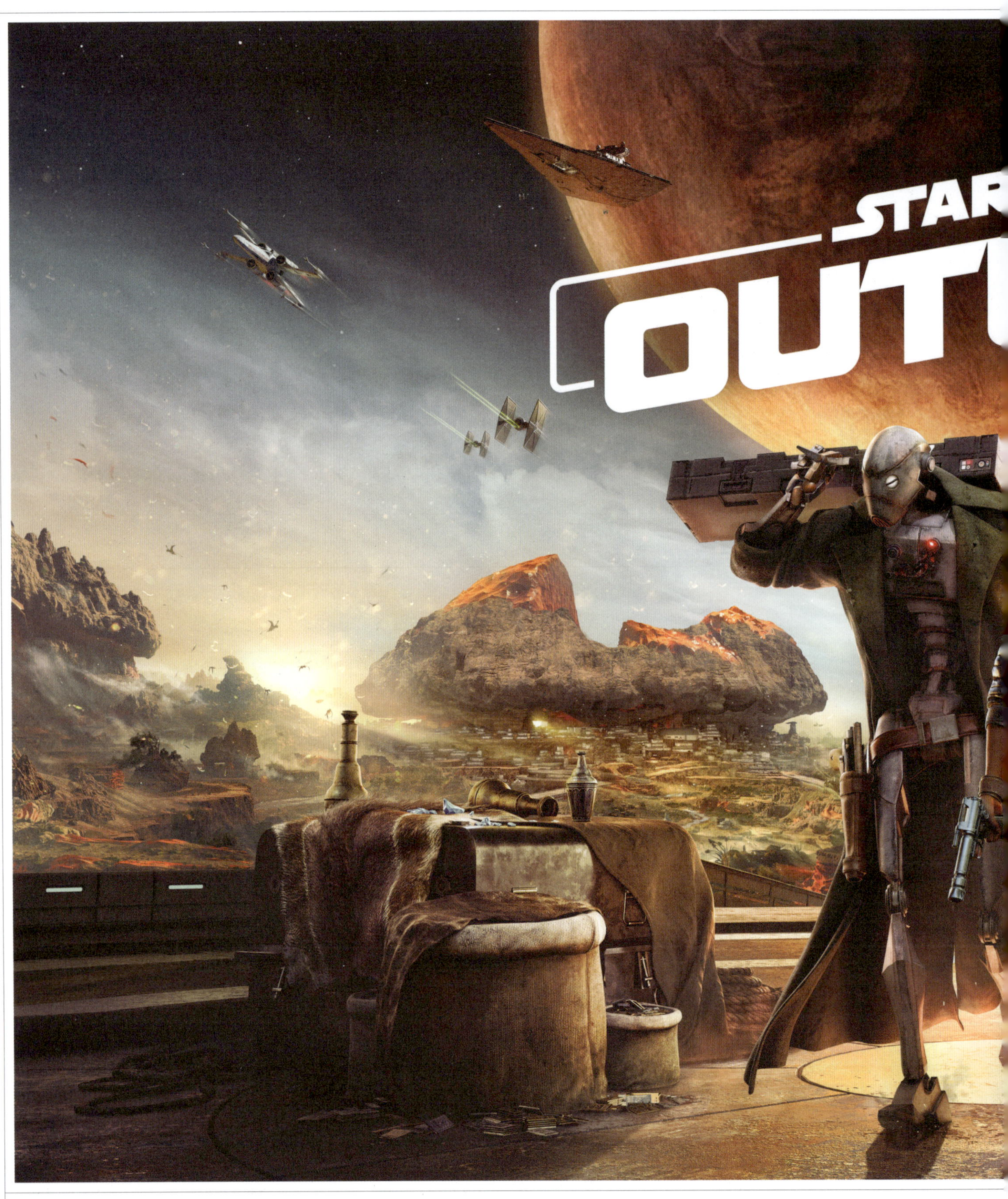

STAR
OUT

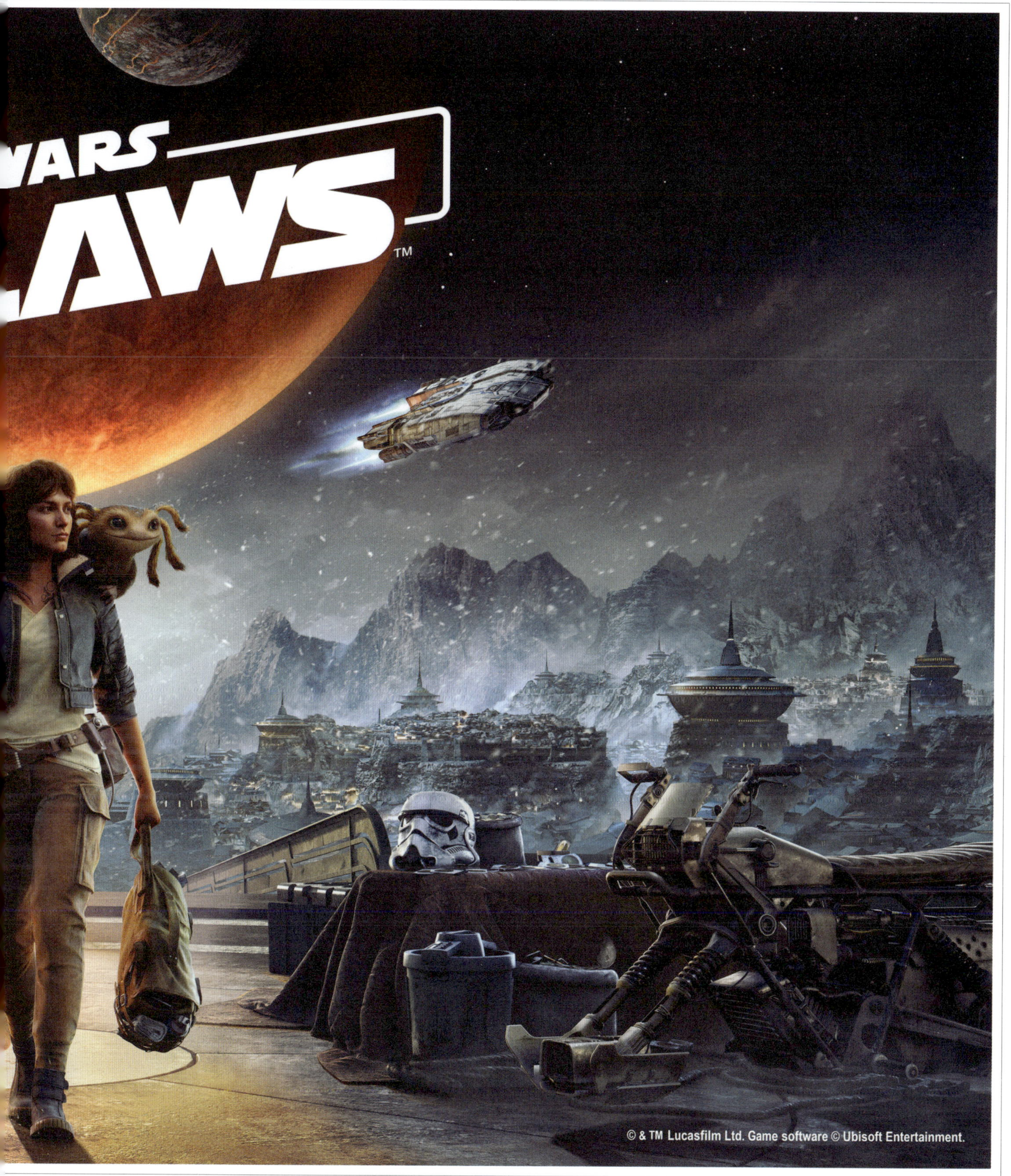

Star Wars Outlaws. Credits: Ubisoft, Massive Entertainment, Lucasfilm, PETROL Advertising.

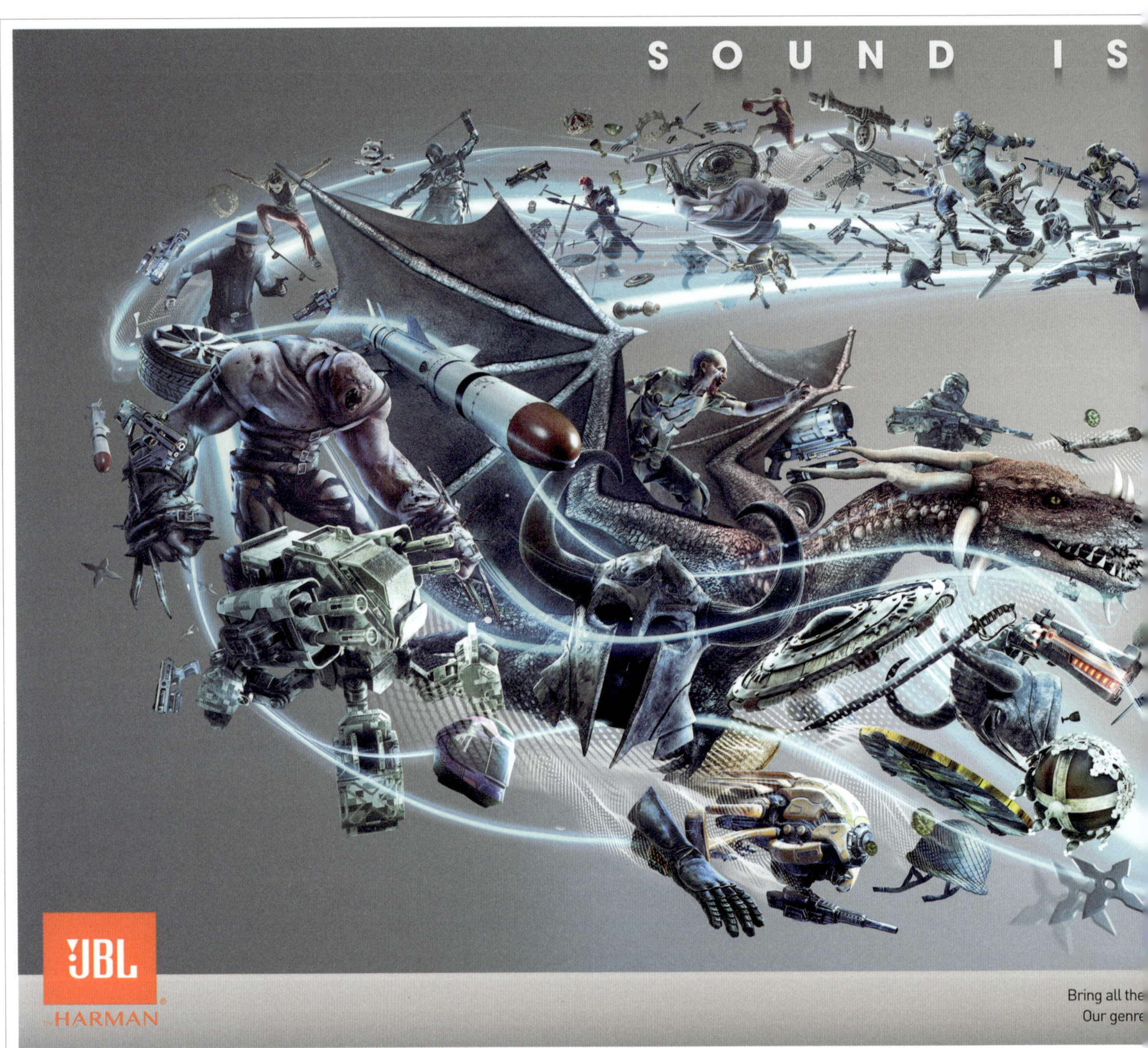
SOUND IS
JBL
by HARMAN
Bring all the
Our genre

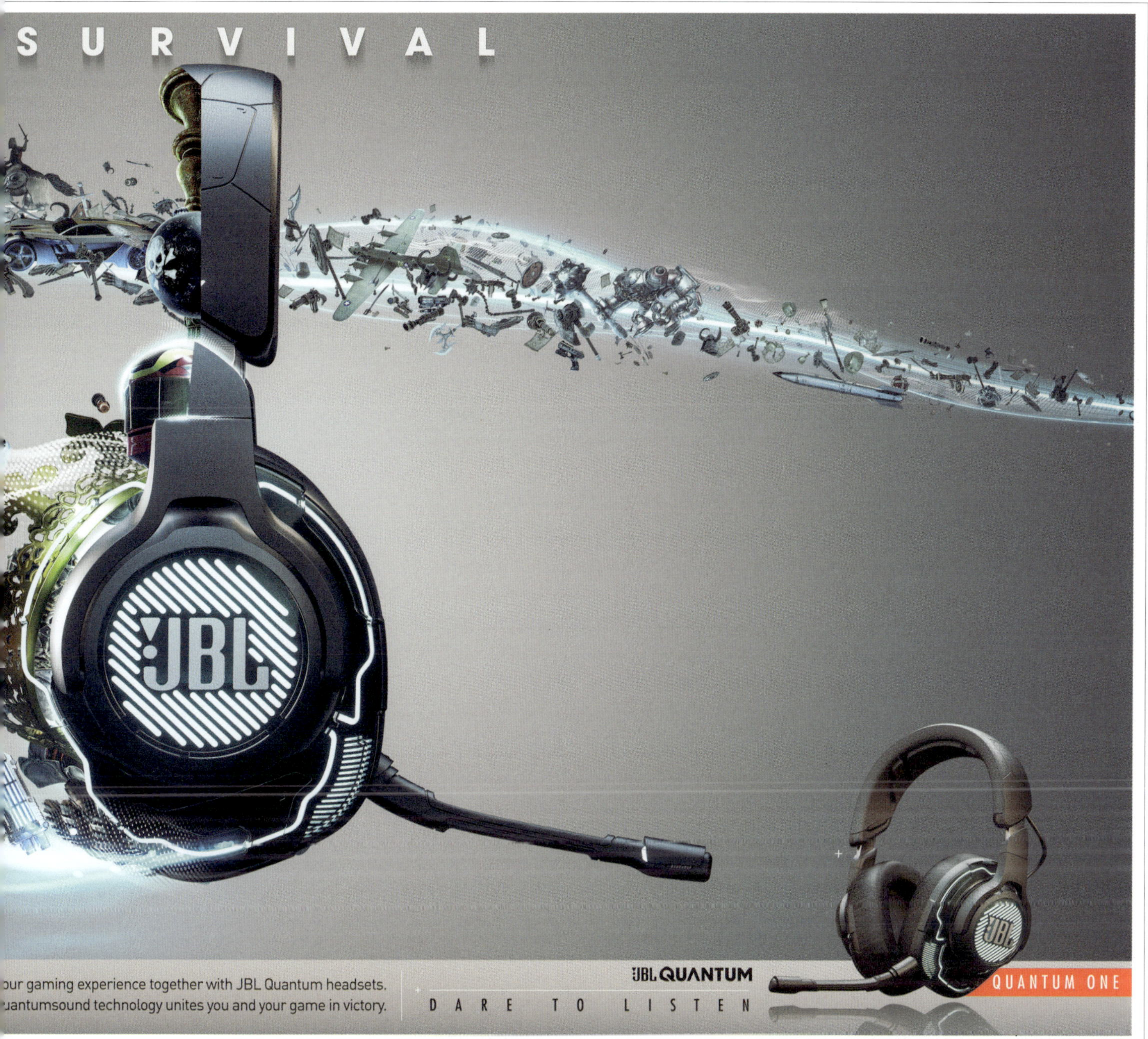

JBL Harman. Credits: JBL Harman, PETROL Advertising.

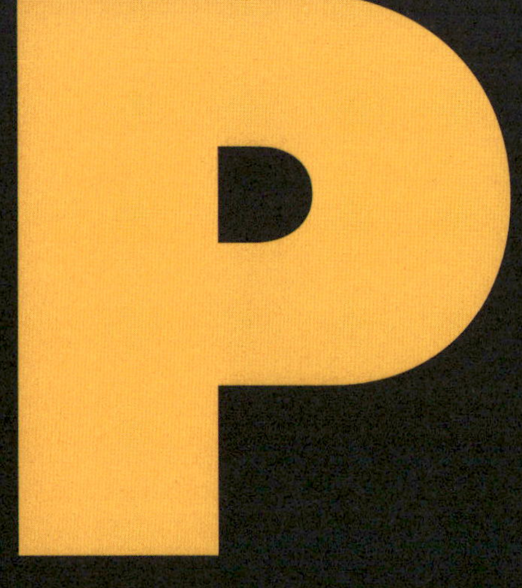

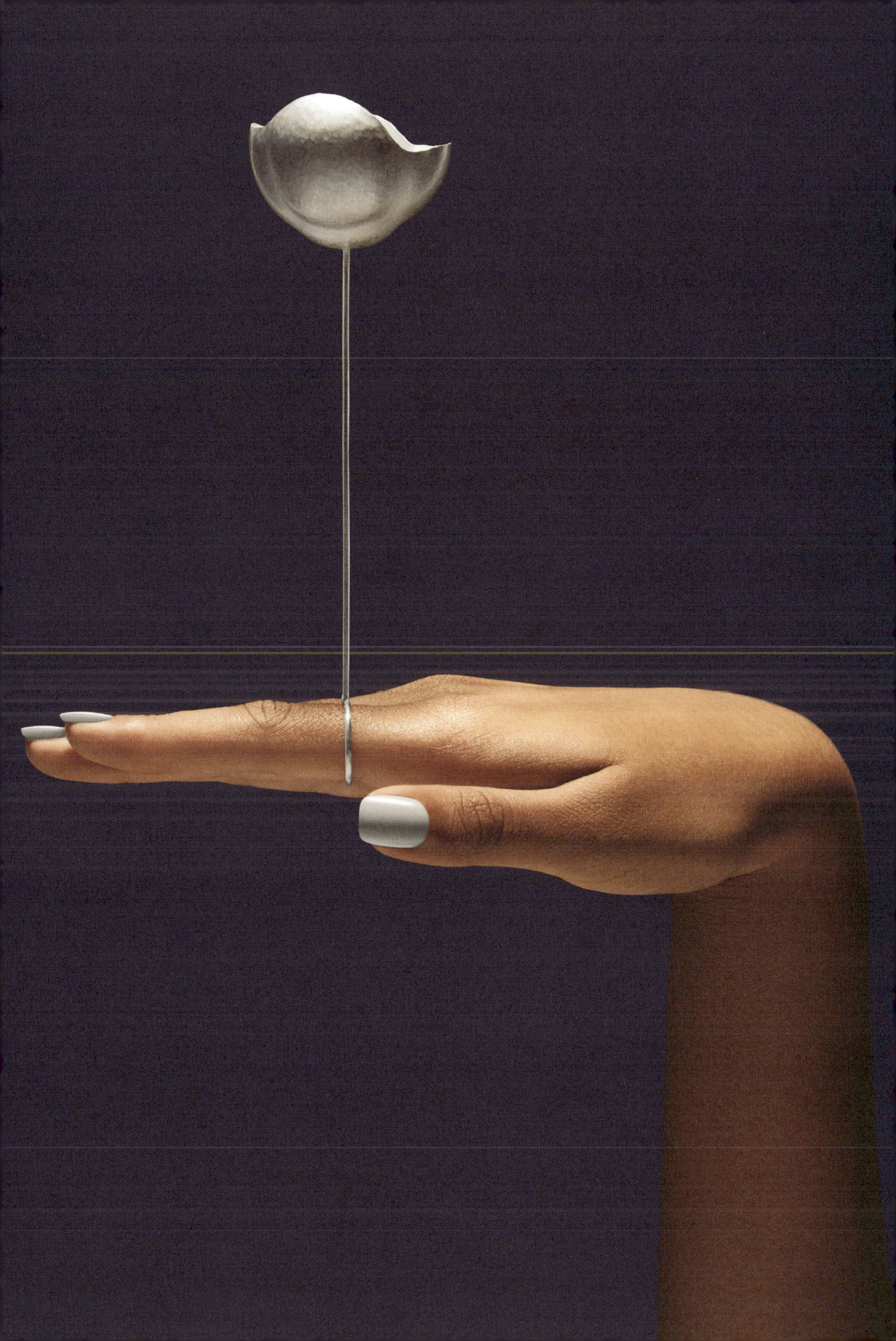

Hadley Stambaugh: Being a Chameleon

HADLEY'S SHARP CURATORIAL EYE AND SWIFT
CREATIVE PROBLEM-SOLVING CONSISTENTLY
ELEVATE EVERY IMAGE SHE IS A PART OF CREATING.

Siobhan Bonnouvrier, *Senior Creative Director of Visual Media, Savannah College of Art & Design*

HADLEY UNDERSTANDS THE FINER POINTS OF
COMPOSING A THOUGHTFUL IMAGE. SHE USES
THESE SKILLS IN HER CREATIVE DIRECTION TO
ACHIEVE THE HIGHEST QUALITY POSSIBLE WHILE
SUPPORTING HER TEAM THROUGH THE PROCESS.

Nick Berryman, *Photographer, Savannah College of Art & Design*

HADLEY MOVES WITH SHARP WIT, CREATIVITY,
AND EFFORTLESS CONFIDENCE. SHE SEES THE
BIGGER PICTURE WITHOUT MISSING THE SMALLEST
DETAILS, WEAVING INSIGHT AND INTENTION
INTO EVERYTHING SHE DOES.

Allison Smith, *Freelance Photographer & Visual Artist*

HADLEY BRINGS A KEEN PHOTOGRAPHER'S
EYE TO ART DIRECTION, LEADING TO SOME OF
THE MOST DYNAMIC AND VISUALLY COMPELLING,
NOT TO MENTION AMBITIOUS, PROJECTS I'VE
HAD THE PLEASURE TO WORK ON.

Jarred Joly, *Photo Retoucher, Savannah College of Art & Design*

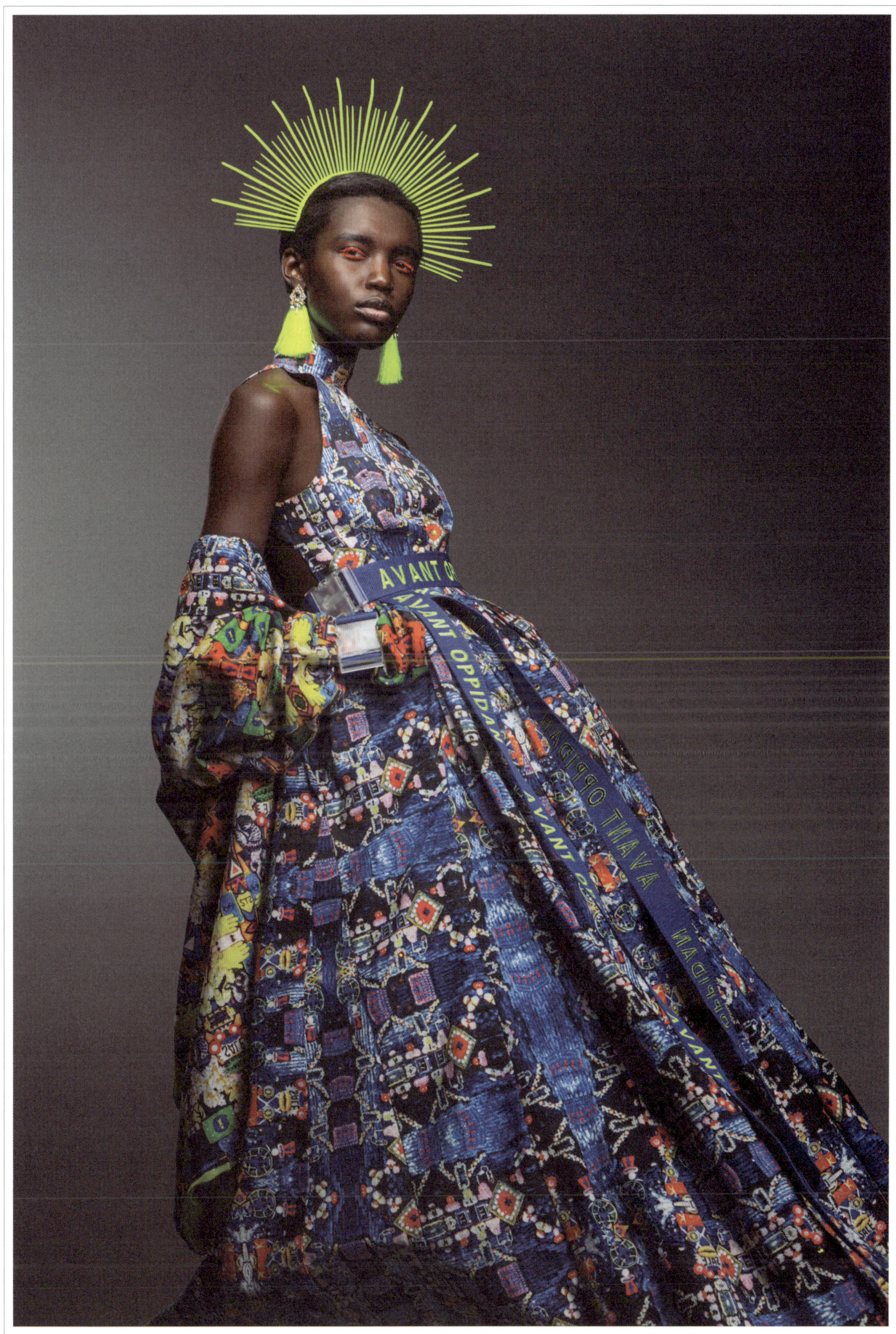

(Page 71) 2020 Fall Susan Grant Lewin Rings / (Above) 2019 Spring Fashion Show Lady Liberty

Introduction by **Paula Wallace** *Founder & President, Savannah College of Art & Design*

Hadley embodies the creative brilliance and entrepreneurial savoir-faire we expect of every graduate of the SCAD School of Visual Communication, with a boundless dedication to her profession and a precisely tuned eye that evokes the unseen. Her professors recall Hadley as a creative force in the classroom, challenging herself to articulate her ideas with passion, clarity, and a love for the enduring beauty of even the most fleeting forms. Her flourishing career in fashion photography was born at SCAD, home to one of the world's elite fashion schools, with a runway show every spring that draws every eye in the industry. Inspiration lives at SCAD! It's no surprise that Hadley's professional accolades just keep piling up. A photogenic career, any way you look at it.

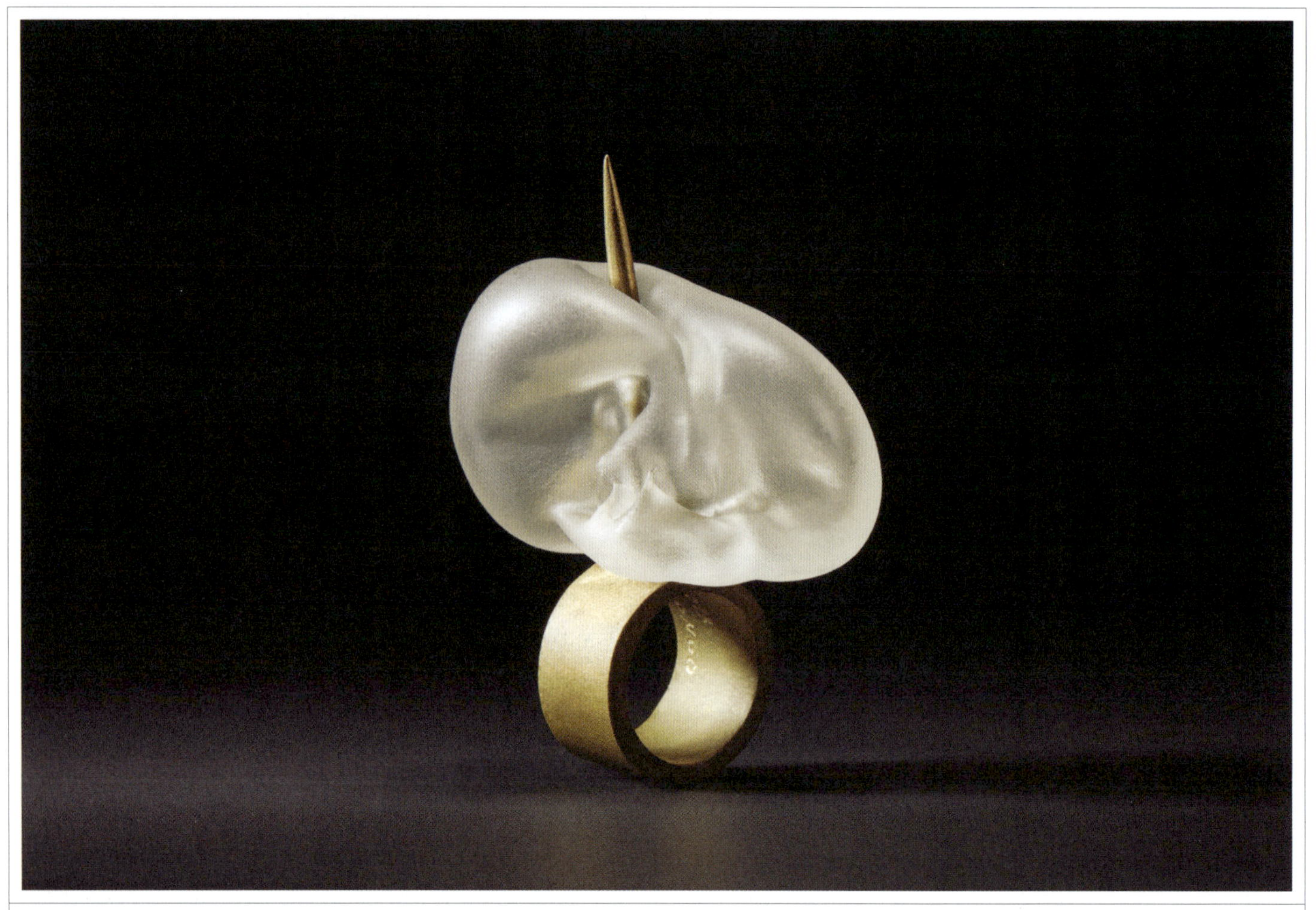

2020 Fall Susan Grant Lewin Rings

LEARNING TO ADAPT TO DIFFERENT ENVIRONMENTS, TIMELINES, AND EVEN CREW EXPECTATIONS CAN BE CHALLENGING IN A GOOD WAY. IT'S BEST FOR GROWTH.

Hadley Stambaugh, *Photographer & Creative Director, Savannah College of Art & Design*

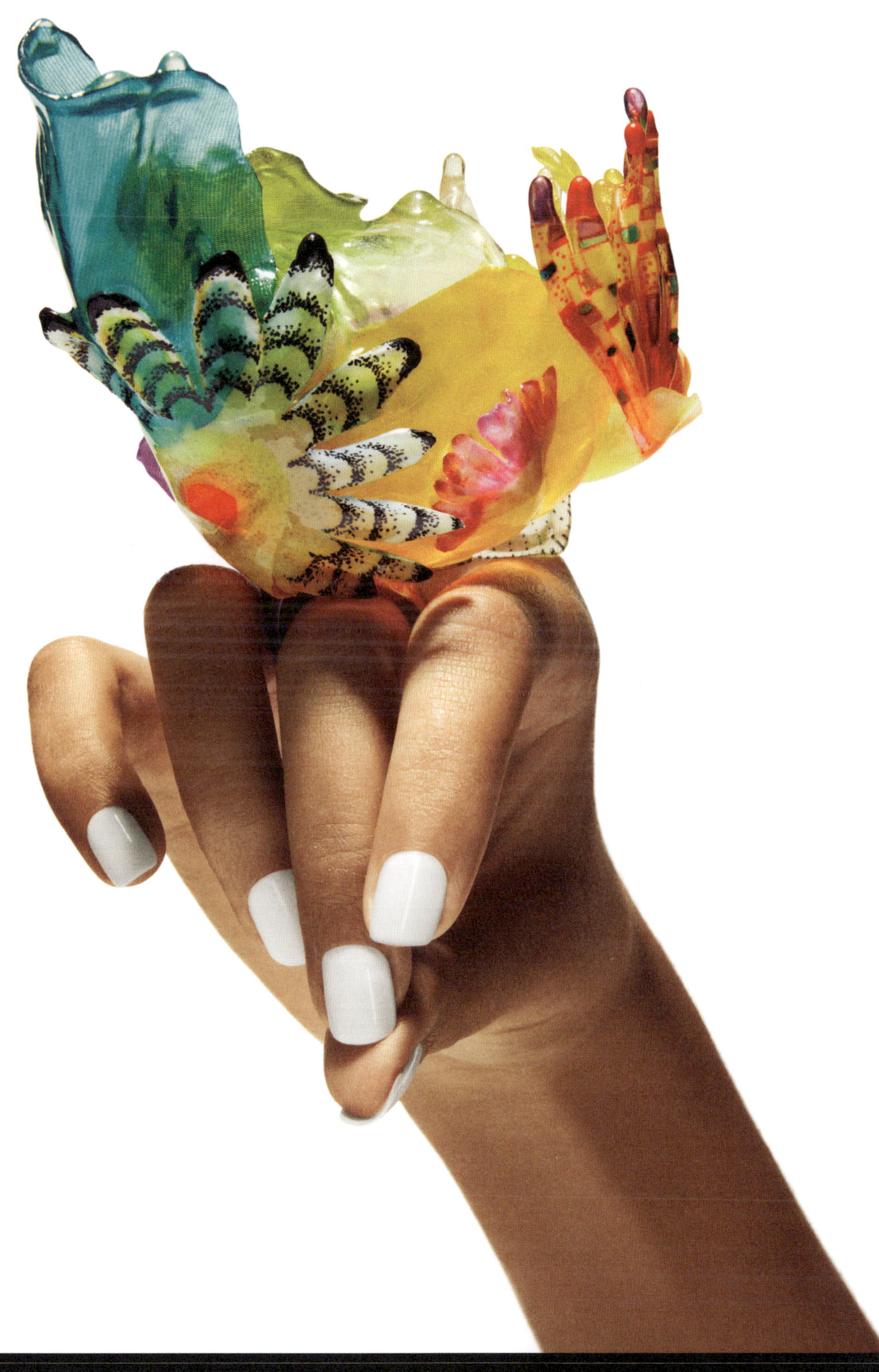

What has inspired or motivated you in your career?
I love sculpting light.

What is your work philosophy?
It takes a village to create the smallest idea; everyone contributes equally.

Who is or was your greatest mentor?
My fellow photographers/crew that I worked with throughout my career. Every set is an opportunity to learn from and create with a multitude of individuals.

What is it about photography that you're most passionate about?
I love visual storytelling and matching a client's ideas and identity. A still can grab someone's attention longer than most forms of media.

What is your favorite type of photography to shoot?
I love a good environmental portrait. It's like a visual puzzle.

What is the most difficult challenge you've had to overcome to reach your current position?
Each set comes with its own challenges and needs. Truthfully, learning to adapt to different environments, timelines, and even crew expectations can be challenging in a good way. It's best for growth. Being a chameleon to better fit the needs of a project is the best path forward.

Who have some of your greatest past influences been?
Most would quote certain photographers, but I love how movies are light and mixing light sources into my work, both as a creative director and photographer on projects.

What would be your dream assignment?
I would adore working with small brands.

What are the top things you need from a client in order to do successful work for them?
Communication, trust, and a good mood board always help.

Much of your photography work is for the Savannah College of Art & Design (SCAD). How did you start working for them, and what's it like working with a university?
I'd worked in New York City for some time and jumped around assisting in Los Angeles and Miami for small stints of time. I'd done some freelance work for SCAD when a position opened. I had fallen in love with Savannah as a home base city, so working full-time there made the most sense. I saw growth potential in the department and quickly learned a lot in the environment. I've adored working for them as a photographer, and now, as a creative director, I get to positively impact the lives of both the students I work with on projects and my crew, who are my colleagues. It's a dream position in a dream department. The pace of work really keeps me on my toes.

What do you consider your greatest professional achievement so far?
I have the pleasure of being published in *Vogue* and a book called *Ring Redux* with a fellow photographer, Colin Gray. I also feel a lot of gratitude when I see young professionals and alumni using my photographs in their portfolios. I love propelling people visually.

What about your work gives you the greatest satisfaction?
Seeing people get excited about the photos I produce and stretching my work or brand in unexpected ways.

What part of your work do you find the most demanding?
The balance of life and work can have a blurred line, especially when you love your environment, crew, mentors, and work like I do.

What professional goals do you still have for yourself?
I'd love to help grow small businesses and SCAD Alumni's branding eventually. I think SCAD has an amazing foundation of talented individuals who give to the creative world every year. It's exceptional to witness the growth of students and alumni alike.

What advice would you give to students starting out today?
Always ask for advice, but know what you are asking specifically. Try things on a small scale, then go big, and look out for potential problems with a workaround. Don't be afraid to work with large groups. As I said, it takes a village to grow and produce an idea.

What interests do you have outside of work?
I love camping, hiking, throwing pottery, mushroom foraging, consuming movies at an unreasonable rate, and reading/people-watching in parks. Life is fascinating.

What do you value most in life?
Time. You never get enough, and you can't earn it back.

What would you change if you had to do it all over again?
I would ask for help more often (even though I'm the stubborn one, moving heavy gear when I shouldn't).

Where do you find inspiration?
Life around me and reading stories. I often read books and wonder what that scene would look like in a photo.

How do you define success?
Comfort and pride in the work you do at the end of the day. Never leave a set feeling bad or like you didn't do your best.

Where do you see yourself in the future?
My ADHD has the hardest time planning for the future, so I can tell you that tomorrow, I will be at work, putting out what I like to call creative fires and building goals for the end of the year. Present moment living gives me balance.

How do you balance your work with your personal life if there is a distinction between the two for you?
I'm a workhorse at heart. I adore working, so in my 30s, I've tried to work on balance. Ask me in five years.

In what ways do you see your field changing over the years?
I see a lot more problem-solving via lighting and inspiration being pulled from a multitude of media. I also see a big shift in the quantity of photography created for social media consumption.

Savannah College of Art & Design www.scad.edu

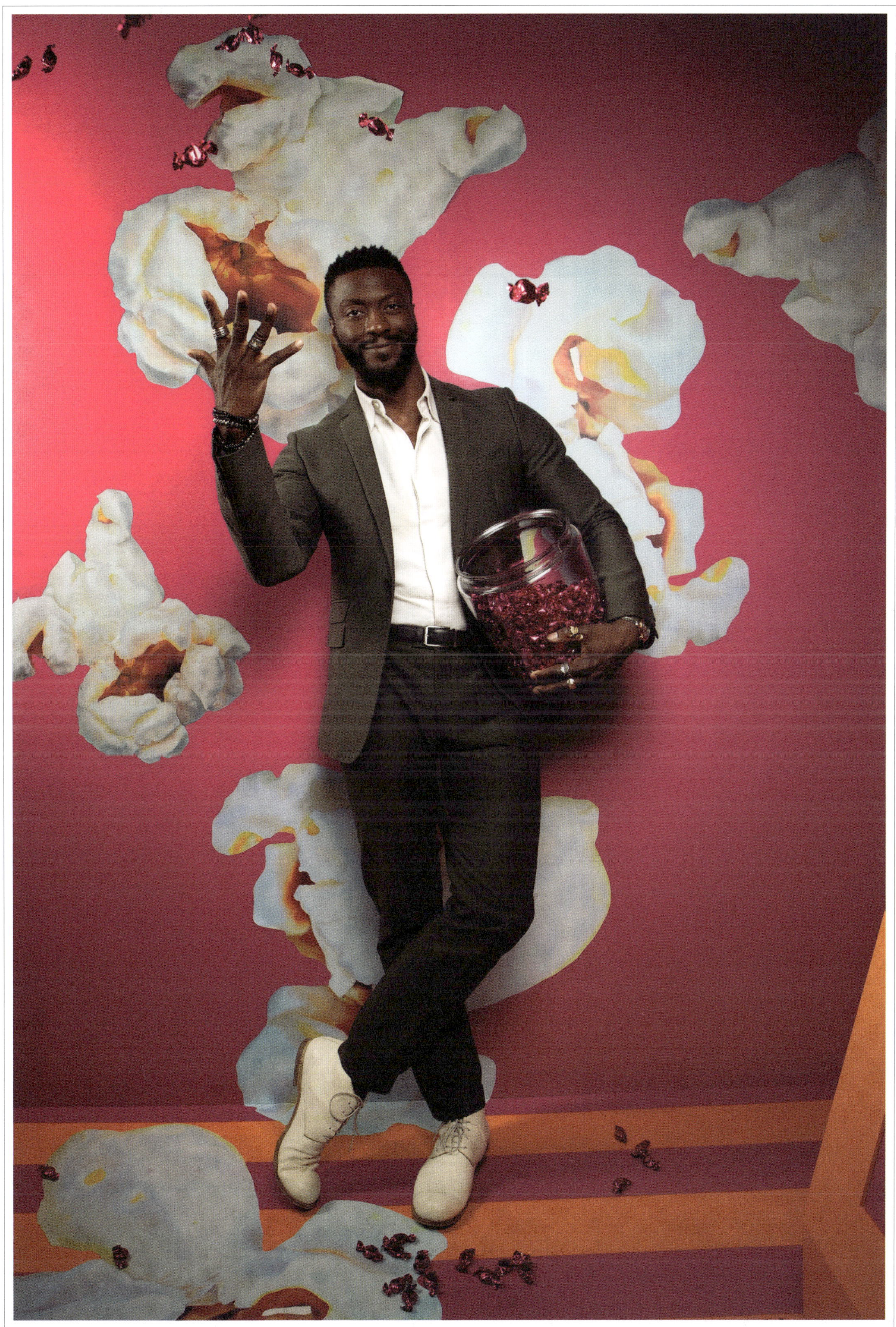

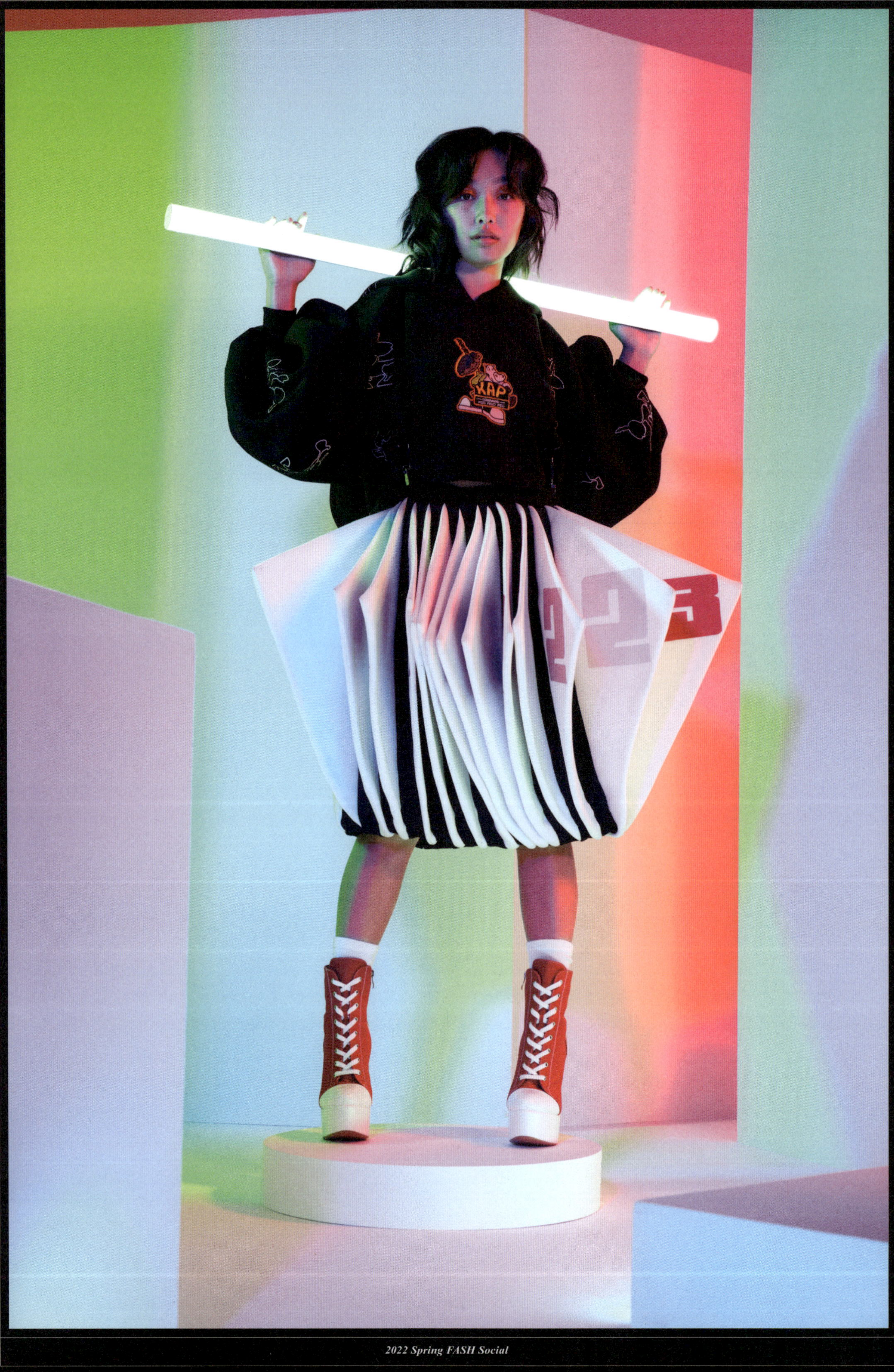

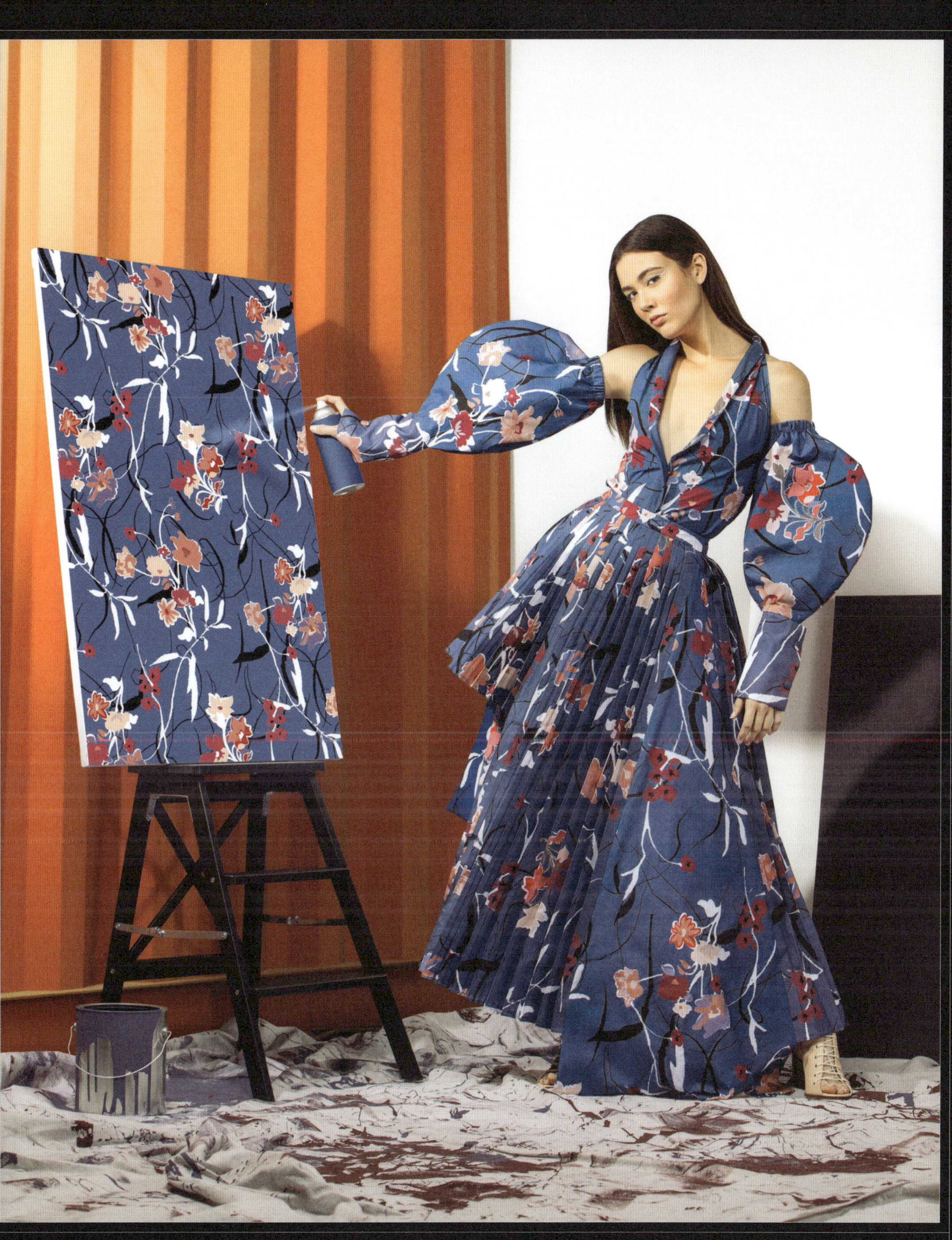

2019 Fall Supima Yoohyeon Kim

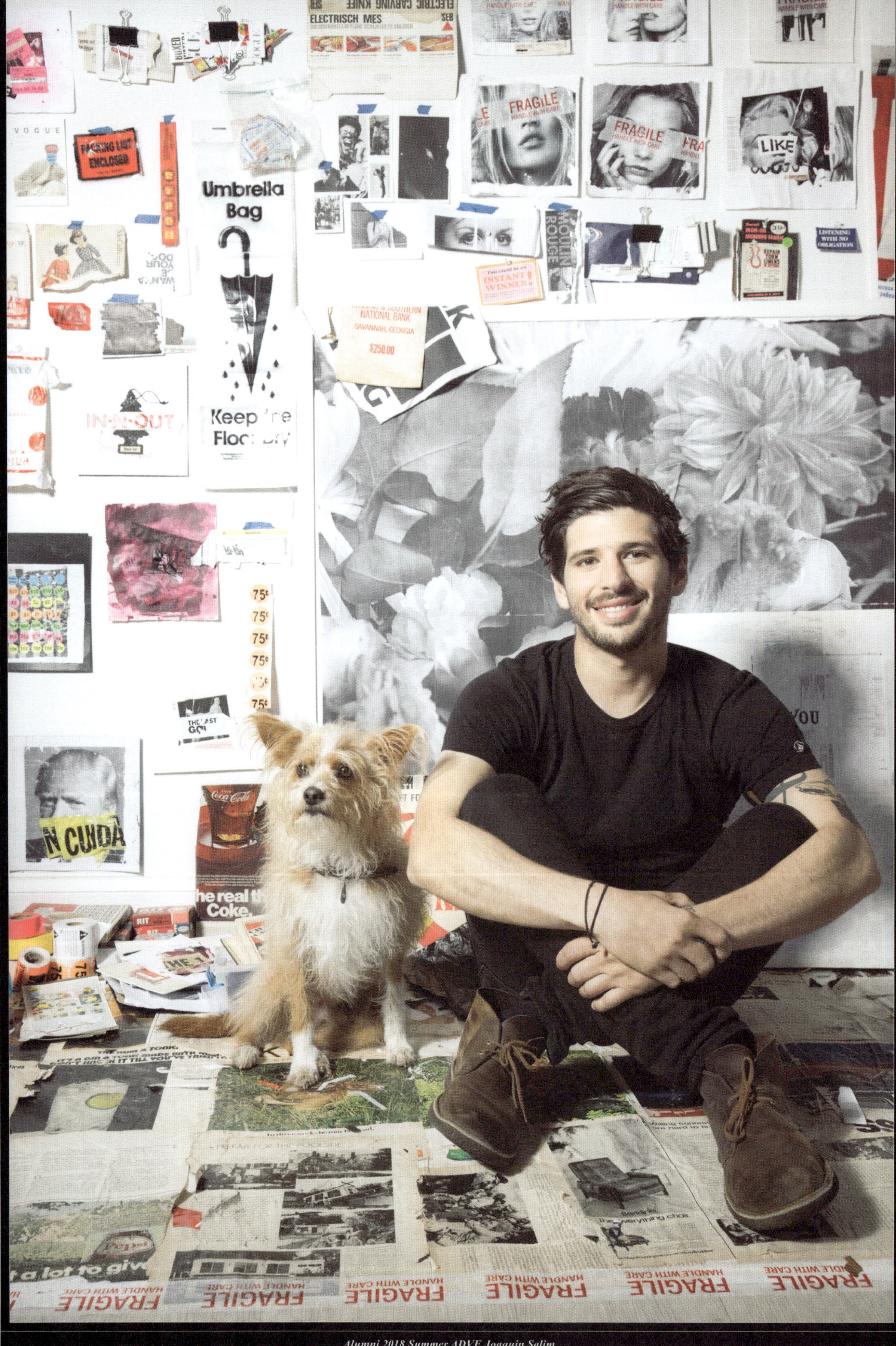

ELECTRIC CARVING KNIFE
FRAGILE HANDLE WITH CARE
Umbrella Bag
Keep the Floor Dry
IN-N-OUT
VOGUE
NATIONAL BANK
SAVANNAH, GEORGIA
$250.00
Coca-Cola
the real thing
Coke.
FRAGILE HANDLE WITH CARE

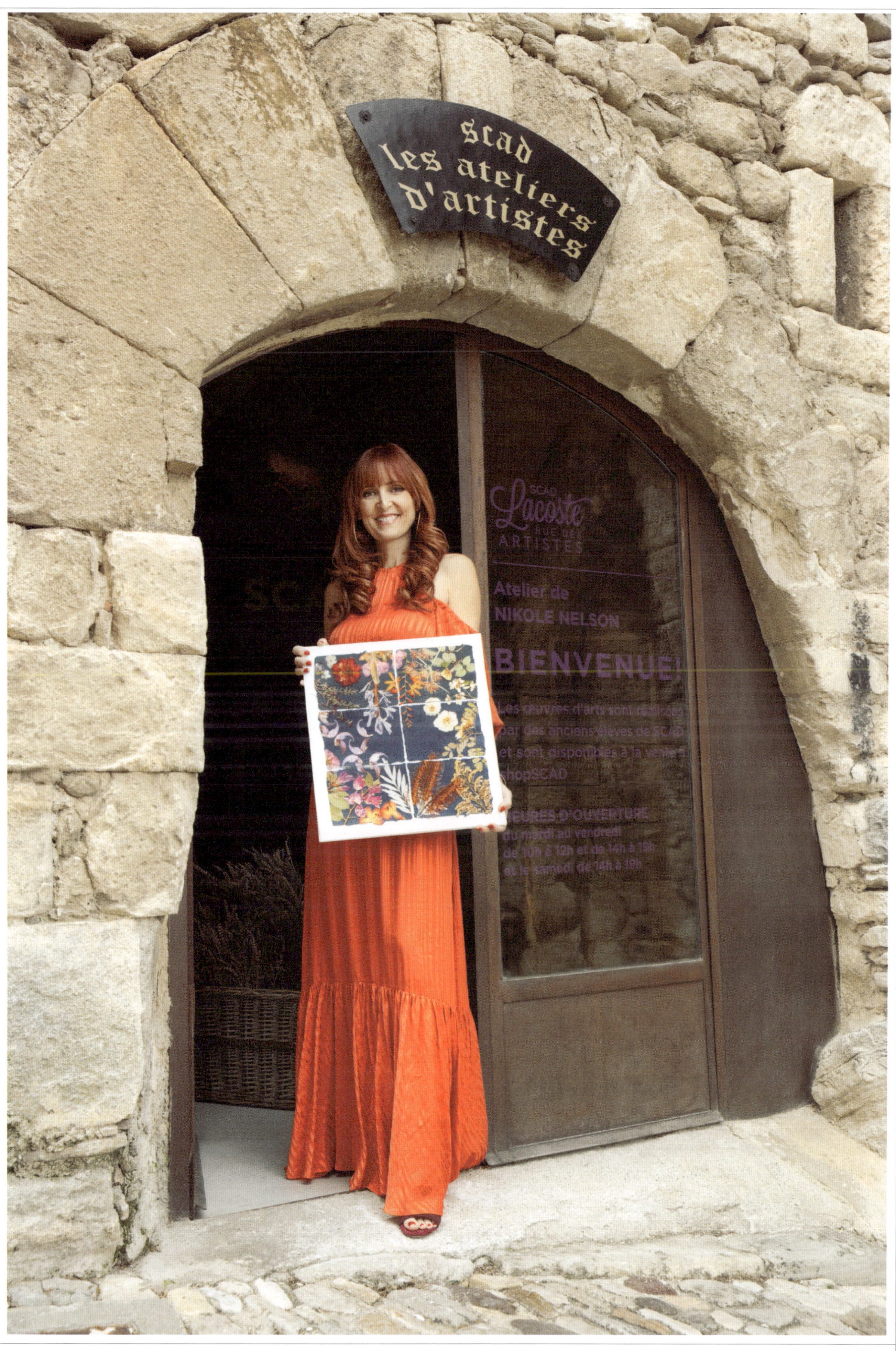

2022 Spring Atelier Nikole Nelson

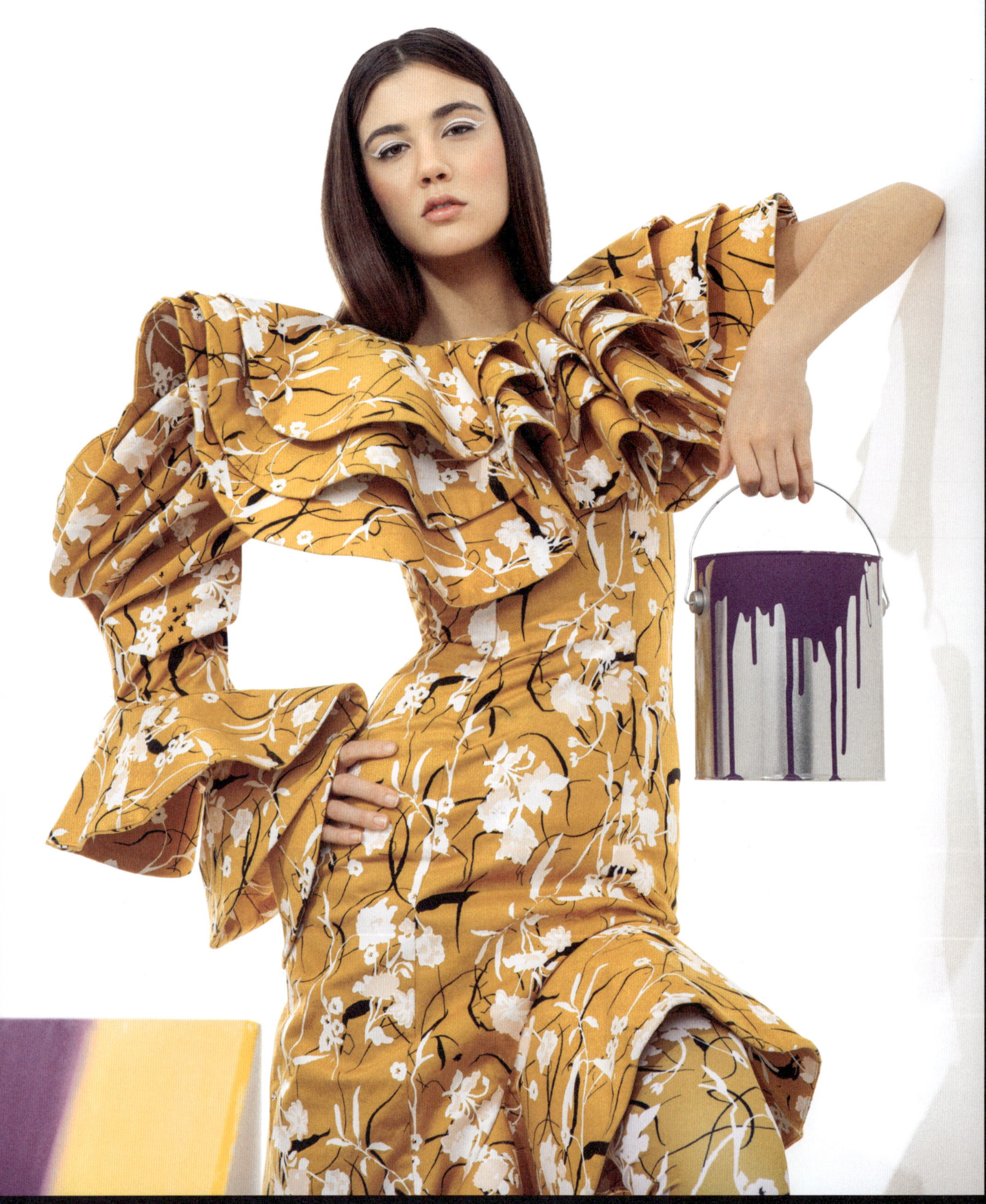

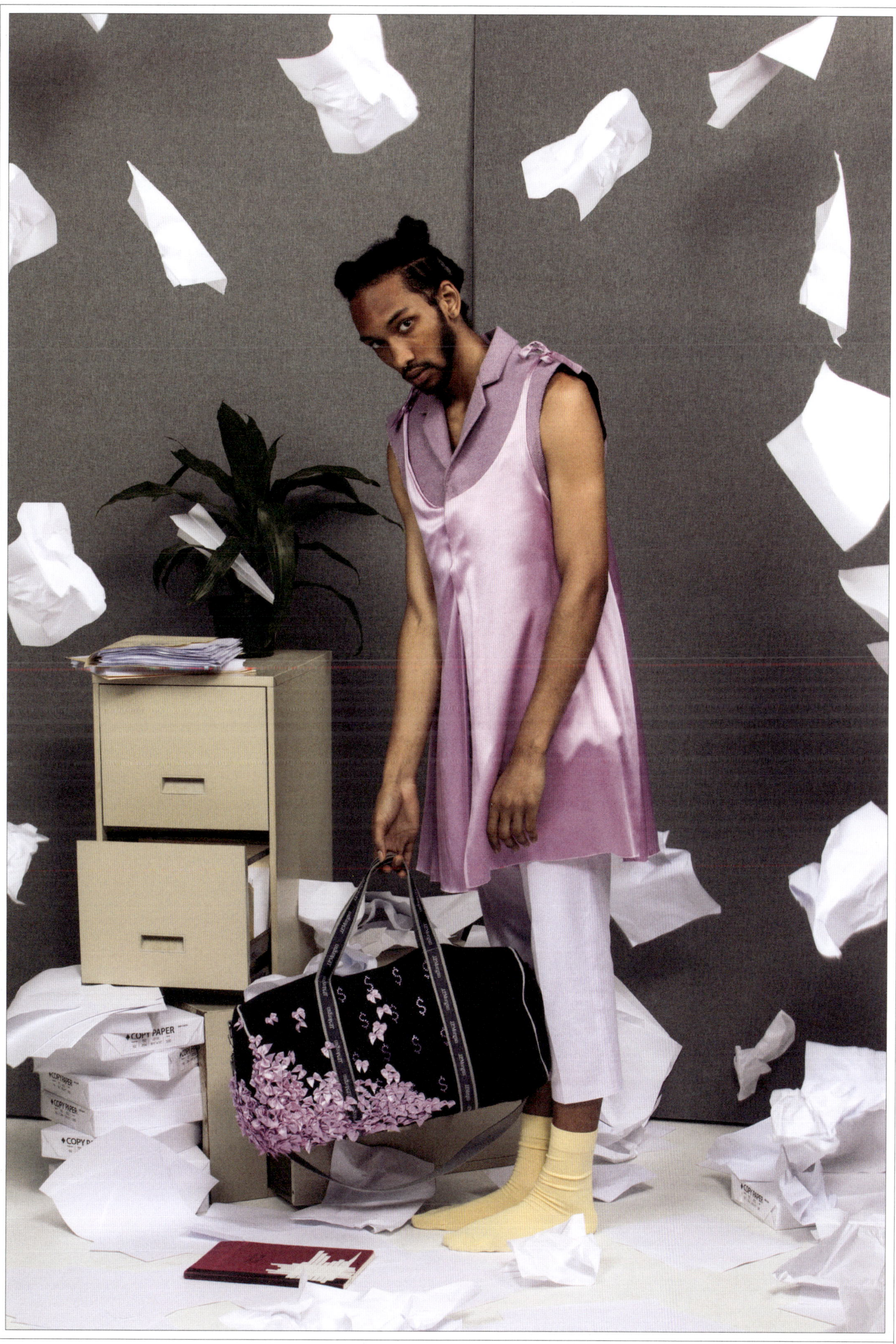

2018 Spring FASH LVMH Jackson Wrenn McCabe

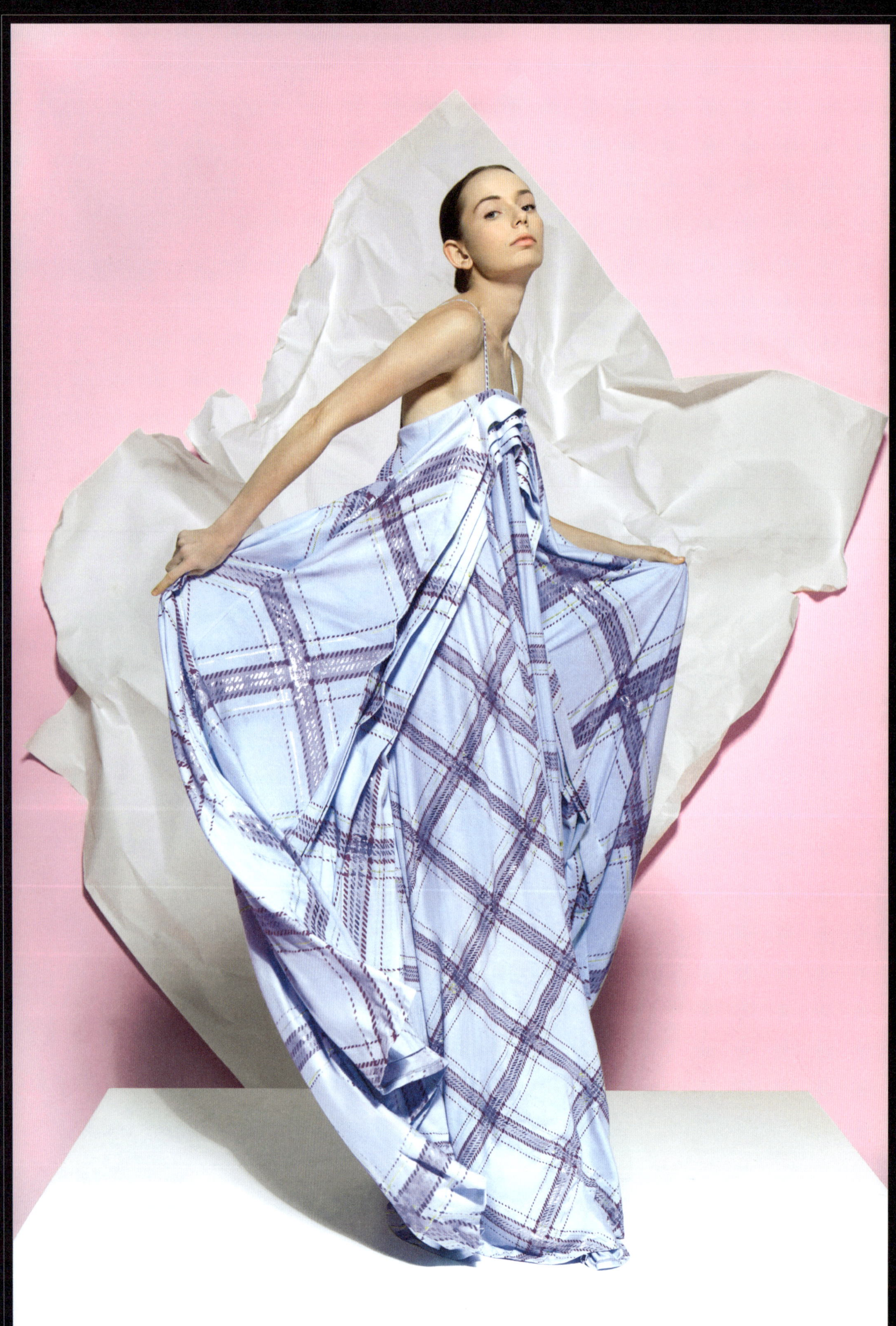

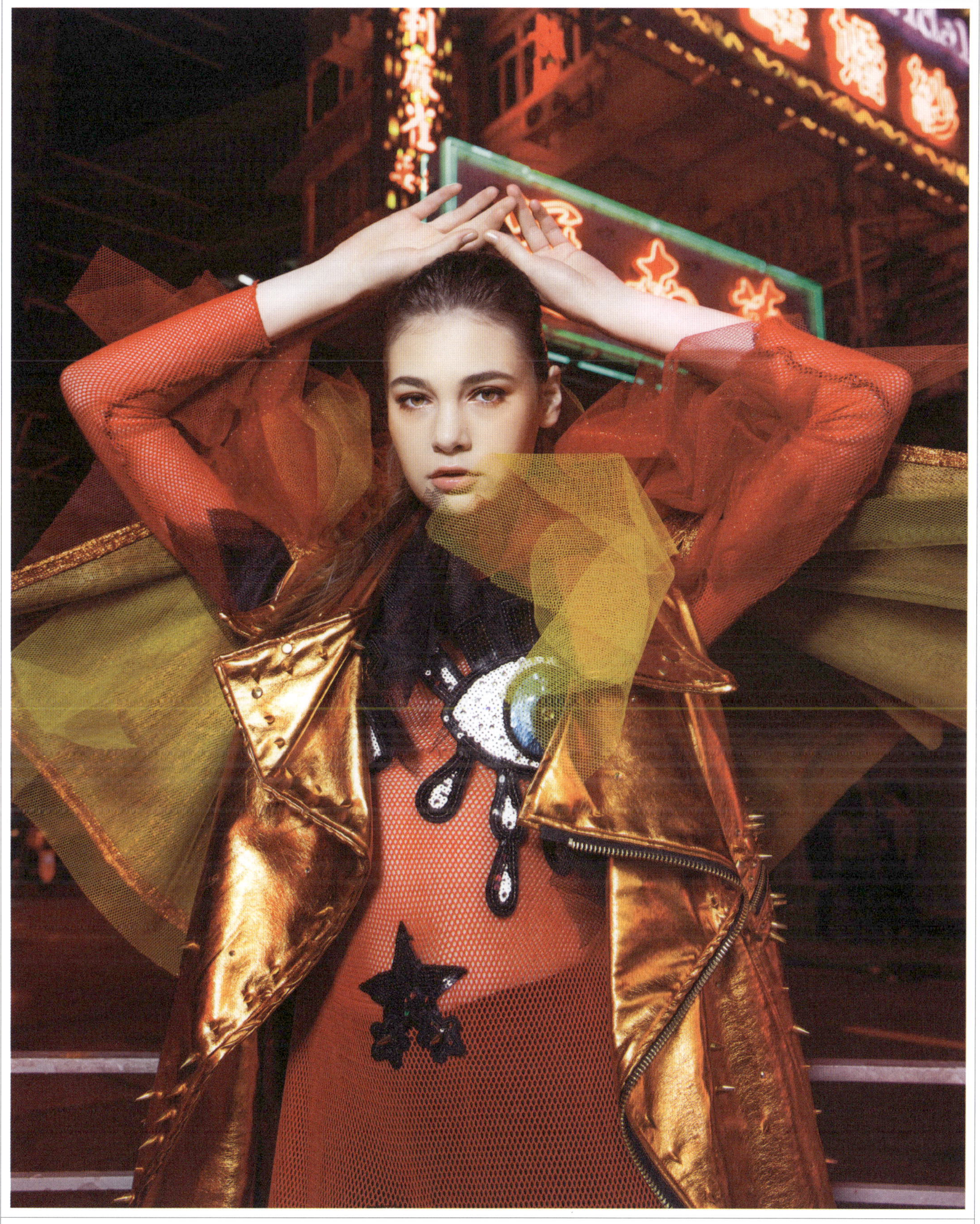

2020 Winter FASH Darren Apolonio

Scott Lowden: The Serendipity of Play

I HAVE KNOWN SCOTT FOR A LONG TIME.
HIS LIFESTYLE PHOTOGRAPHY IS EMBEDDED WITH
HIS AUTHENTIC EMOTIONAL CONNECTION TO
THE PEOPLE OR SITUATIONS HE PHOTOGRAPHS.
Parish Kohanim, *Photographer, Parish Kohanim Fine Art LLC*

SCOTT LOWDEN IS AN EXCEPTIONAL
PHOTOGRAPHER WHO EXPERTLY DIRECTS HIS
SUBJECTS, MAKES EVERY PROJECT SEAMLESS
AND FUN, AND DELIVERS STUNNING RESULTS!
Kristie Ray, *Regional Director of Mixed-Use Marketing & Brand Strategy, Hines*

WORKING WITH SCOTT LOWDEN IS FUN AND
EFFORTLESS. HE CONSISTENTLY DELIVERS
HIGH-QUALITY, PLAYFUL PHOTOGRAPHY THAT
CAPTURES A BRAND'S ESSENCE.
Koble Delmer, *Design Manager, Ashton Design*

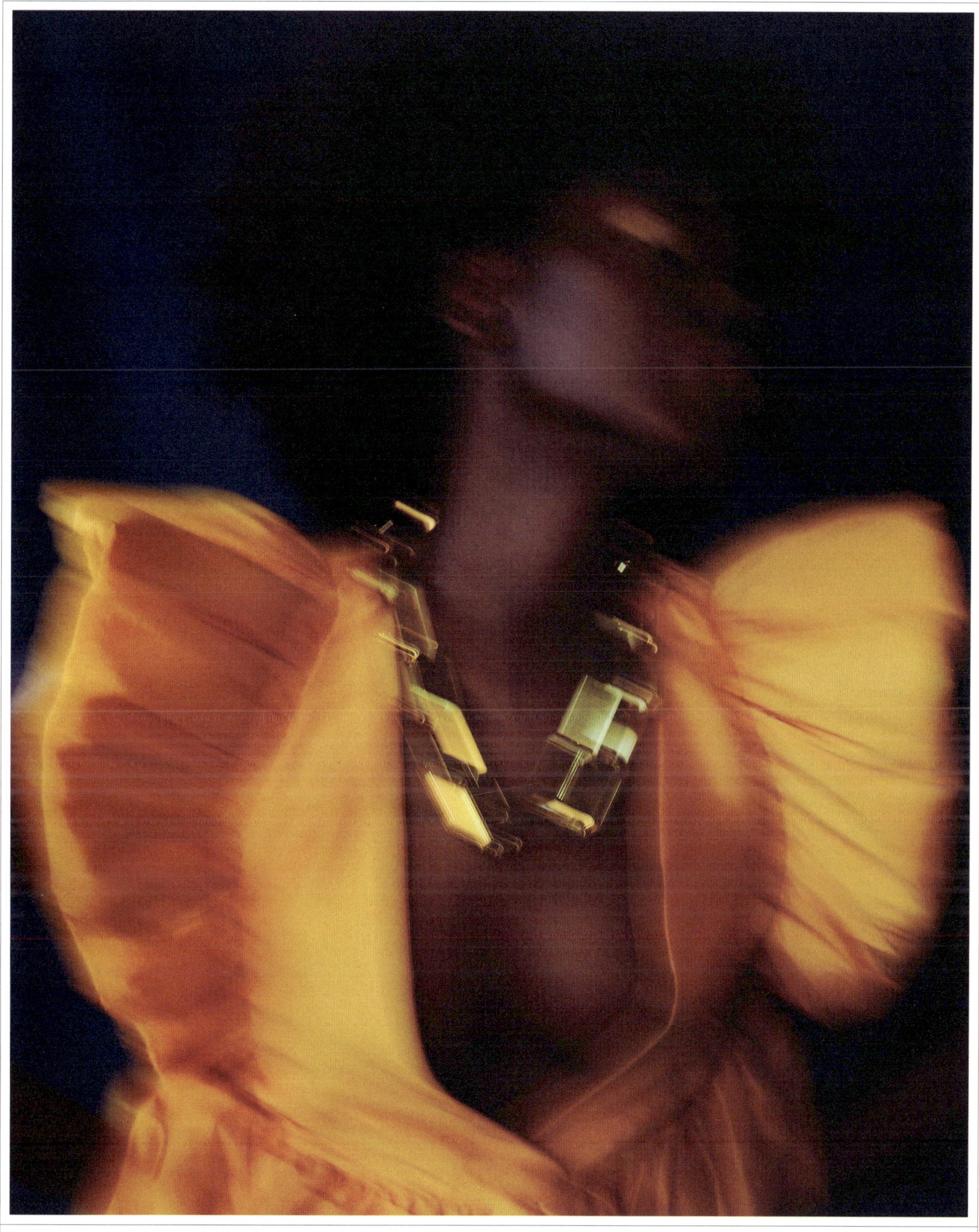

Title: Beauty – Motion, 2024. Client: Self-assigned. Creative Director: Wendy Lowden. Makeup: Destiny Curkendall. Hair: Sara Giraldo. Wardrobe: Jabe Mabrey.

How do you distill down an entire career of collaboration? Not easily, but happily. Scott has worked for me and my clients for over 30 years at various agencies, always bringing his eye, energy, and teamwork to every project, no matter how big or small. On the business side, budgets are always scrutinized by our clients, and Scott does an excellent job explaining everything clearly and managing the entire process seamlessly. He will find creative ways to make almost every budget work and ensure the production value remains high. In truth, Scott is my favorite photographer because he is an extension of our team in every way. And the many awards we have won together don't hurt either! I feel fortunate that our paths crossed early in our careers, and we have been able to "grow up" in this crazy business together. He is a friend and our agency's secret weapon, which turns out to be a winning combination.

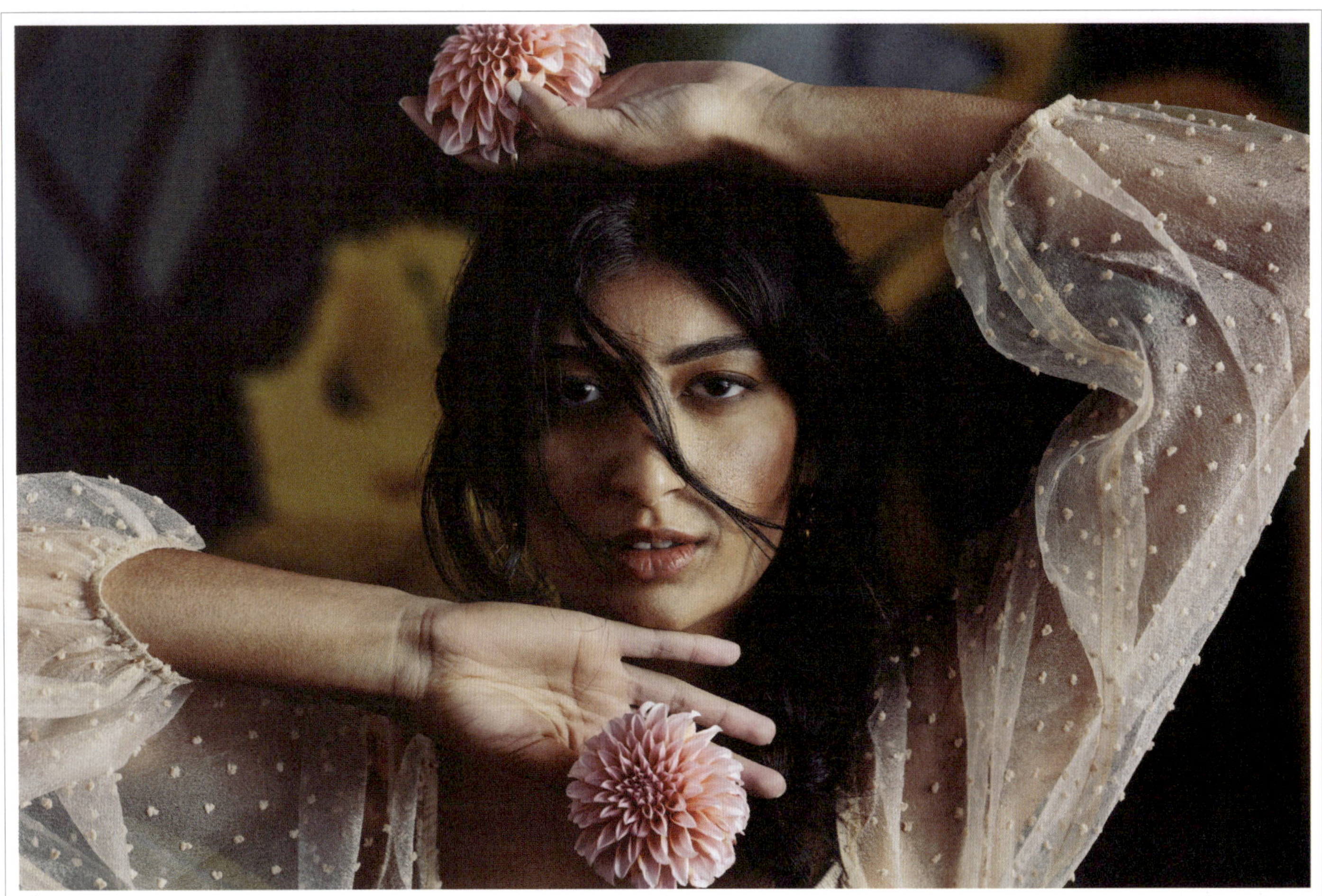

Title/Client: Fenton, 2022. Creative Director: Wendy Lowden. Makeup: Destiny Curkendall. Hair: Sara Giraldo. Wardrobe: Ray C'Mone.

Q&A: Scott Lowden

What has inspired or motivated you to have a career in photography?
What has inspired or motivated me has changed over the years. Earlier, I would have said that my inspiration was light and movement and capturing it in interesting, storytelling ways. But now, I'd say I'm much more inspired by people's mannerisms and faces… I love capturing the subtle changes in a person during a shoot, as well as our relationship, even if it's only for a few minutes at a time.

What is your work philosophy?
I tend not to lean on habits or formulas but look at every project with new eyes. Of course, it's impossible to avoid repeating setups that work, but the serendipity of being open to play can sometimes land on something amazing. Coming from a stereotypical Northeastern blue-collar family, my philosophy is to roll up my sleeves, get into every detail of a shoot, dive deep into an assignment no matter the budget, and keep the vibe positive.

Who is or was your greatest mentor?
Many people have contributed to my growth as a photographer, starting with Parish Kohanim, who I assisted early on. He taught me what advertising photography was all about, the preparation needed, and the flow of a shoot. Liz Von Hoene inspired me to always add style and whimsy to elevate a scenario. Robert Whitman, with his spontaneous nature, showed me that I can light

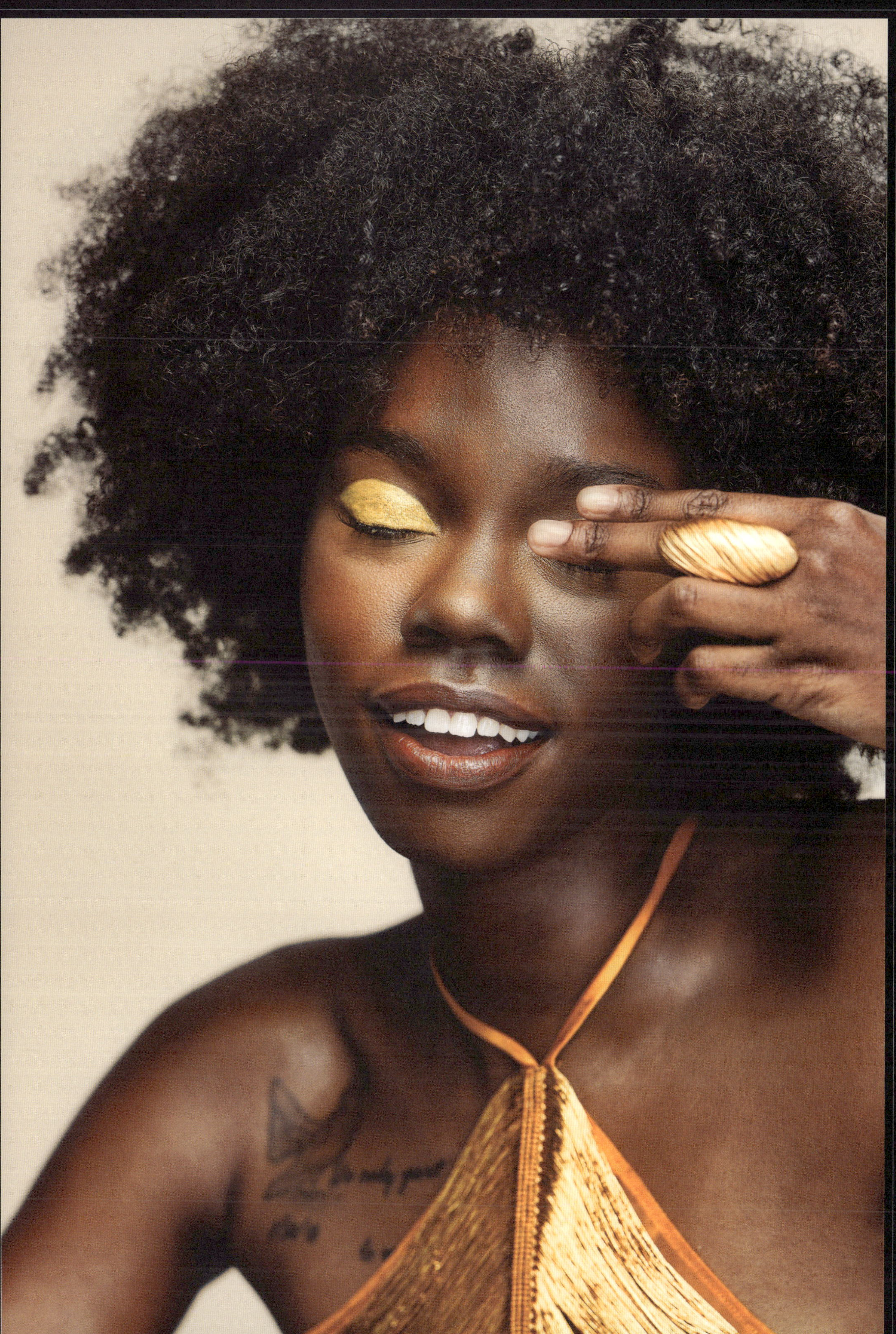

and direct any way I like, that set dynamics are important to creating a great image, and that a little motion blur couldn't hurt.

What is it about photography that you are most passionate about?
It's capturing a memory to revisit later or finding a scene's subtle, nuanced energy. It's capturing the magic of a specific place at a specific time… a sense of place. When some or all of those attributes come together, it's like, wow! It's the same whether it's assignment work or fine artwork.

What type of camera do you typically use, and why?
I've never really been a camera nerd; I go with what feels right for what I'm shooting. Over the years, I've used various cameras, starting with a Kodak 4x5 from an antique shop, then on to Nikon and the infallible F5, Mamiya RZ67, Contax 645, and the Leica M series. Now, the Canon R5 is my workhorse. It allows me to focus on directing the image and not worry about the tool I'm using. But I'm also loving the Fujifilm GFX100S II and hope to spend more time with it soon.

On your website, you describe your photography style as "life-fashionography." Would you explain this term further?
Yes! Life-fashionography best describes what I do. I love to walk the line between documentary and lifestyle, capturing the spirit of life with an eye for style. It's that authentic moment—you're wearing your favorite brand, and the sun is low and glowing. It's your best day ever. I trust collaboration, invention, and a dose of serendipity to help the viewer discover emotion and energy.

What is the most difficult challenge you've overcome to reach your current position?
I'd say the fact that advertising photography budgets are subject to the whims of financial markets. I've been making a living as a photographer long enough to have seen the dot-com crash and the financial crisis of 2008, and I'm still at it after the COVID-19 pandemic. Adjusting to varied production levels was a big challenge for me after 2008, when I reduced my full-time staff to one, and again when I finally gave up my studio in 2020. Of course, making great work for great clients isn't always dependent on the budget. I'm passionate about creating dynamic images, and I aim to get portfolio work from every shoot.

Who have some of your greatest past influences been?
I love Elliott Erwitt's ability to disarm his subjects and capture such authenticity, as well as Peter Lindbergh's seemingly effortless and dynamic images. Masao Yamamoto is great with the way he captures an image as it exists first, almost instinctively, before making changes to what he's shooting or changing angles. I also like Lillian Bassman and how she somehow captured energy in a still image.

Who among your contemporaries today do you most admire?
It shifts over the months, but today, it's Nadav Kander. I love that his assignment work is like fine art and his eloquent way of talking about image-making.

What would be your dream assignment?
I love a long-term project where I can dive into a topic or brand—preferably one that positively impacts society or our natural environment—where I have time to revisit the story again and again and not be rushed by deadlines or budgets, and where I can capture each scenario at just the right time of day rather than when it fits into a schedule. And, of course, it should be somewhere sunny…

Who have been some of your favorite colleagues or clients?
I really do believe that photography is a team sport. I rely on everyone on set to help me push my ideas and bring the images to fruition. However, one colleague stands out: Keith Martin, who was my full-time assistant, digital tech, and confidant for many years. Beyond supporting me, he helped me develop my craft and vision.

And favorite clients! Of course, my creative partner, Wendy Lowden, who works at the agency House of Current. We've created a pile of great work together for many years. We're constantly pushing to get the most interesting and dynamic images out of whatever creative brief we're trying to fill, such as our work for the Royal Hawaiian Center, which continues to take me to Waikiki and challenges me to get closer to that perfect image on each shoot. Also, the work I did for Kodak film was super fulfilling and a blast, especially seeing the pictures on black and white film packaging.

What are the top things you need from a client to do successful work for them?
That's an easy one. To create successful work for a client, I need a clear brief, a partnership mentality, and trust. A good budget helps but isn't the most important ingredient. It's so satisfying looking at the images with a client during the shoot and knowing we've nailed it.

What do you consider your greatest professional achievement so far?
For a few years, I created work with Kodak. It feels like a career achievement to be trusted to develop advertising and packaging for the Kodak brand.

What about your work gives you the greatest satisfaction?
Collaboratively solving creative challenges and delivering images that exceed a client's expectations. There can be so many challenges, even with the simplest of projects. When we've overcome rain, equipment failures, and power outages and still create images to be proud of, it's a good day.

What part of your work do you find the most demanding?
Preproduction and planning are the most demanding but are also necessary for a smooth and creative shoot. Well… that and marketing. I'd much rather be shooting than marketing myself. I'm inherently bad at talking about my work, which I continue working on.

What professional goals do you still have for yourself?
Commercially, I have a few brands that I'd love to work with. For some reason, I'm super into kitchens at the moment. Honestly, my goals are pretty simple: to work with good people to create great work.

Outside of assignment work, a big goal is continuing to commit time to fine artwork. Coming from a mainly commercial background, putting energy into fine art projects where there's no guarantee that I'll walk away with anything good is tough. But that's where the process is so valuable, even if I toss most of the images. Those creative exercises are satisfying and can really inform my commercial work. And, of course, like most photographers, I'd love to have a solo show as well as a book or three.

You have self-published several books and mail art projects such as Sentiment Del Lugar, Peru and Sentiment Del Lugar, Mexico. How did you get into self-publishing?
While I'd love to have my work seen on a larger scale by partnering with an established publisher, self-publishing seems al-

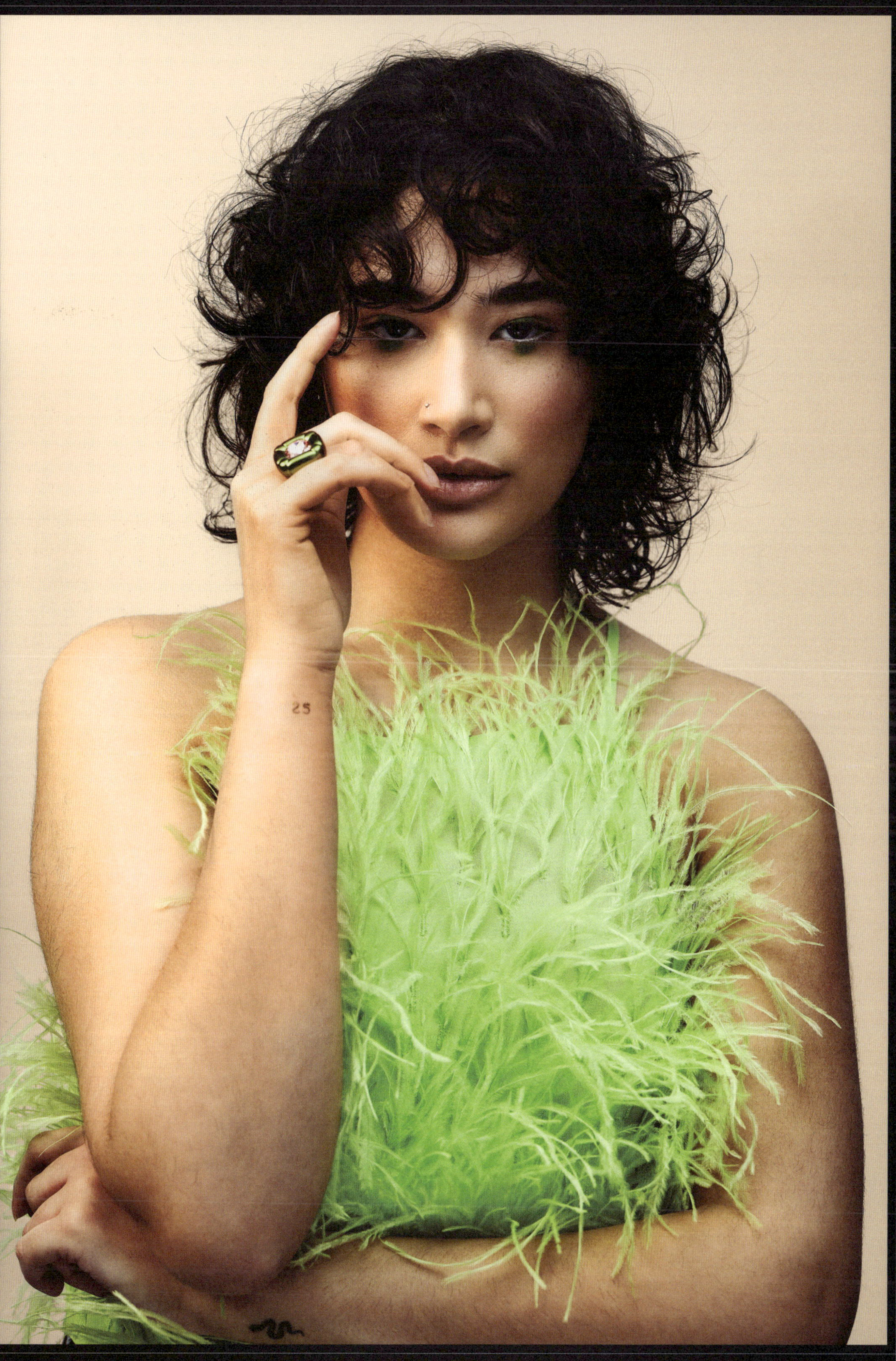

Title: Beauty – Motion, 2024. Client: Self-assigned. Creative Director: Wendy Lowden. Makeup: Destiny Curkendall. Hair: Sara Giraldo. Wardrobe: Jabe Mabrey.

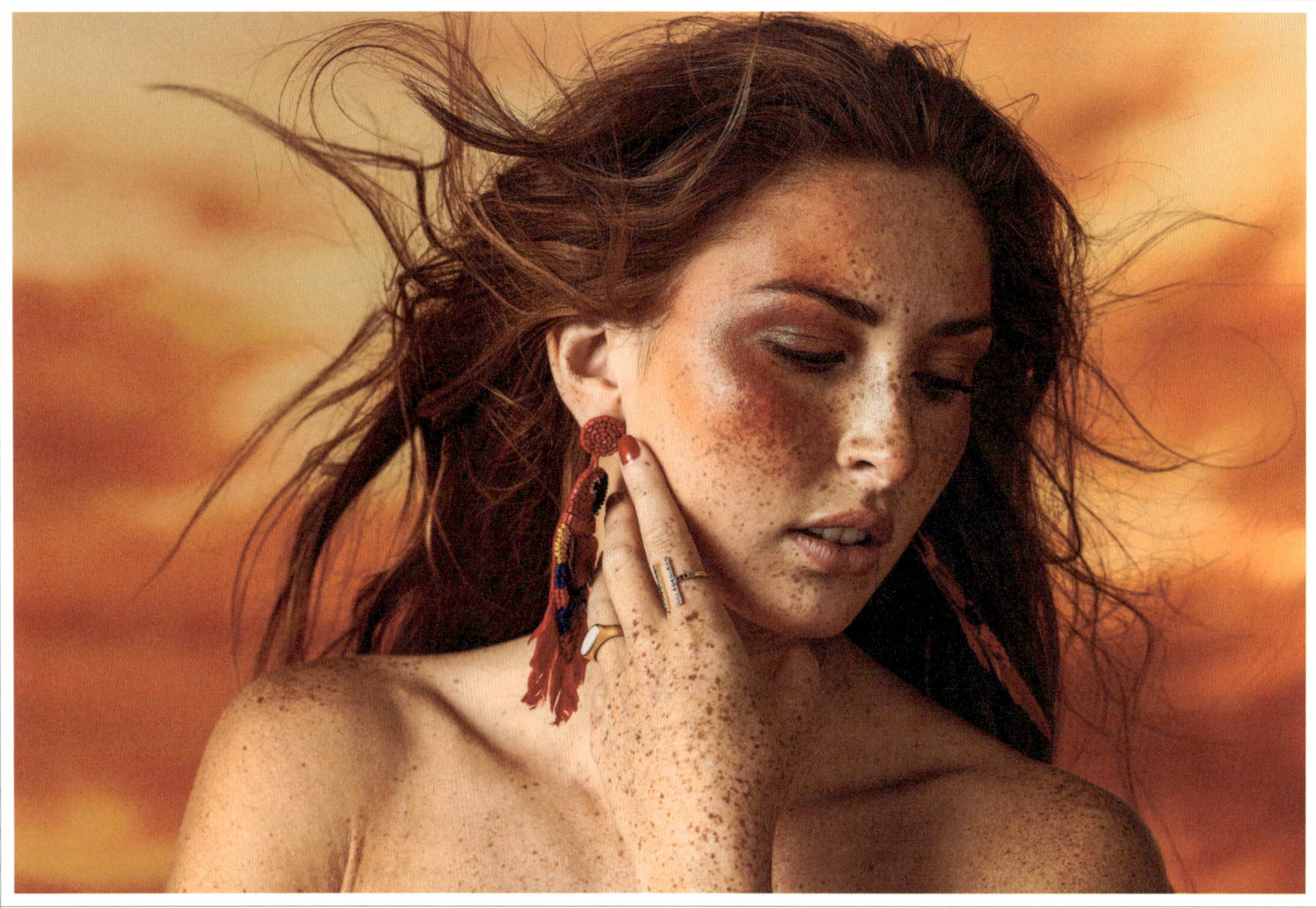

Title/Client: Atlantic Station. Creative Director: Wendy Lowden. Wardrobe: Ray C'Mone. Makeup: Piper Von Hoene.

most an obligation and a necessary way to share the images. Beyond a website, the process of compiling images for a printed piece—the pagination as storytelling—is a satisfying way to do justice to the images. My favorites are short newsprint pieces telling one tight story.

What advice would you give to students starting out today?
I have a few things for students starting out today. Be aware that styles change, so make sure you have an element of authenticity and truth in your images. Creating engaging photos is easy; making a living in photography is all about perseverance and teamwork. There are many ways to put a shoot together, so try to learn from as many different photographers as you can by assisting. Put together a peer group to inspire, and lastly, always be shooting.

What interests do you have outside of work?
It used to be long-distance mountain biking, but that takes its toll! Now, it's yoga, traveling as much as possible, and keeping my 100-year-old home from looking 100 years old.

What would you change if you had to do it all over again?
I would have believed in myself earlier and not worried about the impostor syndrome that we all have from time to time.

Where do you find inspiration?
I find it difficult to answer this question without sounding corny. I'd say I find inspiration in light, mannerisms, and our natural and built environment. And those in-between moments.

Where do you see yourself in the future?
Wow, I plan to continue making images for clients for as long as they'll have me. However, I also want to continue creating more fine artwork and sharing it with a larger audience.

How do you balance your work with your personal life if there is a distinction between the two for you?
Of course, the lines blur, but there is definitely a distinction between work life and personal life. I'm much fresher and more inspired after time spent pursuing other creative interests. I used to always carry a camera, but now it's with more intention. Even when traveling, it's sometimes better to simply experience a place than to capture a postcard version of it.

How do you define success?
To be busy enough, but not too busy.

In what ways do you see your field changing over the years?
There's a much lower barrier to entry to being a professional photographer now than when I began, which is both good and bad. The democratization of who can be a photographer is certainly beneficial in showcasing more varied points of view. The explosion of quality photographers can be tough for those who have been making images longer, but it also inspires us to stay fresh and to have something to say.

Another change I've seen and continue to see is the reduction of value that clients place on photography. While some clients recognize the impact that professional photography can bring to their brand, many are comfortable with low-production-value imagery. While that type of work has a place, in my opinion, it creates a sea of sameness and does little to elevate a brand or message.

Scott Lowden Photography www.scottlowden.com

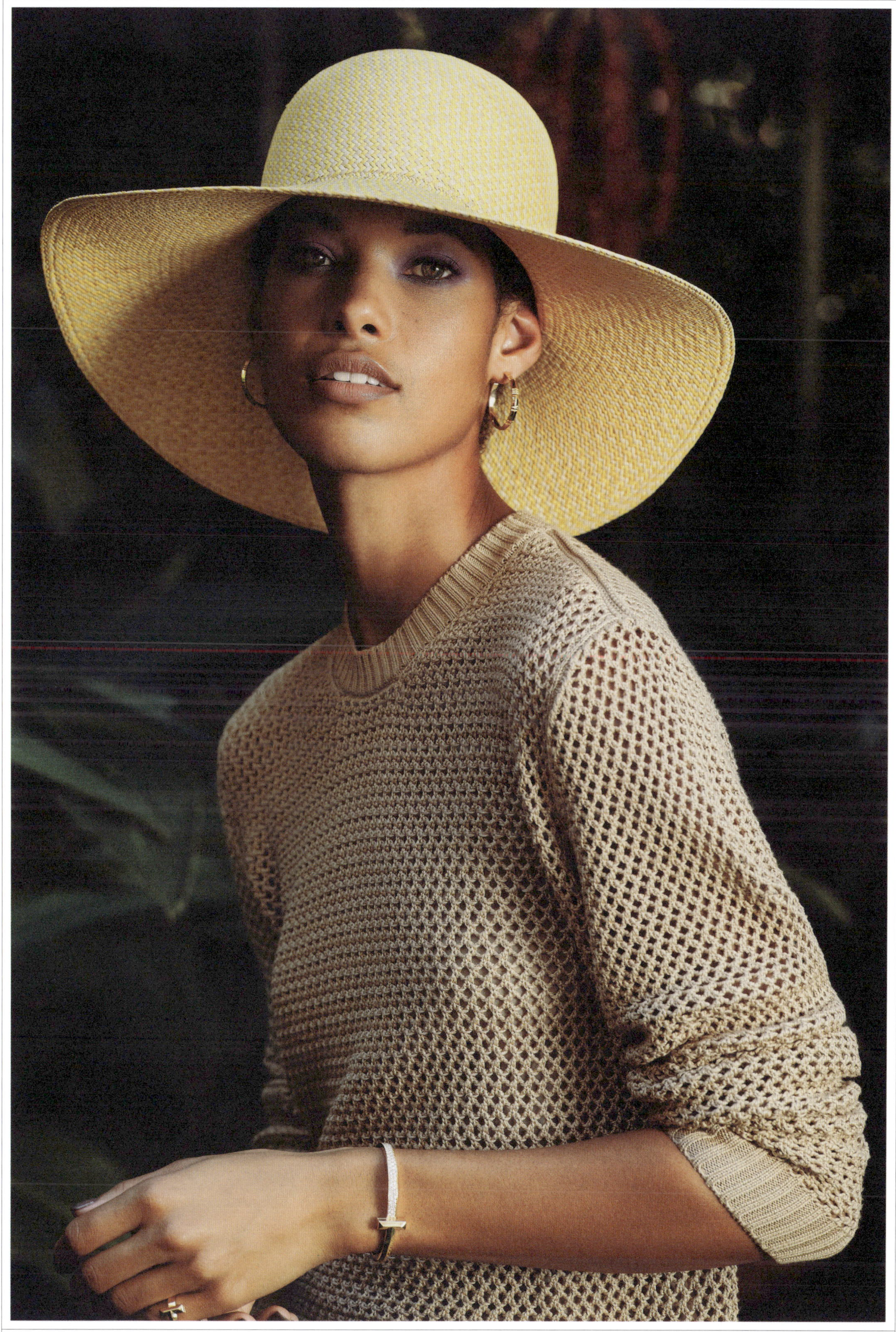

Title/Client: Royal Hawaiian Center, 2021. Creative Director: Wendy Lowden. Wardrobe: Rebecca Weinberg. Makeup Artist: Kecia Littman. Hair Stylist: Shaina Nakahara.

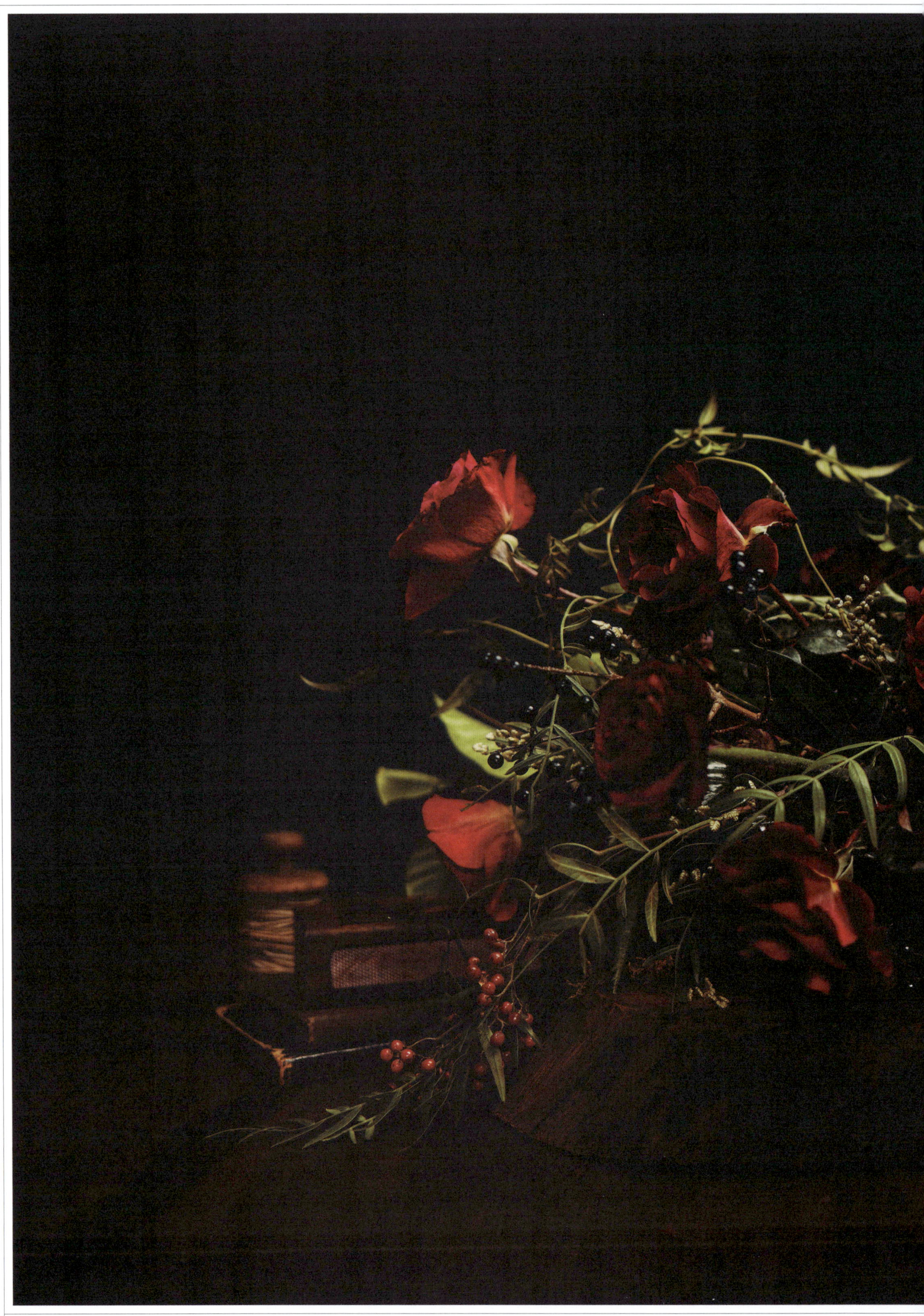

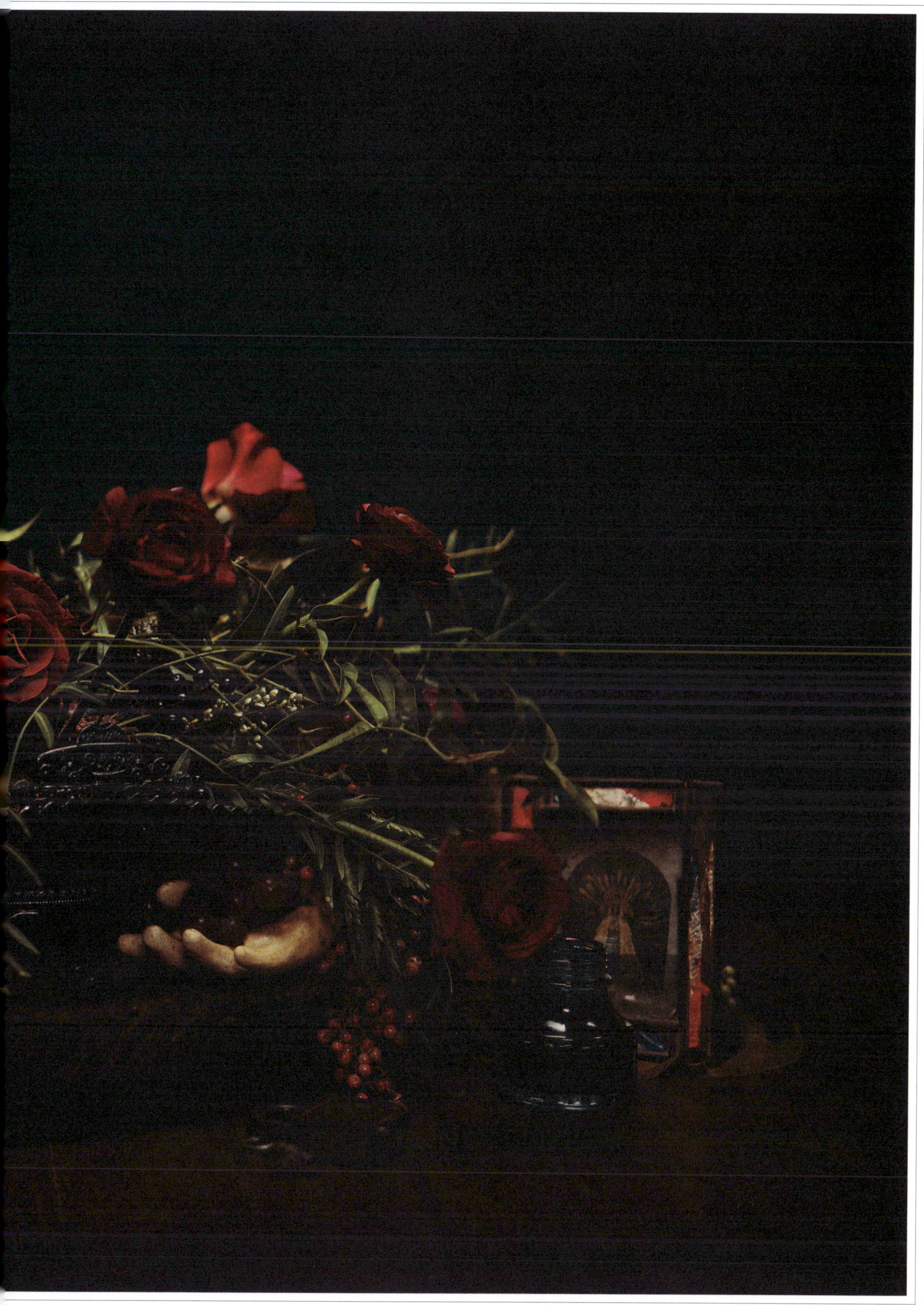

Title: Botanical No. 2. Client: Self-assigned. Floral Styling: Katie Benson.

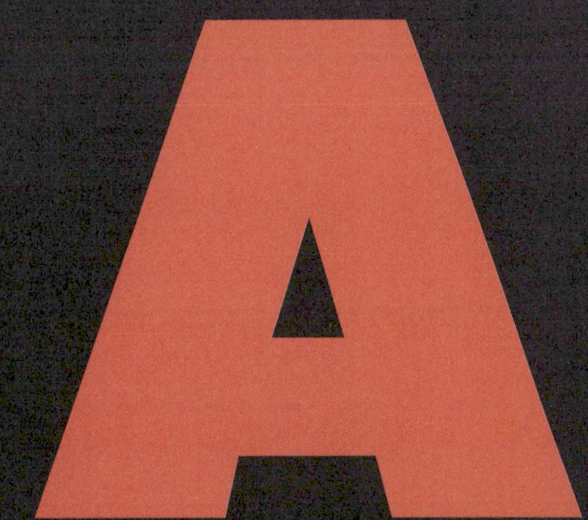

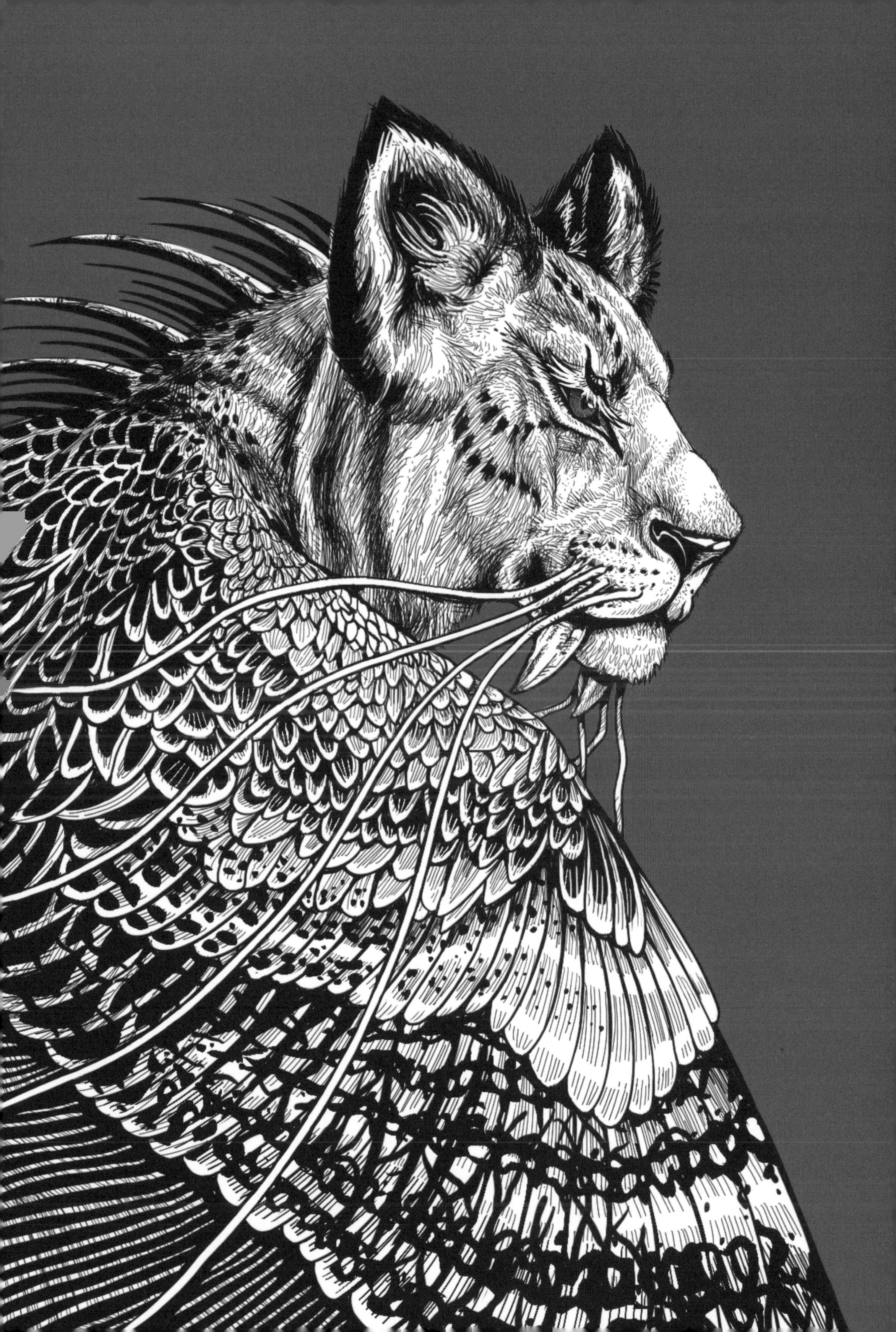

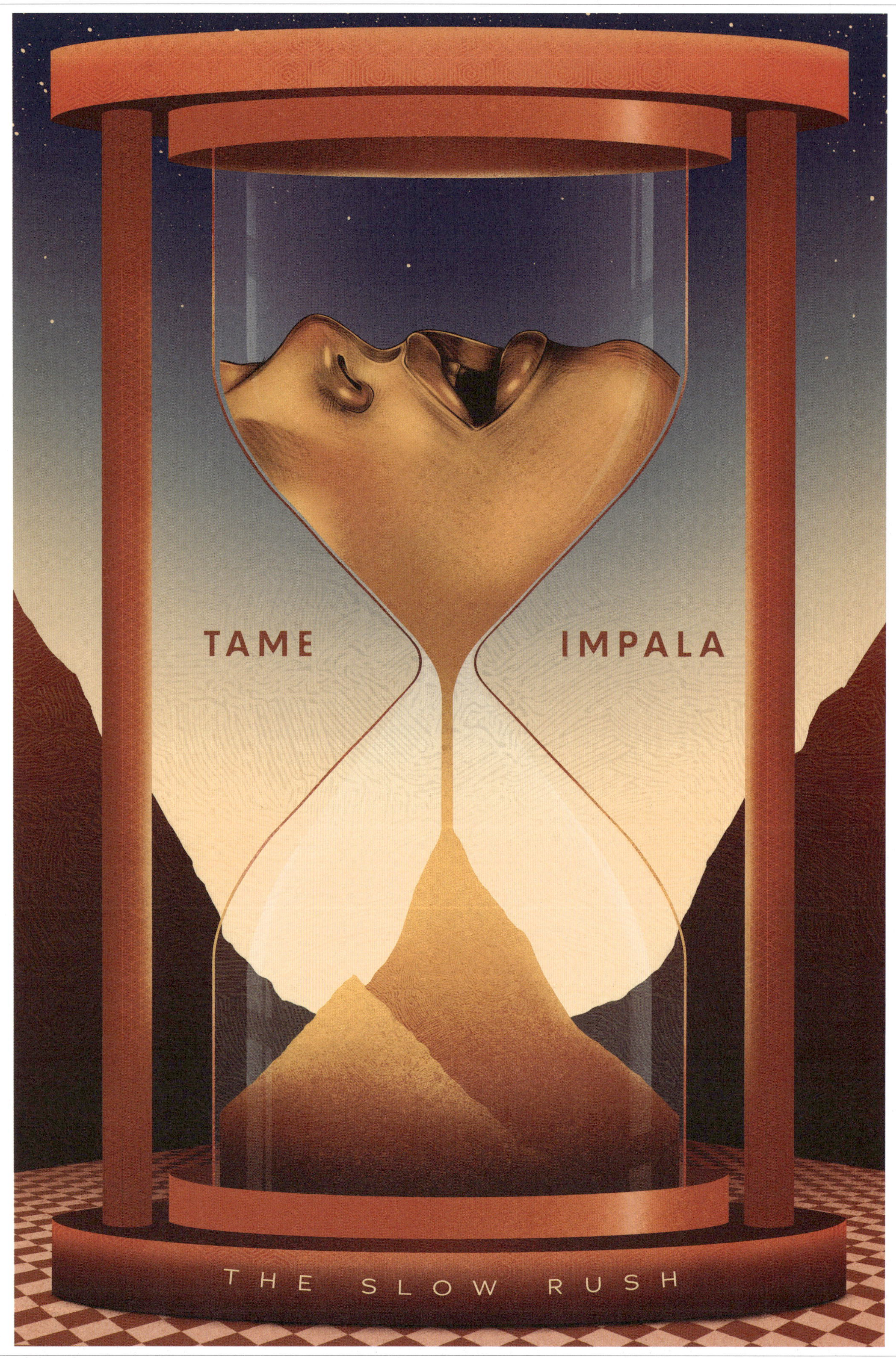

(Page 97) Qiong Qi, New Talent Annual 2023. School: ArtCenter College of Design. Professor: Gayle Donahue. Platinum-winning student: Lauren Chen
(Above) The Slow Rush, New Talent Annual 2024. School: ArtCenter College of Design. Professor: Jim Salvati. Gold-winning student: Maria Dzulfayan

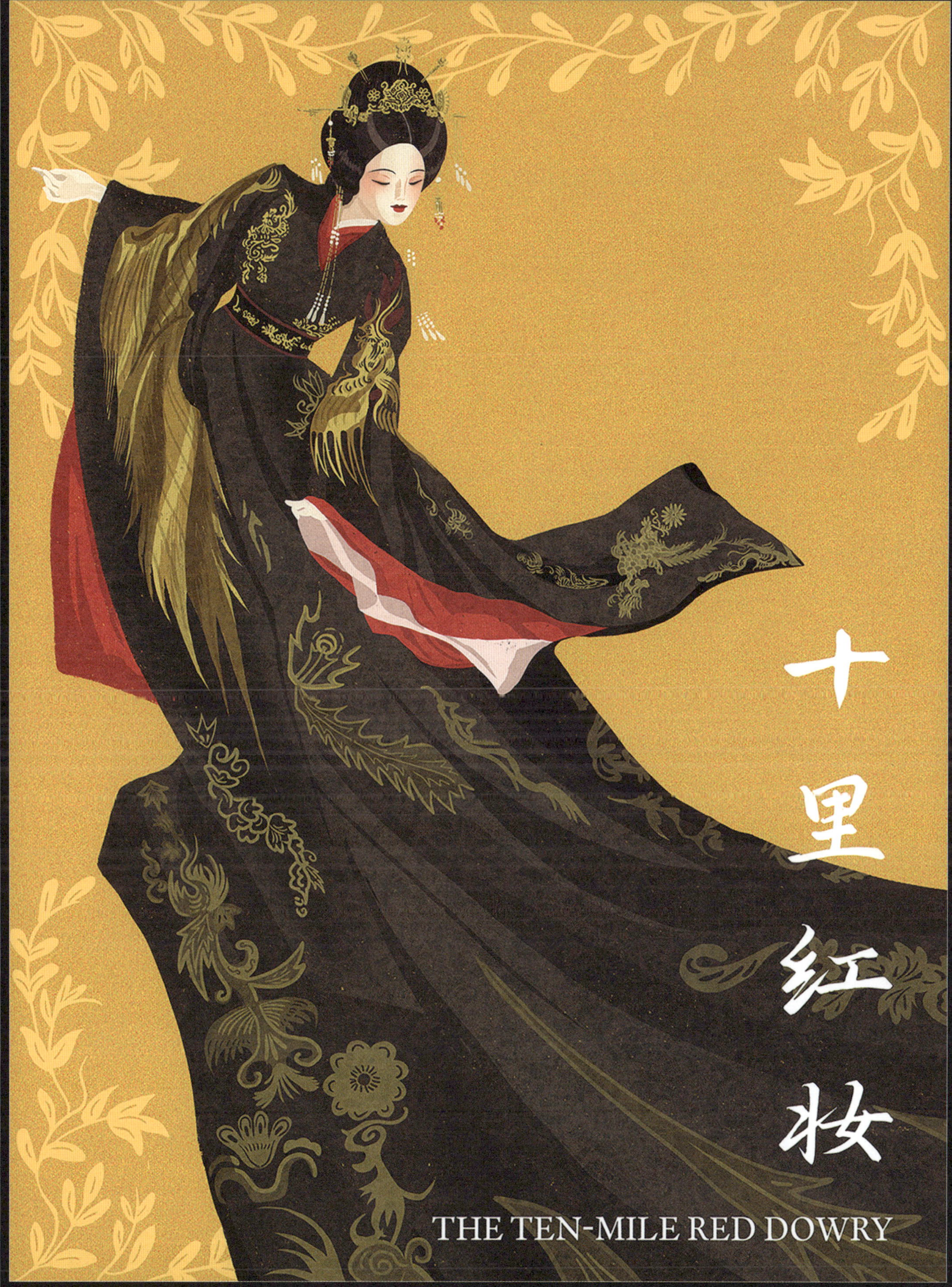

The Ten-Mile Red Dowry, New Talent Annual 2023. School: Pratt Institute. Professor: Unattributed. Gold-winning student: Dexin Chen

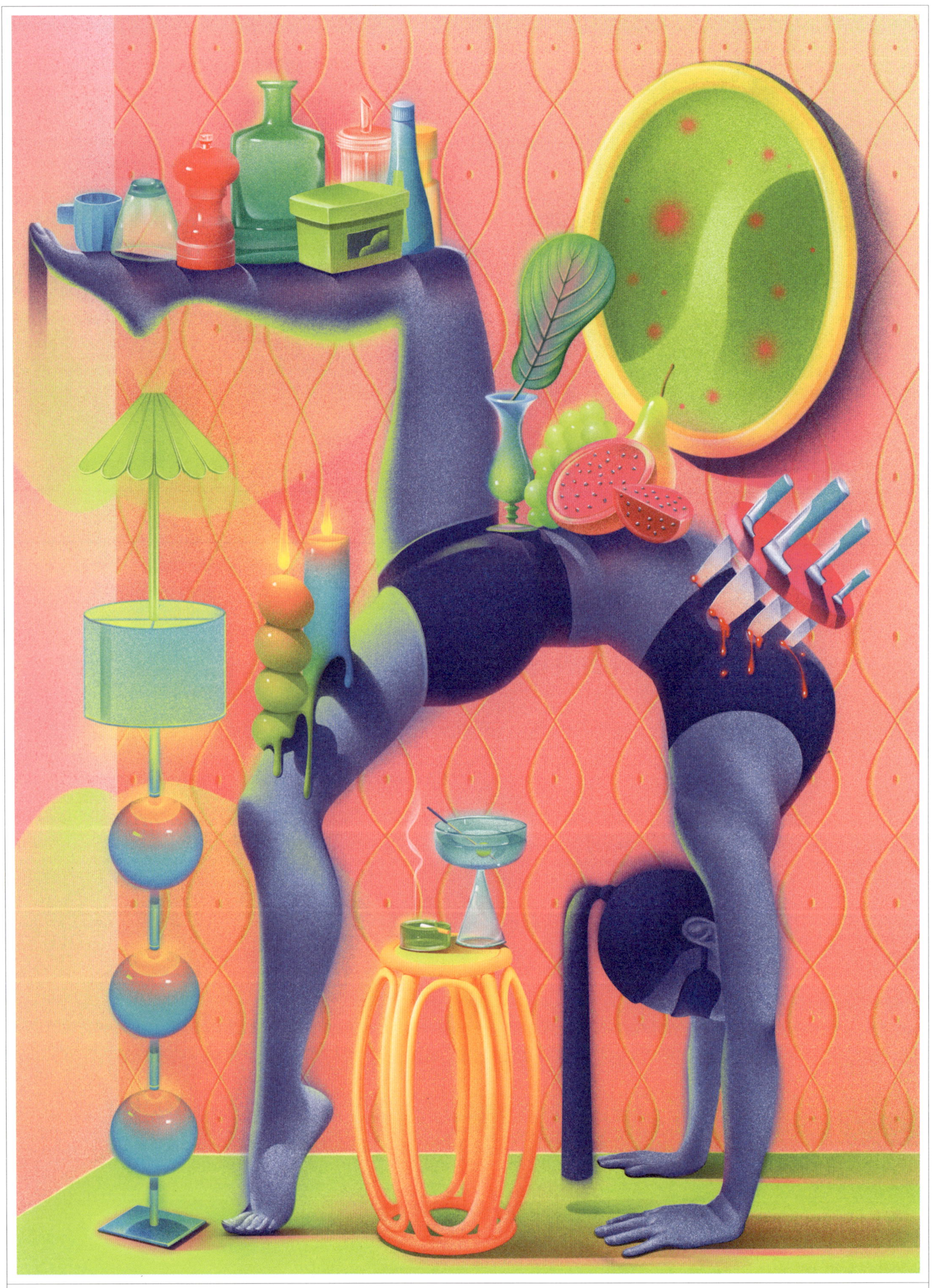

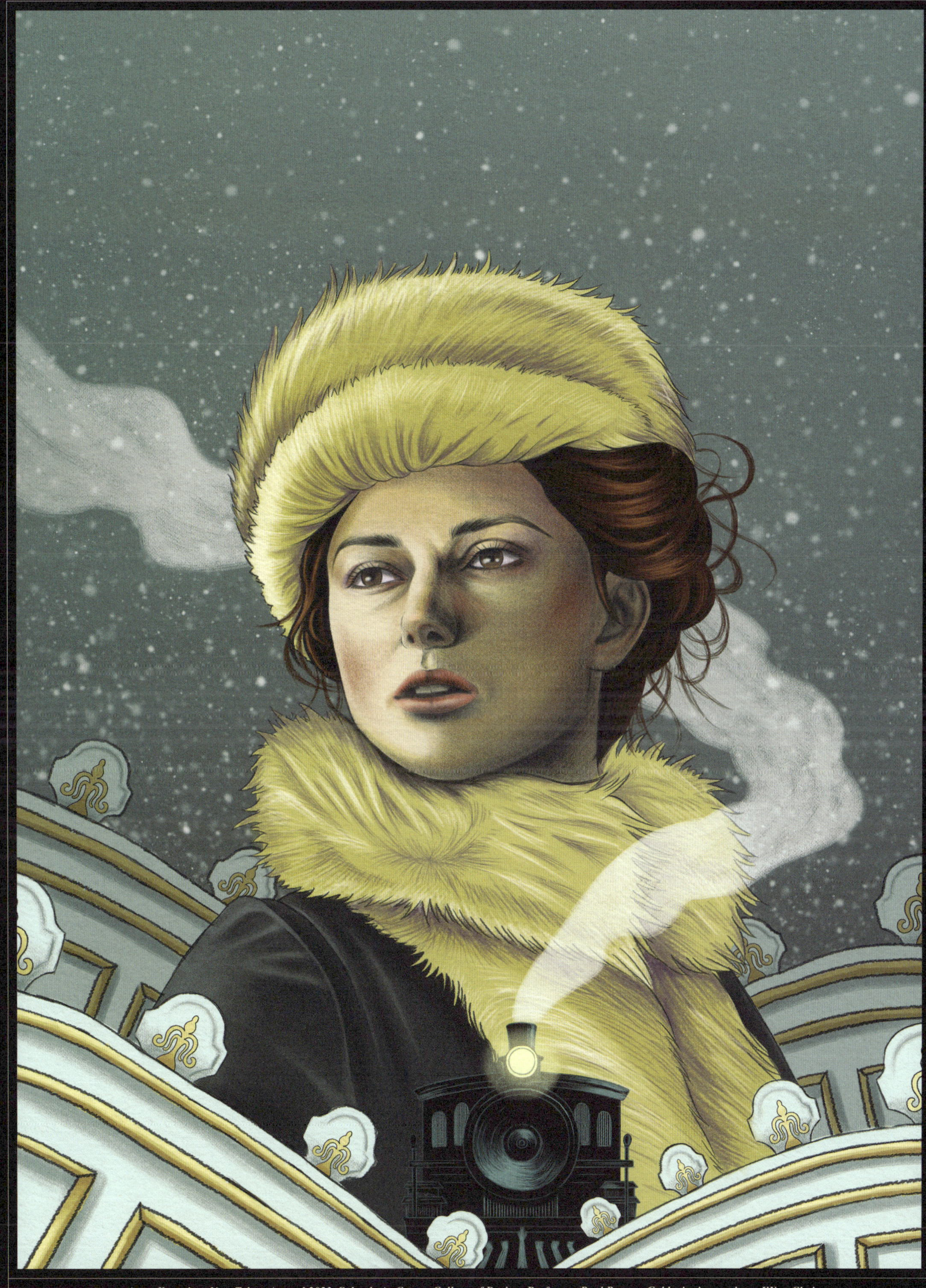

Anna Karenina, New Talent Annual 2023. School: ArtCenter College of Design. Professor: Paul Rogers. Gold-winning student: JiYun Choi

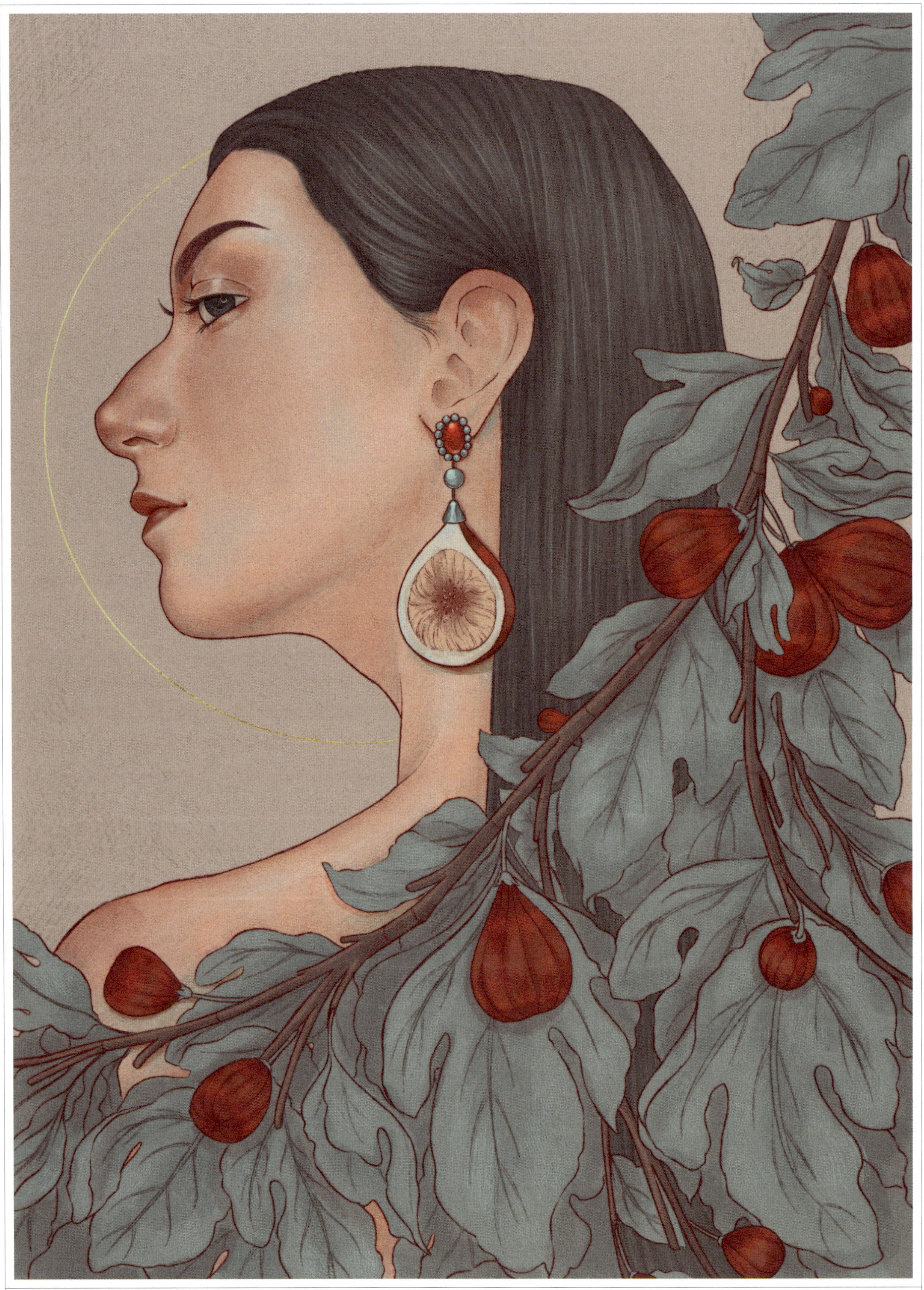

Fig, New Talent Annual 2024. School: ArtCenter College of Design. Professor: Adam Ross. Gold-winning student: Jess Martinez

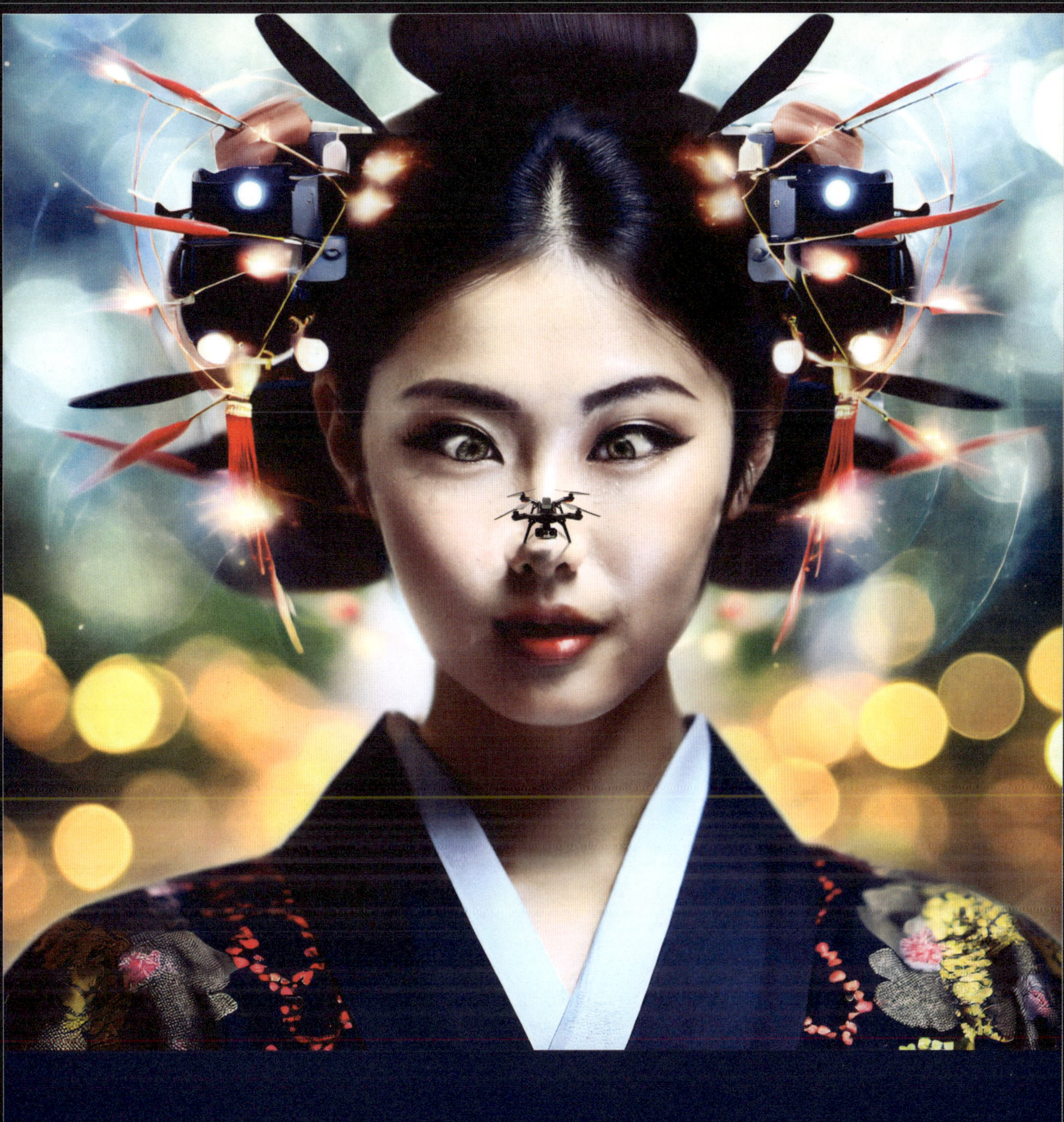

Japan Drone, New Talent Annual 2024. School: Texas State University. Professor: William Meek. Platinum-winning student: Brandy Compton

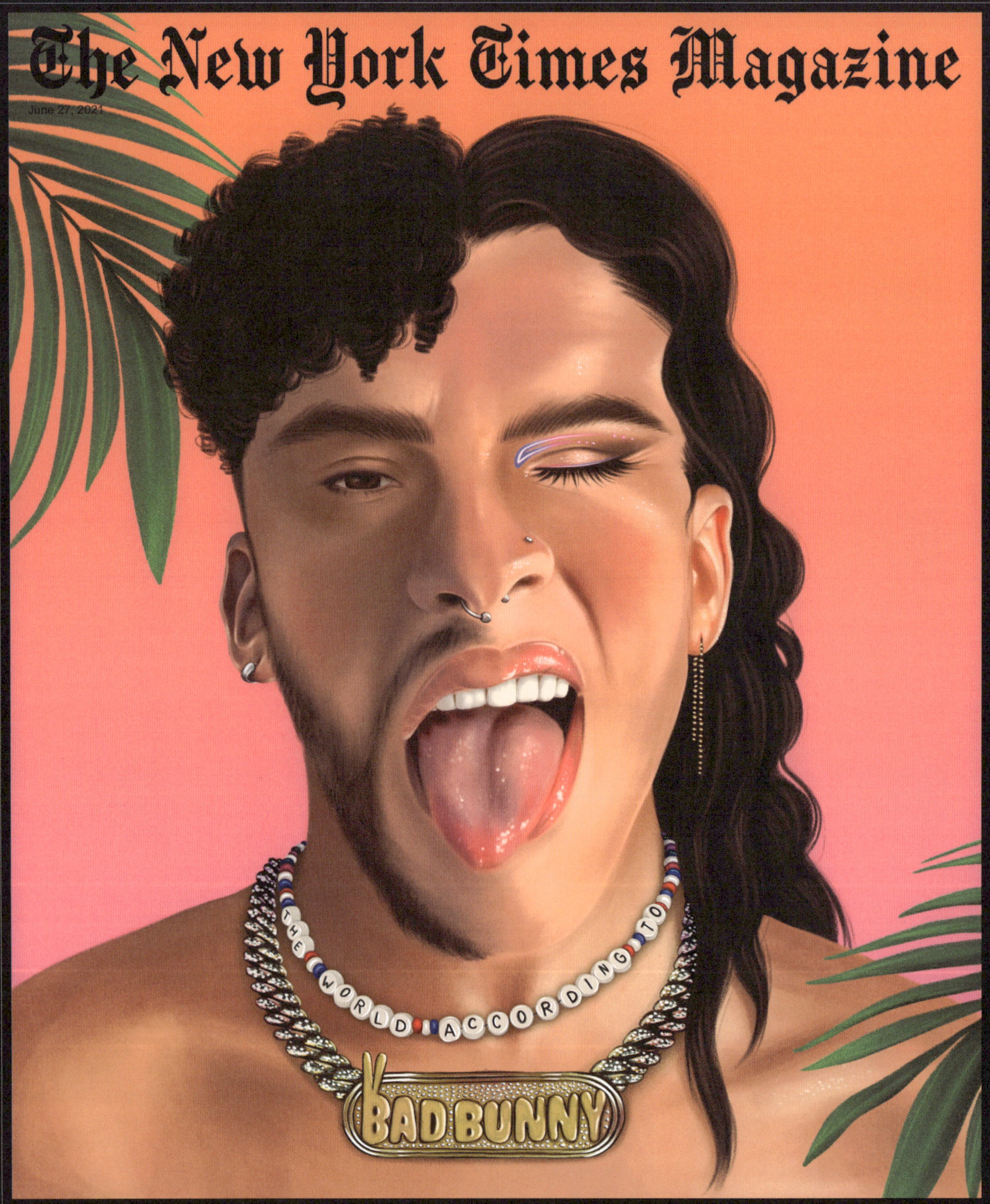

The World According to Bad Bunny, New Talent Annual 2023. School: ArtCenter College of Design. Professors: Paul Rogers and Brian Rea. Platinum-winning student: Maria Dzulfayan

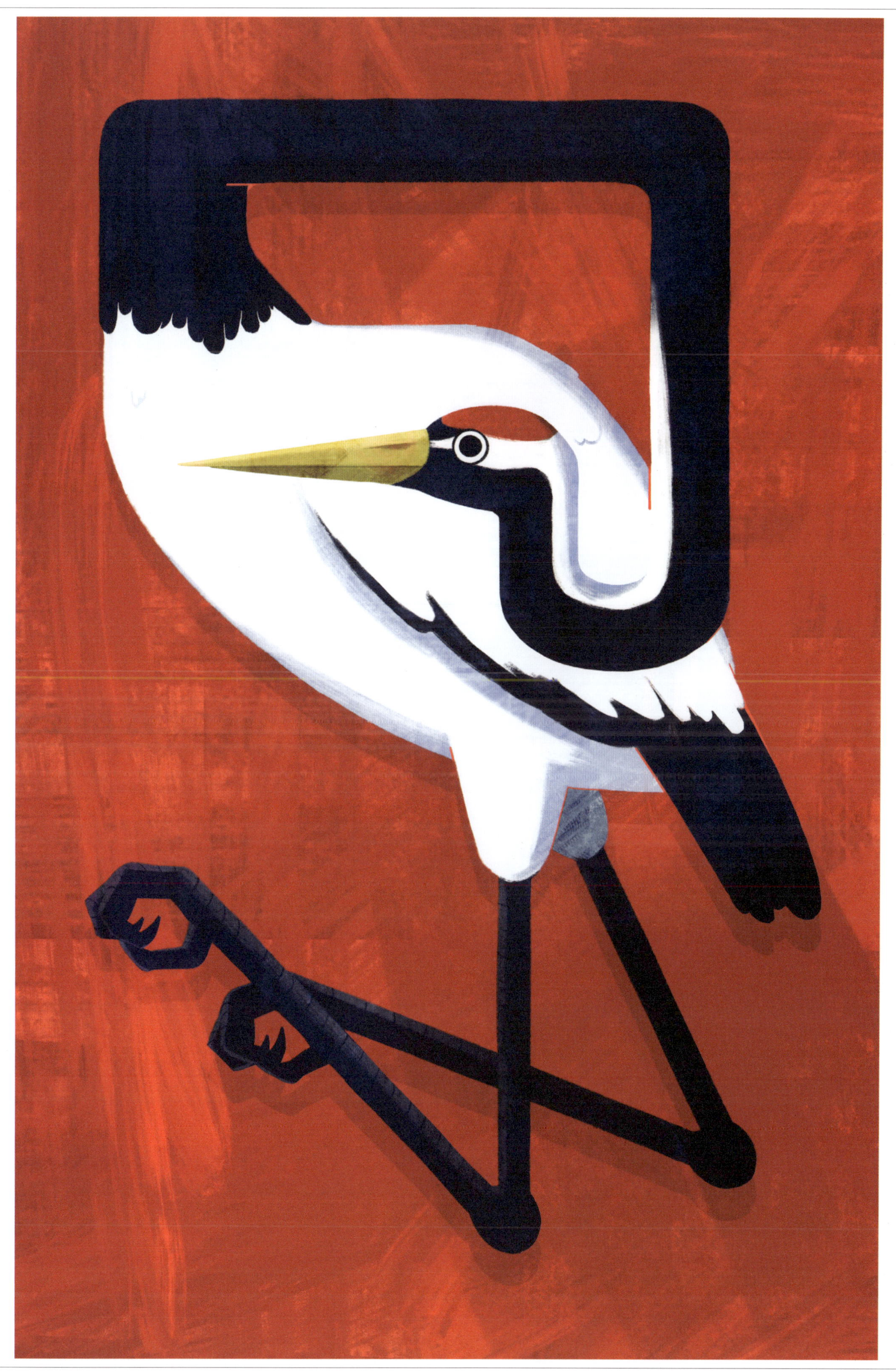

Animal Designs, New Talent Annual 2024. School: ArtCenter College of Design. Professors: David Tillinghast and Rob Clayton. Platinum-winning student: David J. Lee

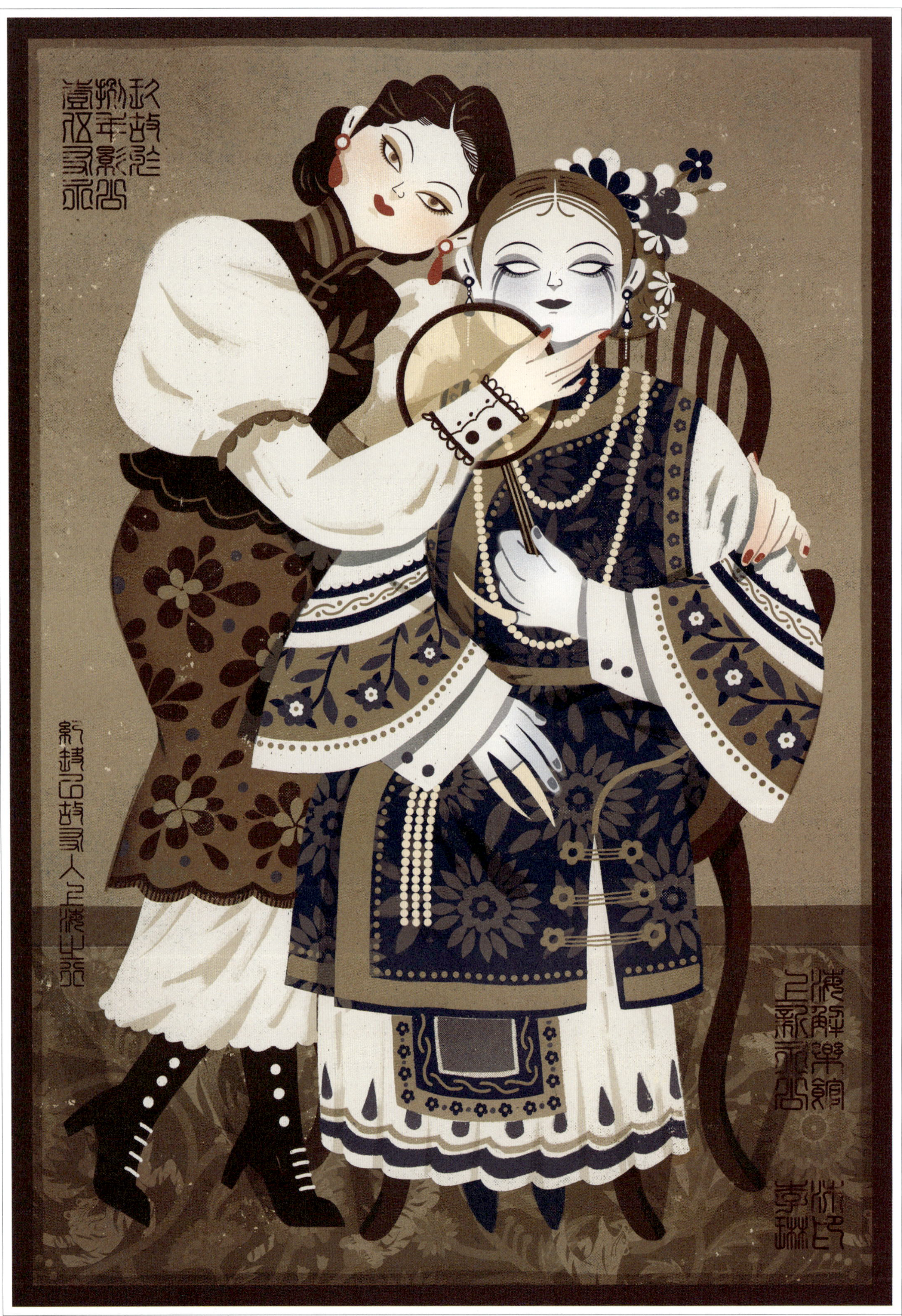

Horror, New Talent Annual 2023. School: School of Visual Arts. Professor: Lisk Feng. Gold-winning student: Peilin Li

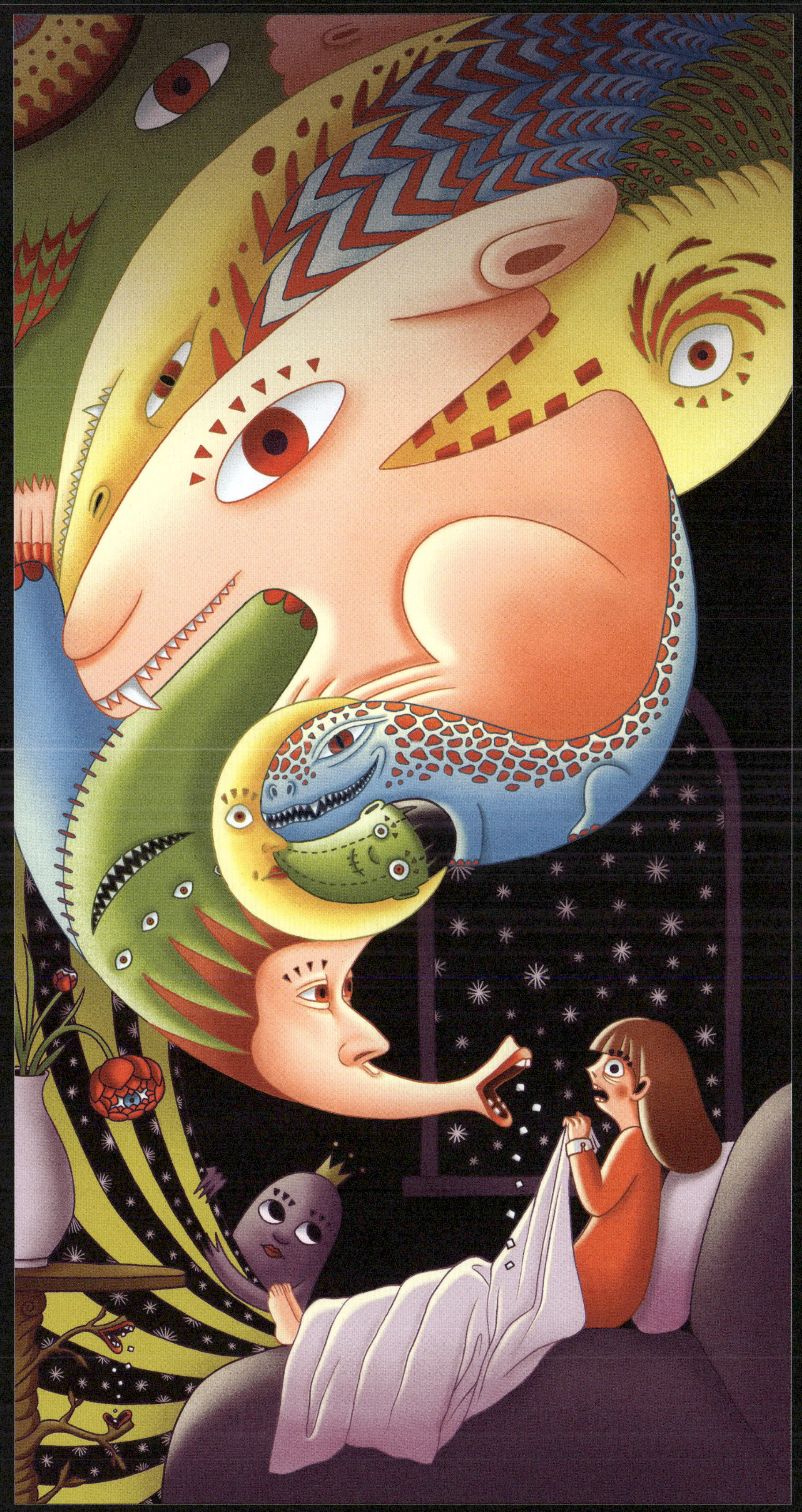

Bedtime Visitors, New Talent Annual 2023. School: ArtCenter College of Design. Professors: Paul Rogers and Brian Rea. Gold-winning student: JiYun Choi

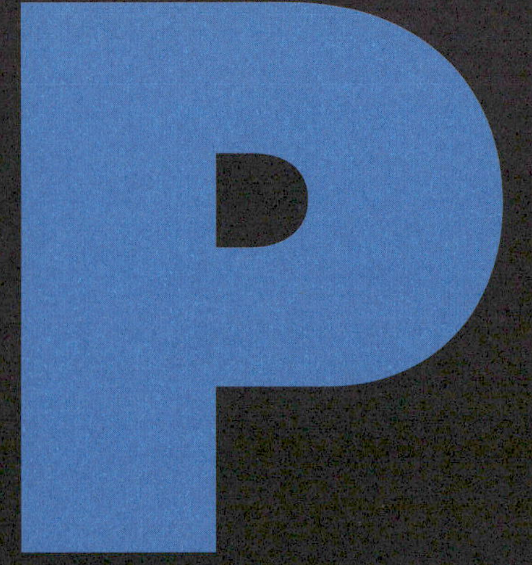

PRODUCT DESIGN

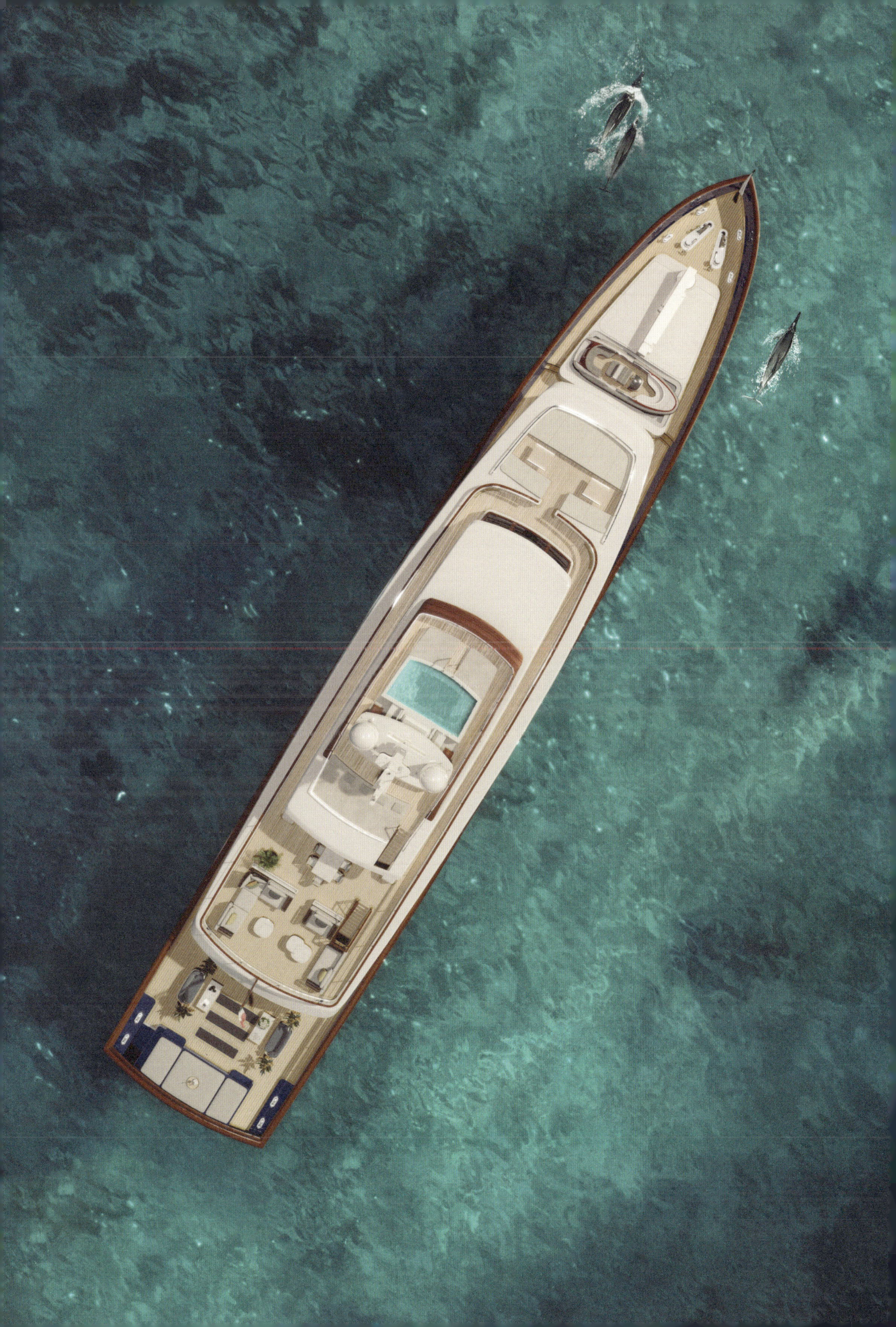

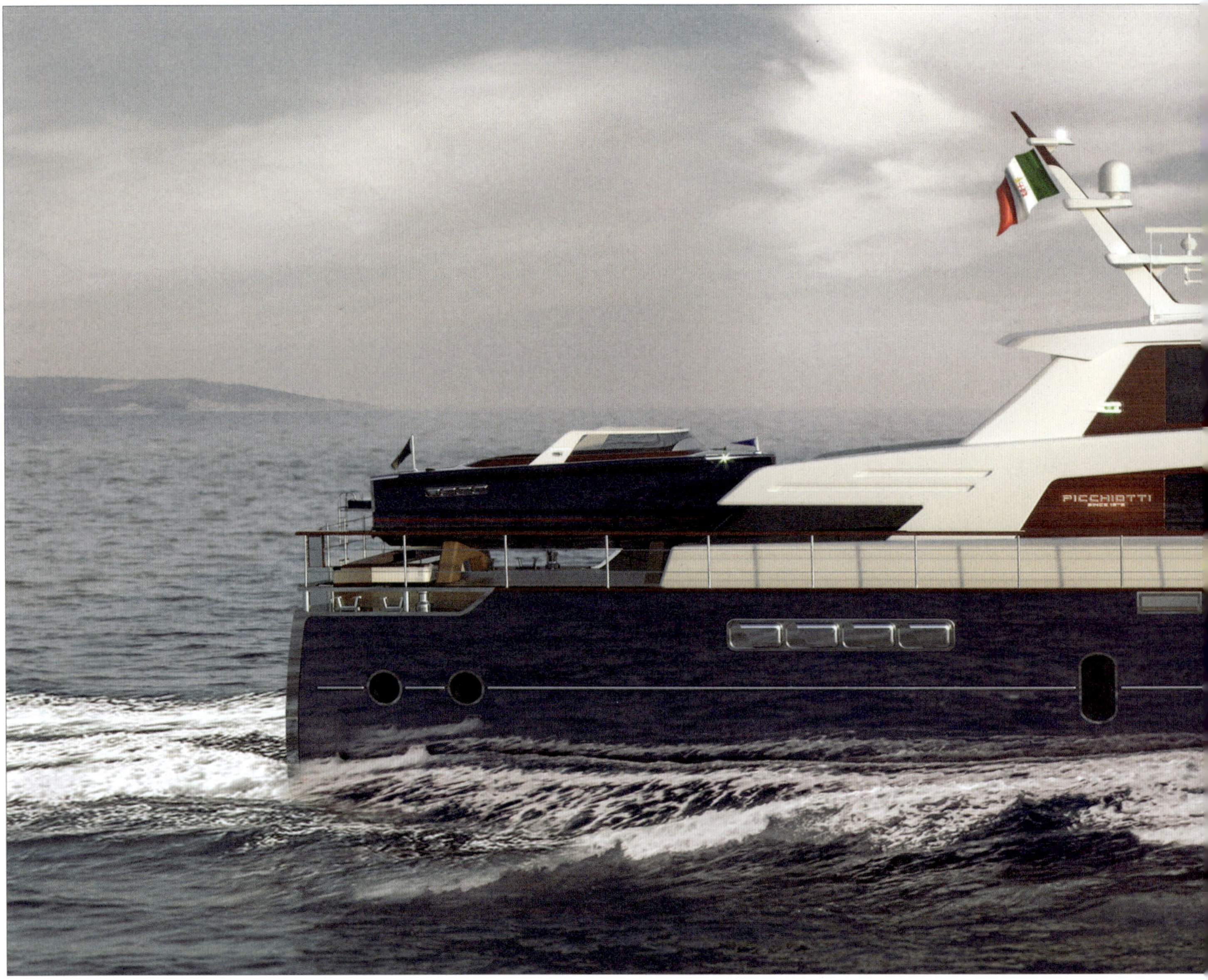

GENTLEMAN'S YACHT 24	**Superstructure material:** Aluminium alloy	**Max beam:** 6.5 m	**Generators:** 2 x 35 kW 400 V / 50 Hz / 3 ph
Hull: Aluminium alloy	**LOA:** 24 m / 79 ft	**Main engines:** 2 x MAN D2862 LE446 V12-1400	**Max speed:** 19 kn

The Gentleman's Yacht, with its striking dark-hulled presence, emerges as a refined expression of nautical design, shaped through a collaboration between the Italian Sea Group, LUCA DINI Design & Architecture, and Kurt Lehmann's Yacht Moments. This semi-displacement yacht line reinterprets a classically inspired silhouette into a softer, more modern form, embodying Italian elegance across five sizes—24m, 30m, 33m, 44m, and 55m. The fleet stands as a testament to the artistry of yacht-making, where heritage and innovation converge on the open water.

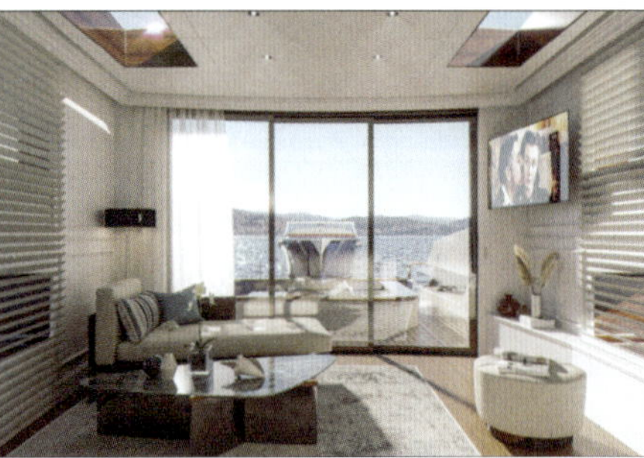

The exterior captivates with its distinctive lines, where a deep blue hull accented by a red beauty line—a historical nod to classics like the M/Y TM Blue One—lends a bespoke character that feels both nostalgic and contemporary. Luca Dini's timeless vision integrates polished mahogany along the elegant flanks, its rich grain catching the light with a warm glow, while wide side corridors invite seamless walks from bow to stern, evoking the grandeur of the iconic yachts of the 1960s. Crafted from aluminum, the hull balances weight and strength, its sleek form gliding through waves with understated grace, the wake trailing behind like a delicate brush stroke on the ocean's canvas.

Inside, the cabin unfolds as a gallery of contemporary design, where sustainable woods and high-grade metals, enriched by the warmth of polished mahogany, honor yacht-building's artisanal heritage while embracing an environmental ethos. Accommodating up to 12 guests, the cabin's layout opens to natural light through expansive panoramic windows, their glass surfaces reflecting the sea's ever-changing hues. The cockpit, framed by these views, transforms from a space for lively gatherings to a quiet retreat under the stars, its versatility blending nature with design in a way that feels intimate and boundless.

Performance and aesthetics intertwine through hydrodynamic principles that shape the hull, its wake revealing a harmony of efficiency and stability. Hybrid and fully electric propulsion systems introduce sustainable seafaring, their quiet hum complementing the vessel's elegance, allowing the sounds of the waves to take center stage. Navigation systems, with their intuitive interfaces, reflect a fusion of art and science, simplifying the complexities of the open water while maintaining a minimalist aesthetic that prioritizes clarity and function.

Each Gentleman's Yacht stands as a bespoke creation; its indi-

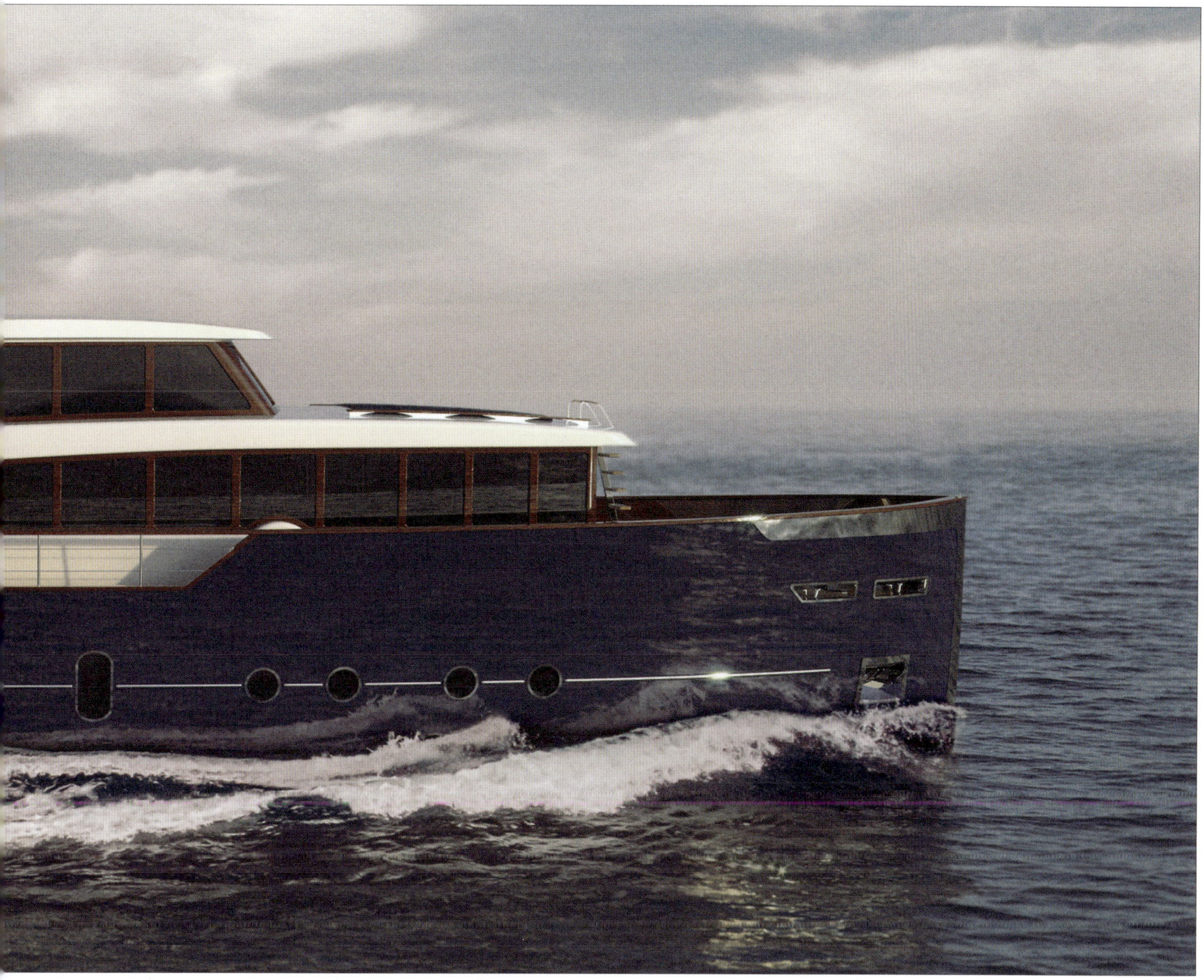

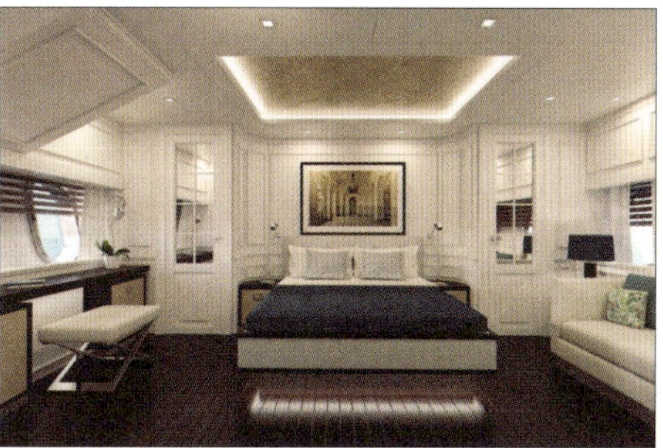

24m @ TISG, LUCA DINI, Yacht Moments

| **Cruising Speed:** 16 kn | **Propellers:** 2 x FPP | **Stabilizer:** Gyroscopic stabilizer | **Max crew accomodations:** 3/4 (2 cabins) |
| **Fuel capacity:** 10,000 lt approx. | **Bow thruster:** 1 x 30 kW electric | **Max guest accomodations:** 6/8 (3/4 cabins) | |

viduality is mirrored in a custom-made tender limousine that echoes the yacht's lines and finishes in miniature form. This personal expression captures the spirit of maritime exploration, rooted in a legacy of craftsmanship that feels alive with every voyage. The Picchiotti Fleet invites reflection on the dialogue between tradition and modernity, where every curve, material, and detail tells a story of design evolution.

In an industry where detail reigns, the Gentleman's Yacht presents a thoughtful synthesis of art, engineering, and heritage. It stands as a moving canvas of modern design, its form gliding across the sea with quiet confidence, inviting admiration for the vision that shapes its aesthetic and purpose—a testament to the enduring beauty of innovation on the water.

THE PROJECT IS INSPIRED BY THE SILHOUETTE OF THE AMERICAN YACHTS OF THE '60S, INTERPRETING TIMELESS CLASSIC LINES WITH EXCLUSIVITY AND ELEGANCE AND FEATURING INNOVATIVE ENGINEERING SOLUTIONS AS WELL AS UNIQUE AND DISTINCTIVE DESIGNS. **Sophie Spicknell,** *SuperYacht Times*

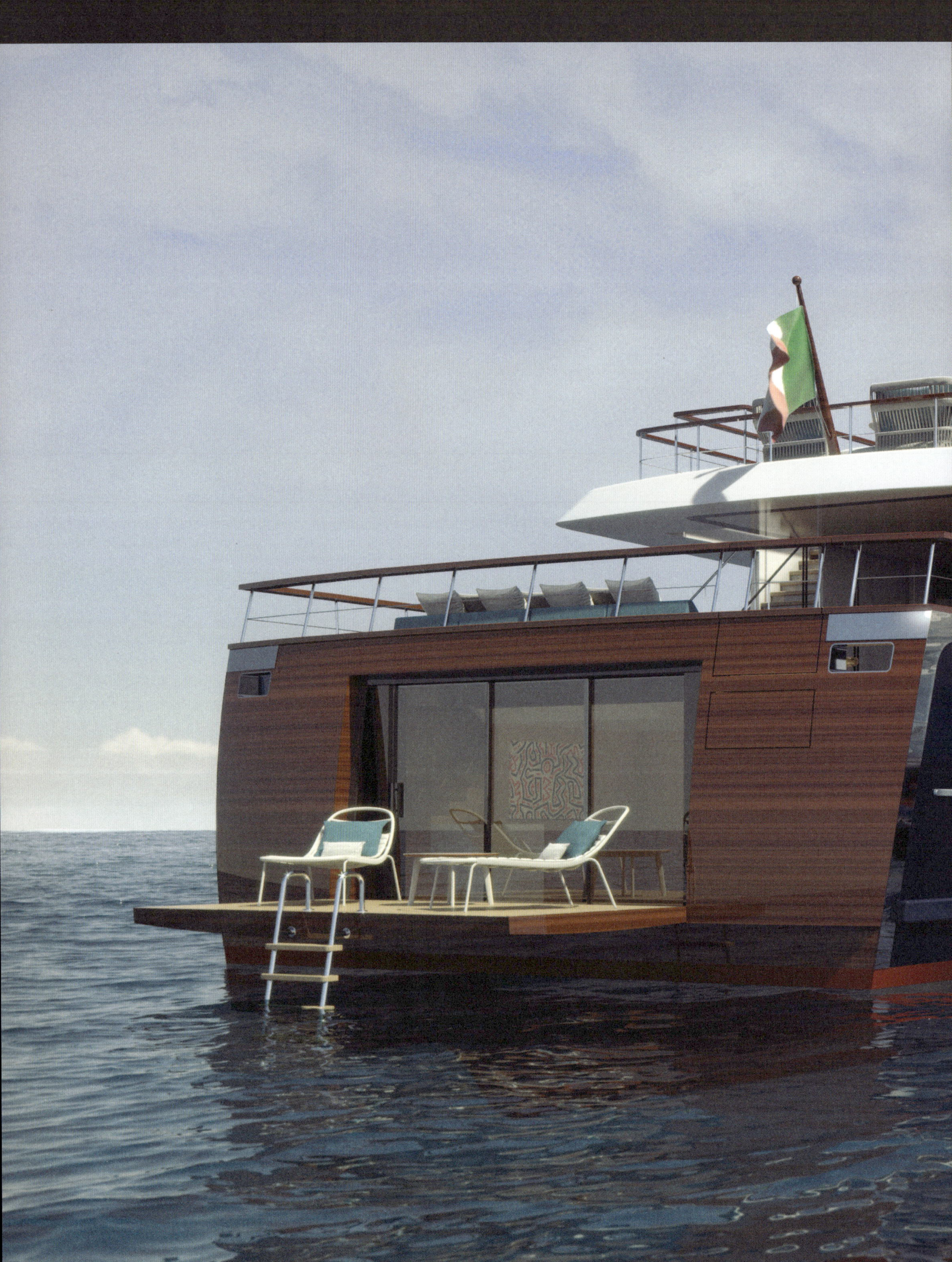

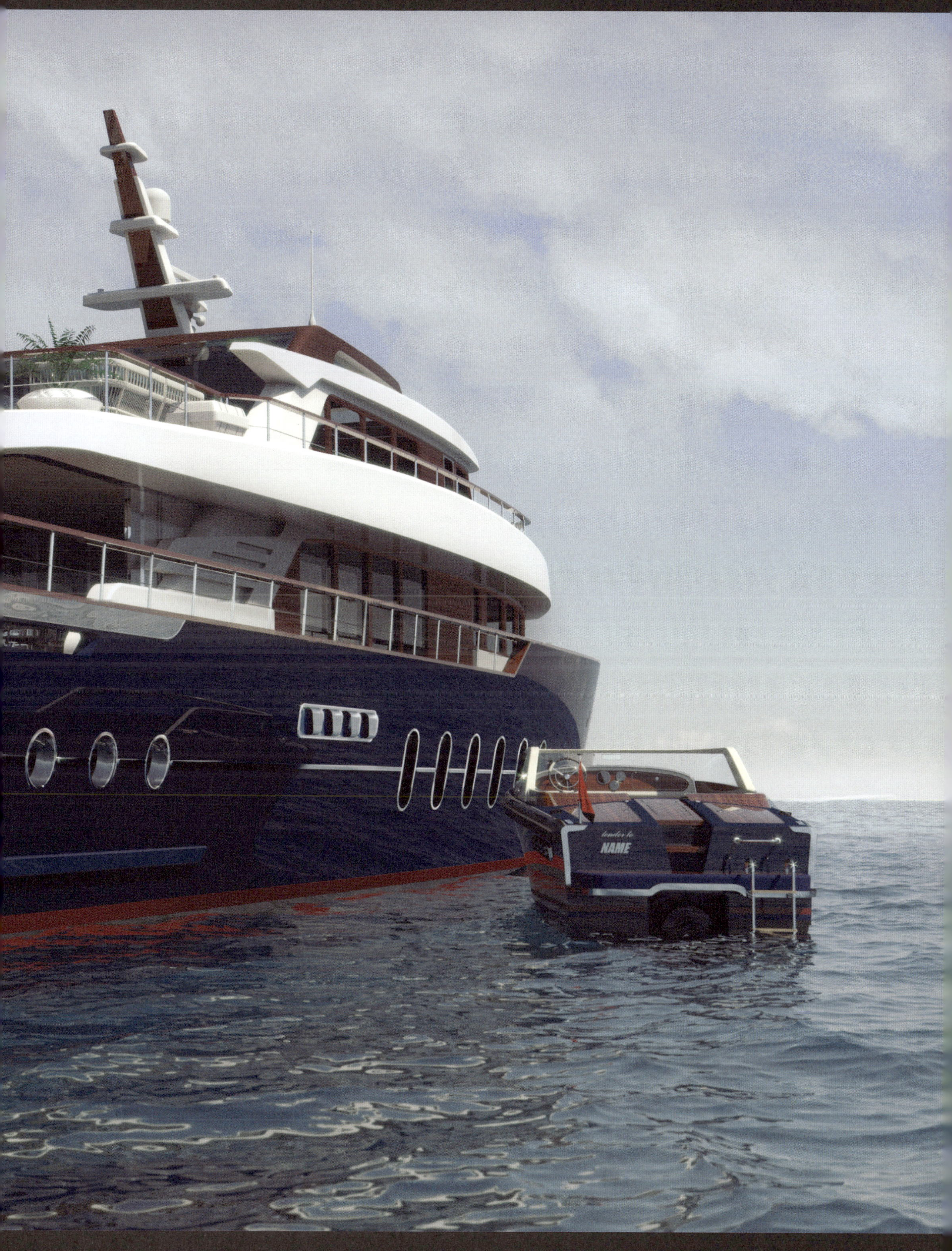

tender to
NAME

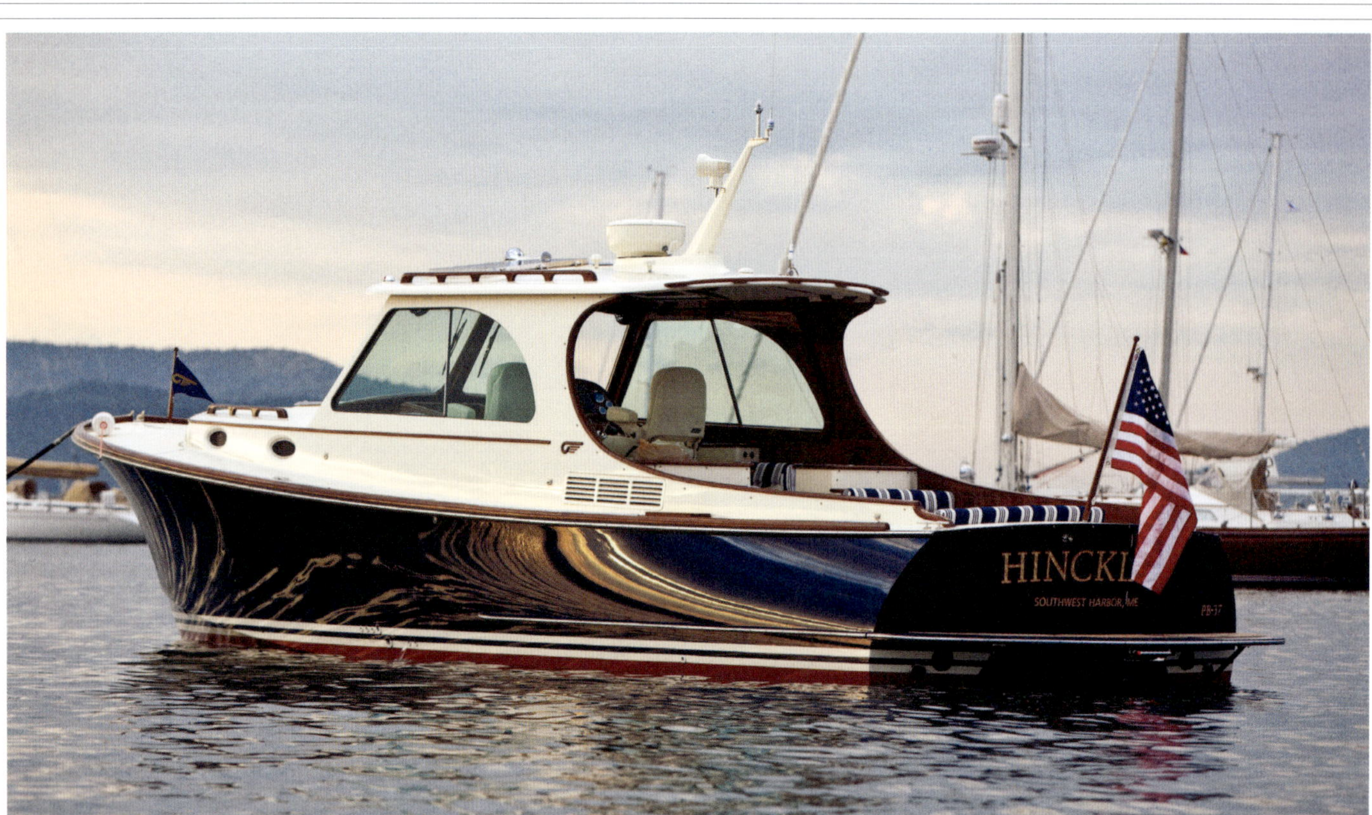

Picnic Boat 37

Length, overall: 38 ft, 8 in	**Draft:** 2 ft, 1 in	**Engines:** Twin Volvo Penta D6 440HP V8 diesel	**Cruising speed:** 35 kn
Length, hull: 36 ft, 11 in	**Displacement (cruising):** 19,000 lbs'	**Jets:** Twin Hamilton HTX Series	**Top speed:** 37 kn
Length, waterline: 33 ft, 10 in	**Fuel capacity:** 220 US gal	**Construction:** DualGuard™ SCRIMP® carbon E-glass composite hull with epoxy	**Transom deadrise:** 19°
Beam: 11 ft, 3 in	**Water capacity:** 40 US gal		

The Hinckley Picnic Boat 37 is a stunning testament to the marriage of innovative design and timeless craftsmanship. Built with an epoxy-infused carbon composite hull, this vessel combines remarkable strength with a lightweight structure, ensuring both durability and agility. At 38 feet 8 inches overall, with a hull length of 36 feet 11 inches and a waterline length of 33 feet 10 inches, the Picnic Boat 37 is meticulously engineered for performance and elegance. Its 11-foot-3-inch beam and shallow 2-foot-1-inch draft make it versatile for coastal cruising, while its 19,000-pound cruising displacement strikes a perfect balance of stability and speed.

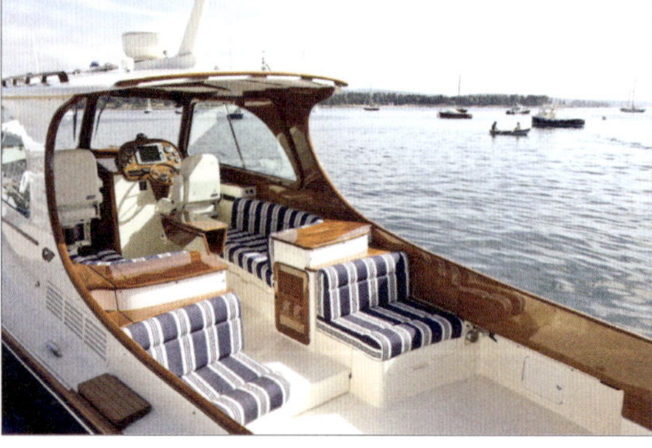

One of the boat's most striking features is its aesthetic finesse, exemplified by the eight pieces of solid Burmese teak that crown the deck. Hand-selected in Hinckley's Maine finish carpentry shop, these pieces are masterfully joined and shaped into a glossy, languid curve that defines the boat's iconic silhouette. The teak toe rail, sanded and varnished with up to ten coats, follows the sheer line with a subtle radius—neither too flat nor too pronounced—enhancing the boat's graceful bow and timeless appeal.

Functionality is elevated by Hinckley's cutting-edge Jet-Stick 4® system, a technological marvel that redefines intuitive control. This patented feature integrates fly-by-wire steering with military-grade hardware, offering effortless precision. With a single button, owners can deploy a virtual anchor to hold position anywhere in the world or engage Dockhold to lock the boat in place while securing lines. The improved G-lock feature maintains heading and position, freeing the captain to enjoy moments like a yacht race start or a sunset with guests.

Performance is where the Picnic Boat 37 truly shines. Powered by twin Volvo Penta D6 440HP V8 diesel engines and Hamilton HTX Series jets, this boat achieves a cruising speed of 35 knots and a top speed of 37 knots. Hinckley has shaved 1,000 pounds off its predecessors by leveraging advanced coring materials and laminate techniques, resulting in a ride that's smoother, quieter, and more exhilarating than ever. With a 220-gallon fuel capacity and 40-gallon water capacity, it's built for extended adventures.

Constructed with a DualGuard™ SCRIMP® carbon E-glass composite hull and a 19-degree transom deadrise, the Picnic Boat 37 blends breathtaking speed with enduring beauty. It's not just a boat—it's a Hinckley masterpiece designed to thrill and inspire.

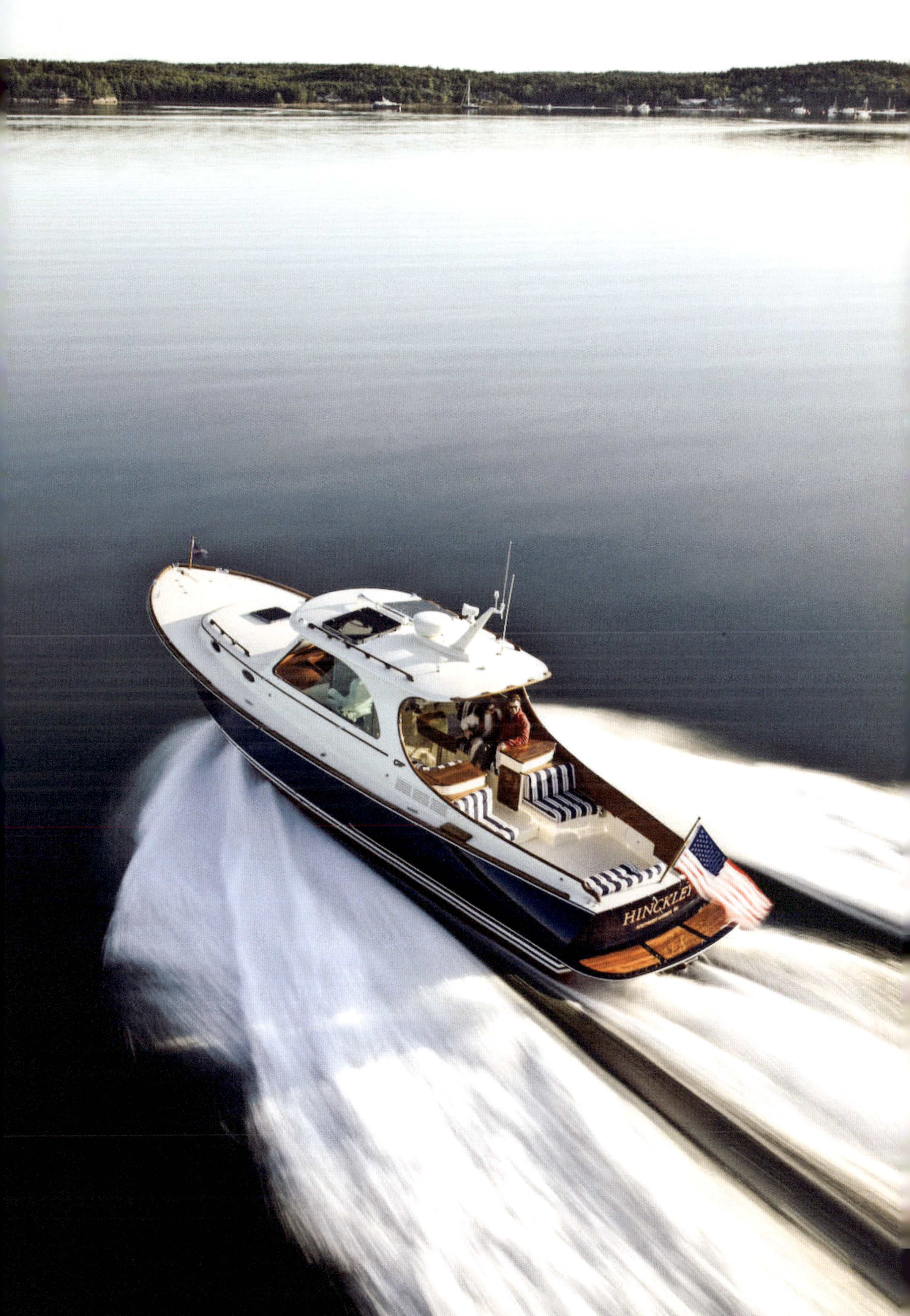

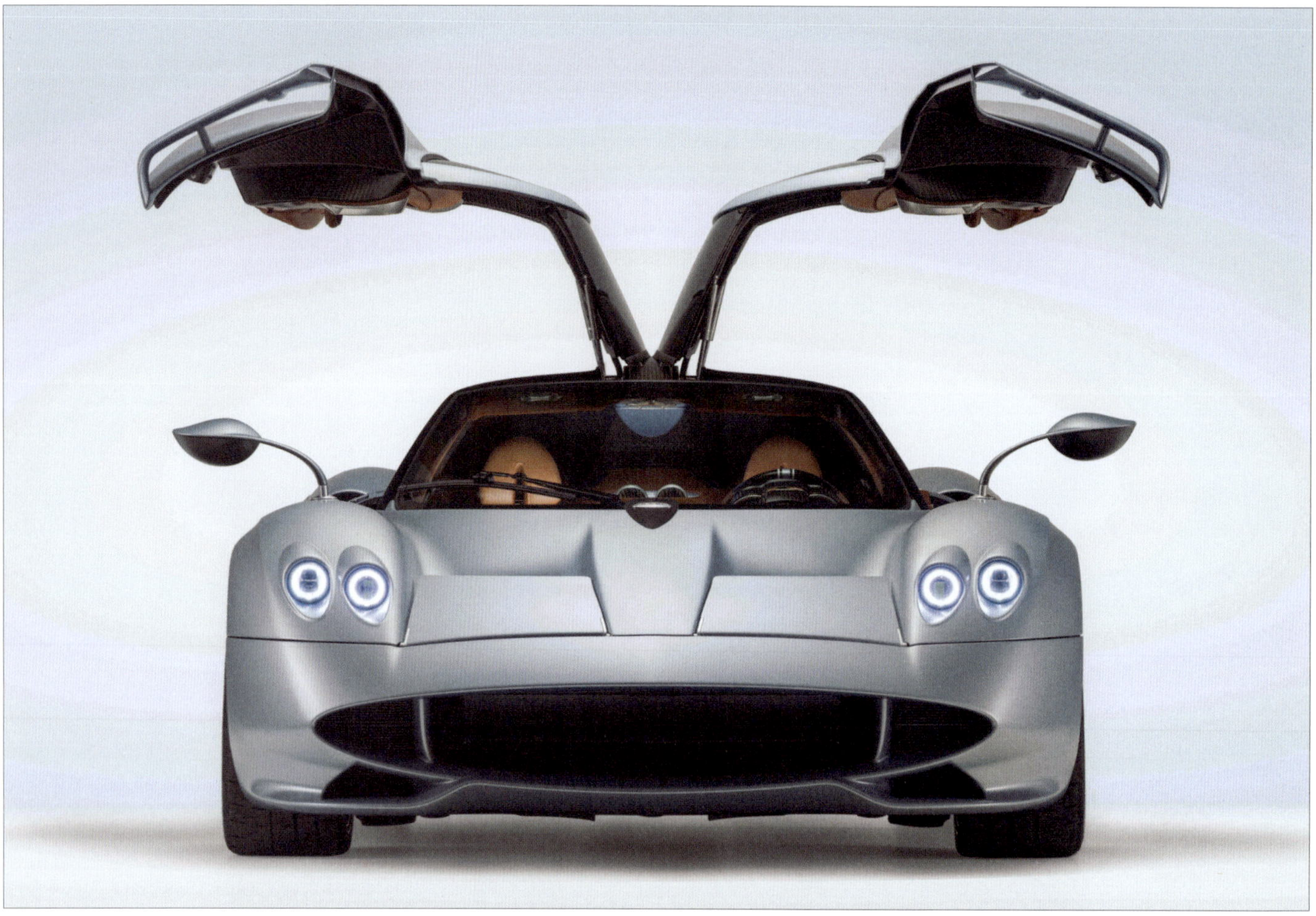

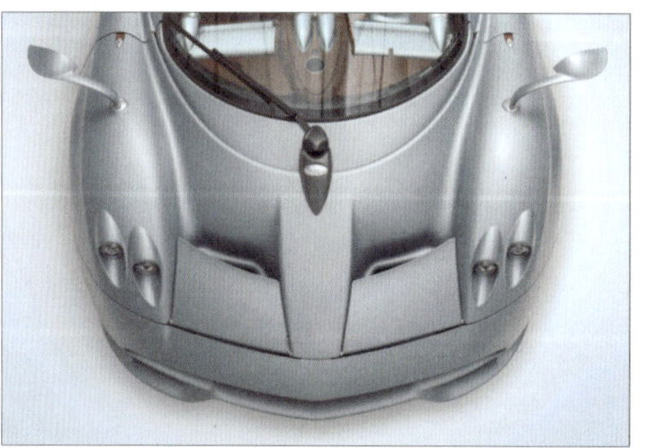

Huayra Codalunga by Pagani

Engine: Pagani V12 60° 36 valves 5,980 CC, twin turbo
Power: 840 CV (628 kW) at 5,900 RPM
Torque: 1,100 Nm from 2,000 RPM to 5,600 RPM
Transmission: Pagani by Xtrac, transverse mounted 7-speed sequential

Brakes: Pagani by Brembo carbon-ceramic self-ventilated disc brakes: diameter 410x38 mm with 6-piston 1-piece calliper at the front; diameter 390x34 mm with 4-piston 1-piece calliper at the rear
Wheels: 1-piece tech in forged avional, 20 in at the front and 21 in at the rear
Tires: Pirelli P Zero Corsa 265/30 R20 at the front and 355/25 R21 at the rear; Pirelli Sottozero for driving in low temperatures
Suspension: Active forged aluminium alloy, independent double wishbone with variable-pitch helical springs and coaxial dampers
Chassis: Carbon-titanium HP62 and carbon-triax HP62 monocoque
Dry weight: 1,280 kg (2.822 lb)

The Pagani Huayra Codalunga stands as a pinnacle of automotive design, where artistry and engineering converge to create a breathtaking masterpiece. Unveiled in June 2022, this limited-edition hypercar—Italian for "long tail"—stretches the Huayra lineage into a realm of timeless elegance, drawing inspiration from the sleek, aerodynamic racers of the 1960s, such as the Porsche 917. With only five units produced, each starting at €7 million, the Codalunga is a bespoke creation born from the vision of two dedicated Pagani collectors and executed by the marque's Grandi Complicazioni special projects division.

At its core, Codalunga's design philosophy is one of subtraction rather than addition. Horacio Pagani, the visionary founder, describes it as a form "caressed and molded by the wind," resulting in a silhouette that exudes simplicity and grace. The car extends 14.2 inches longer than the standard Huayra Coupé, with a rear engine cover spanning over 3.7 square meters. This elongated tail, free of rear grilles, exposes a titanium exhaust system weighing just 4.4 kilograms, its ceramic coating a nod to Le Mans heritage. The absence of a prominent wing amplifies its streamlined aesthetic, while four variable-profile flaps—Pagani's signature active aerodynamics—ensure high efficiency without compromising the clean lines.

Crafted from advanced composite materials, the Codalunga weighs a mere 1,280 kilograms, a testament to Pagani's relentless pursuit of lightweight perfection. Its exterior eschews the brand's typical flamboyant carbon-fiber finishes for neutral, semi-matte paints that evoke a vintage charm. The sculpted bonnet, raked windscreen, and minimalist front grille with split projector headlights further refine its understated elegance, while gull-wing doors and subtle side vents maintain a balance of form and function.

Inside, the Codalunga is a sanctuary of craftsmanship. The cabin blends handwoven leather and nubuck upholstery with machined aluminum accents, evoking the coachbuilding era of the 1960s. The ergonomic layout prioritizes driver focus, with a minimalist dashboard and polished gear knob that fuses wood and carbon, a process that takes days to perfect. Every detail, from the exposed carbon-fiber structure to the bespoke luggage set, reflects Pagani's devotion to artistry.

The Huayra Codalunga is not merely a car—it's a rolling sculpture. Powered by an 840-horsepower twin-turbo V12, it marries its exquisite design with exhilarating performance, embodying Leonardo da Vinci's ideal of art and science in harmony. For its fortunate few owners, it's a timeless icon of automotive design.

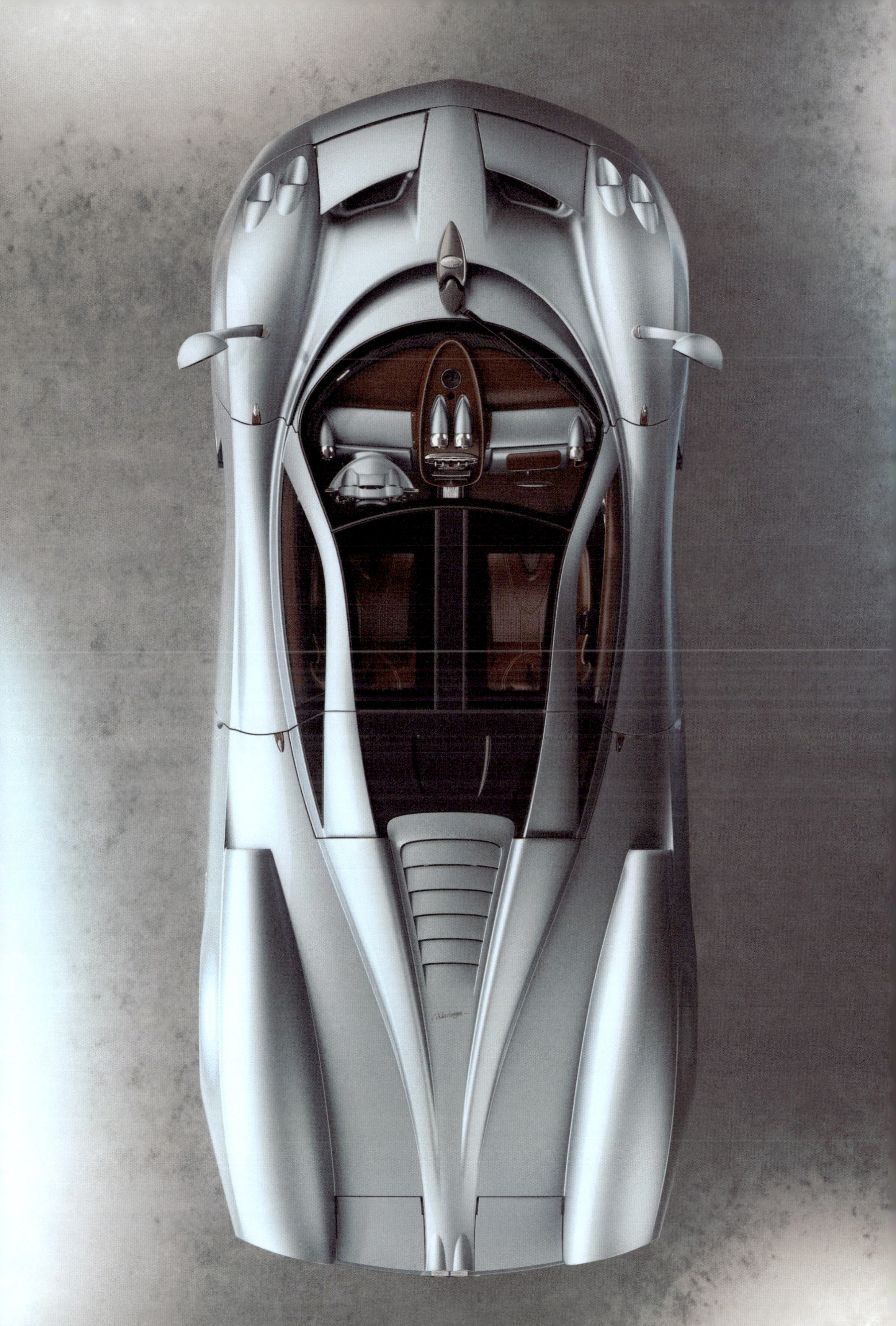

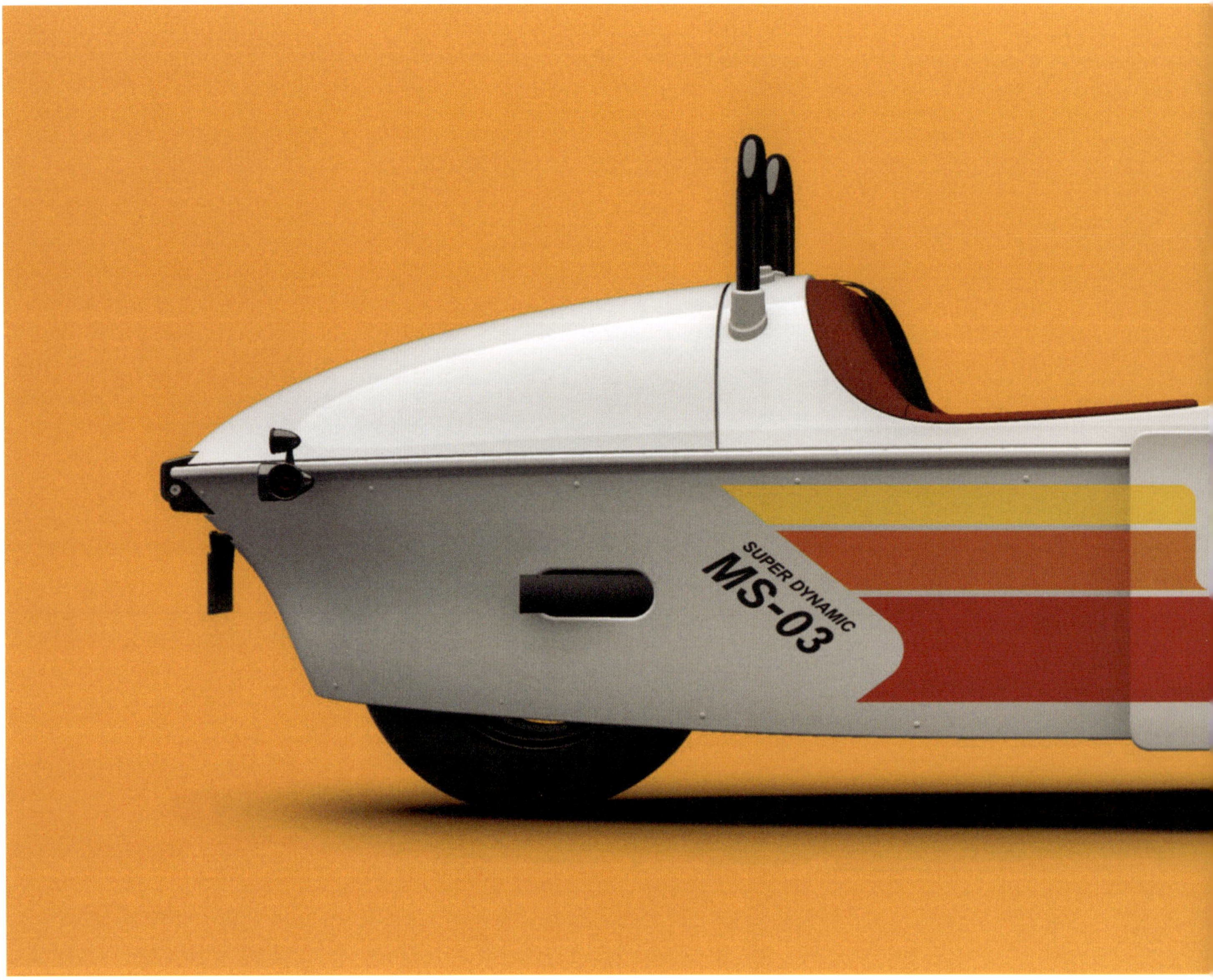

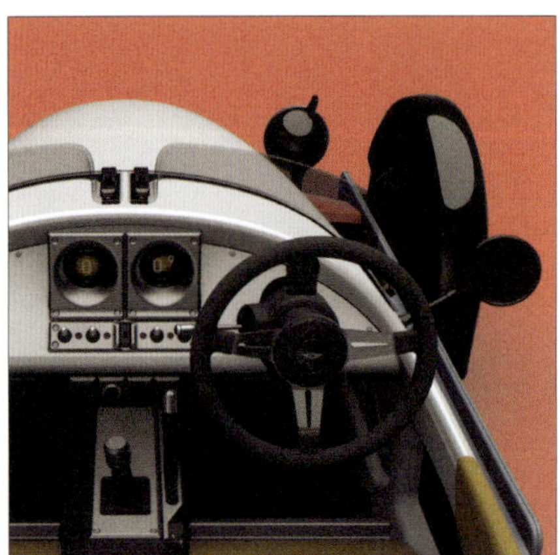

Engine: Ford Dragon 1.5L in-line 3 cylinder naturally aspirated	**Platform:** Aluminium modular monocoque	**Torque:** 110 ft/lbs (150 Nm)
Gearbox: 5-speed manual	**Power:** 118 bhp (87 kW)	**Dry weight:** 635 kg

The Morgan Super 3 is a striking reimagination of the three-wheeler, blending retro-futuristic design with the artisanal soul of Morgan Motor Company's 113-year legacy. Launched in February 2022, this clean-sheet creation departs from its V-twin forebears, embracing a jet-age aesthetic that fuses mechanical honesty with bespoke charm. Measuring 151 inches long, 65 inches wide, and 49 inches high, with a featherlight dry weight of 1,400 pounds, the Super 3 is a compact marvel of proportion and purpose. Built on Morgan's first-ever CX generation-bonded aluminum monocoque platform, it abandons the traditional wooden substructure for a modern, rigid foundation that enhances both strength and agility.

The Super 3's design is a captivating interplay of form and function. At the front, cast aluminum structures frame a square grille, housing a 1.5-liter Ford three-cylinder engine that delivers 118 horsepower to the single rear wheel through a Mazda-sourced five-speed manual gearbox. These exposed components double as suspension mounts and airflow guides, channeling cooling to side-mounted radiators with unapologetic transparency. Flanking the fuselage, two "sideblades"—reminiscent of jet engine diffusers—manage thermal dynamics while offering mounting points for bespoke panniers or custom graphics. The tail tapers into a sleek, minimalist curve, its subtle ribbed detail echoing mid-20th-century aircraft seams,

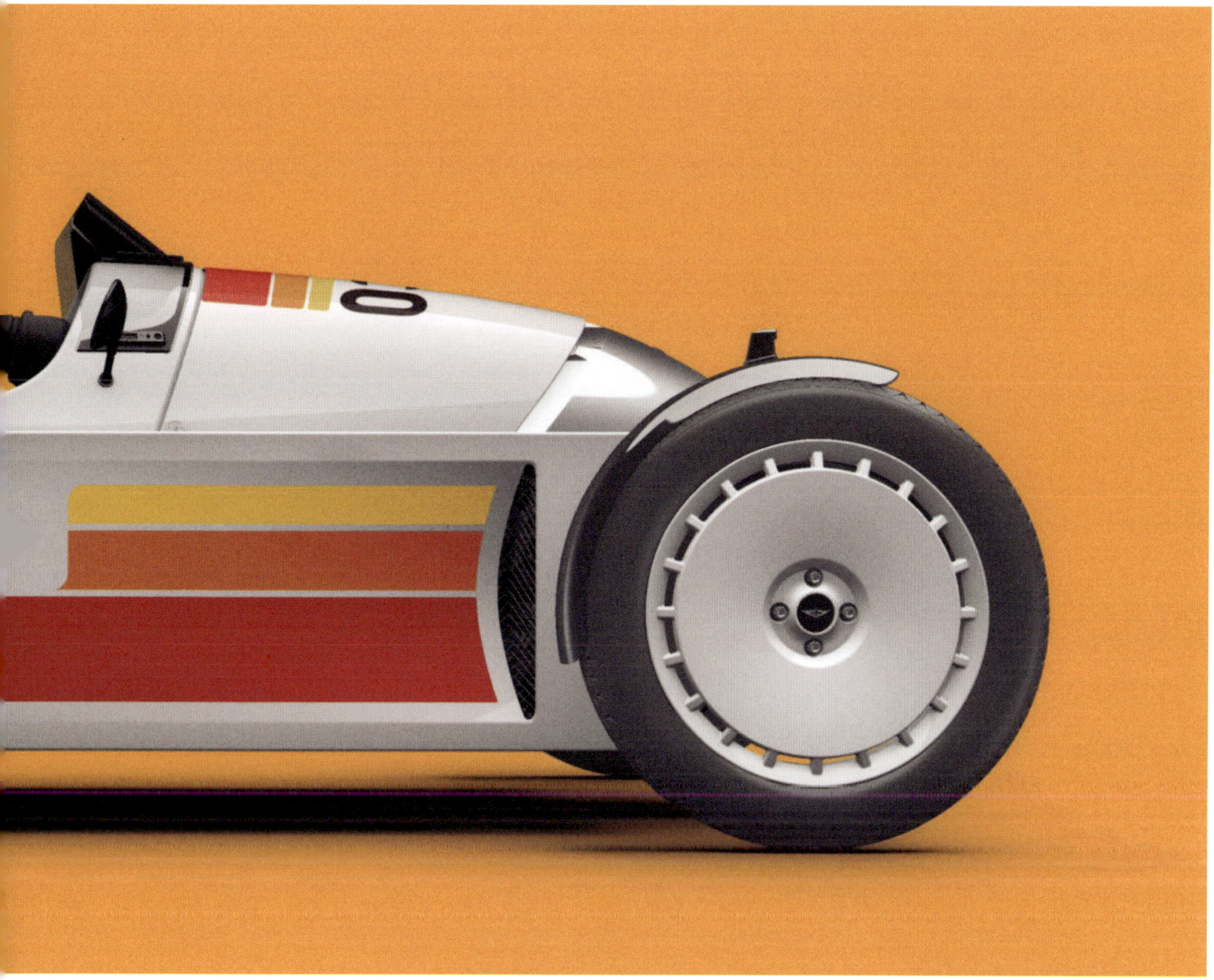

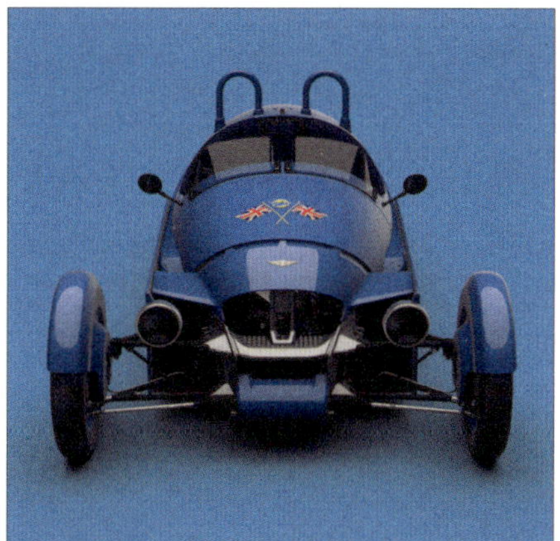

Super 3 by Morgan Motor Company

0-62 MPH: 7 seconds (pending final certification)
Top speed: 130 mph (209 kph)

Fuel economy: Combined: 40 mpg (7.0 L/100 km)
CO2 emissions: Combined: 100 g/km

a deliberate nod to the jet-inspired ethos that defines the Super 3's silhouette.

Inside, the cockpit is a driver's haven, rugged yet refined. Built to IP64 water- and dust-resistant standards, it features fixed seats with adjustable pedals and steering, ensuring a tailored fit for every owner. Digital gauges with a vintage aesthetic, anodized aluminum accents, and optional heated seats merge heritage with contemporary comfort. The absence of a soft top and reliance on minimal aeroscreens amplify the visceral, open-air experience—every vibration, sound, and scent of the road becomes part of the journey. It's a space that invites connection, stripping away excess to focus on the essentials of driving.

Customization is the Super 3's beating heart. From luggage racks to bold paint schemes, Morgan offers endless options, ensuring each vehicle reflects its owner's personality. Powered to a top speed of 130 mph and a 0-60 mph sprint in seven seconds, it delivers a spirited performance that matches its striking design. Priced from £41,995 in the UK—approximately $52,750 USD as of March 2025, based on current exchange rates—the Super 3 is more than a vehicle; it's a rolling canvas of individuality.

Hand-assembled in Malvern, England, the Super 3 embodies Morgan's ethos of crafting adventure-ready icons. It's a testament to design that prioritizes experience over convention, a three-wheeled masterpiece that invites owners to not just drive but to live the journey.

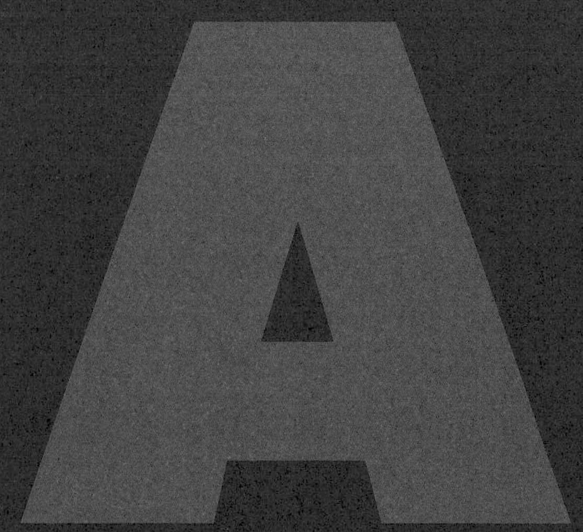

ARCHITECTURE & EXHIBITS

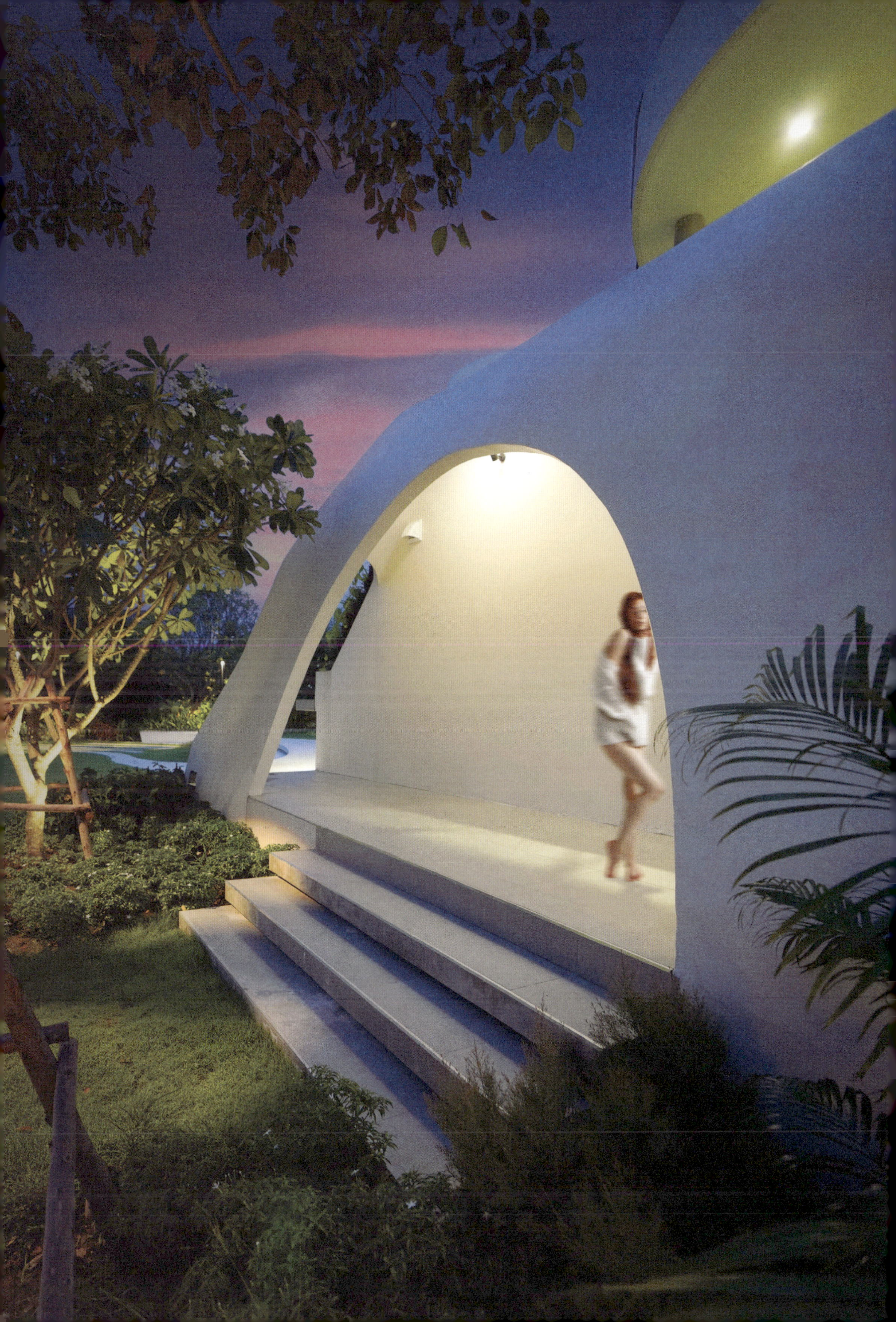

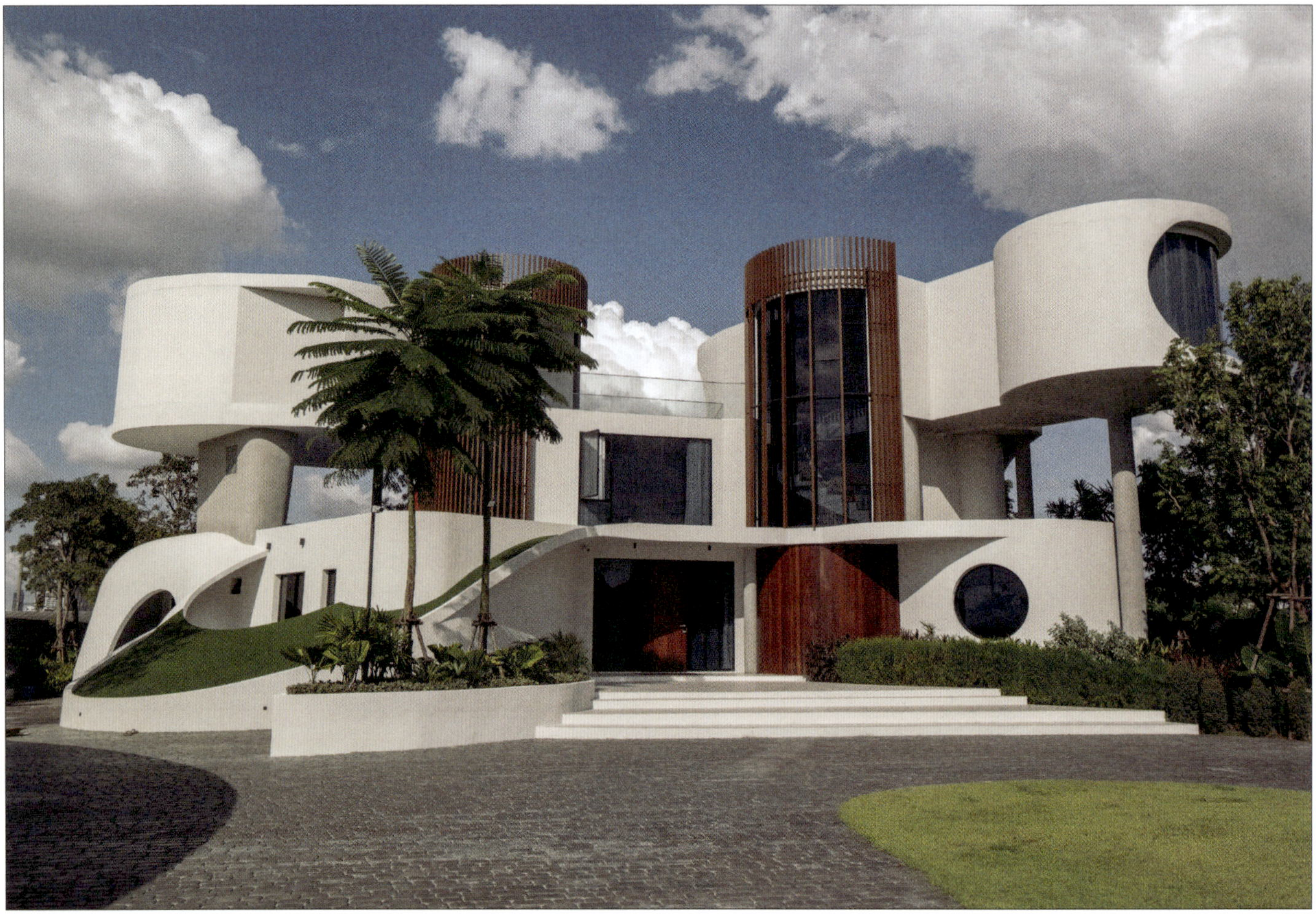

The Nest by The Collective Studio Co., Ltd. / www.thecollectivestudio.co.th

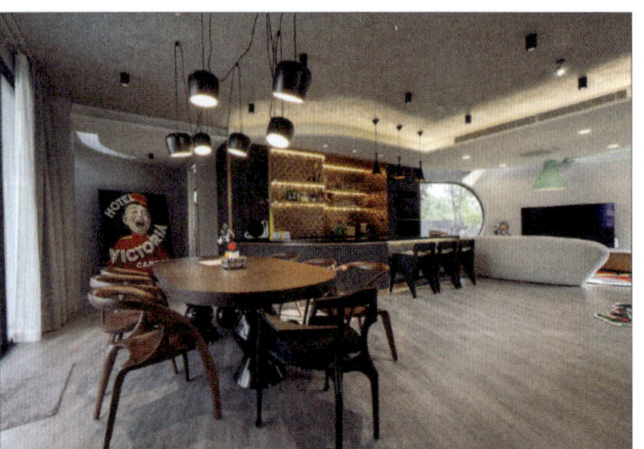

Nestled within Bangkok's verdant Bang Kachao, often dubbed the city's "green lung," The Nest by The Collective Studio Co., Ltd. is a riverside residence that redefines architectural harmony with nature. Spanning 4,305 square feet, this futuristic home, completed in 2024, draws inspiration from the concept of a nest—a protective refuge seamlessly woven into its surroundings. Designed along the Chao Phraya River, The Nest balances legal constraints like height limits and setbacks with a playful, curvilinear form that mirrors the organic flow of its environment.

The exterior is a symphony of smooth, flowing lines, with a concrete garage elevated beneath a modern-retro roof clad in artificial grass, extending the lush landscape skyward. Circular skylights puncture the structure, casting dynamic patterns of light and shadow. The landscape design integrates trees and greenery to frame the home, enhancing privacy while transforming the riverside into a multifunctional retreat. Polished stone benches emerge naturally from the ground, blurring the line between built and natural elements.

Inside, The Nest prioritizes both relaxation and connection. A wooden deck terrace, cooled by a vertical garden, serves as a social hub, while a curvaceous swimming pool echoes the building's contours, offering river views with seclusion. A double-sided spiral staircase, wrapped in aluminum wood-patterned slats, anchors the interior, channeling sunlight across multiple levels. This interplay of light, texture, and form creates an airy, expansive feel despite the home's modest footprint.

The Nest is more than a residence—it's a dialogue between modernity and nature. The Collective Studio Co., Ltd. has crafted a space that feels intimate and boundless, a testament to innovative design that respects its ecological context while offering a serene escape from Bangkok's urban sprawl.

THE NEST IS A RIVERSIDE RESIDENTIAL PROJECT THAT REDEFINES THE RELATIONSHIP BETWEEN ARCHITECTURE AND ITS NATURAL SURROUNDINGS.

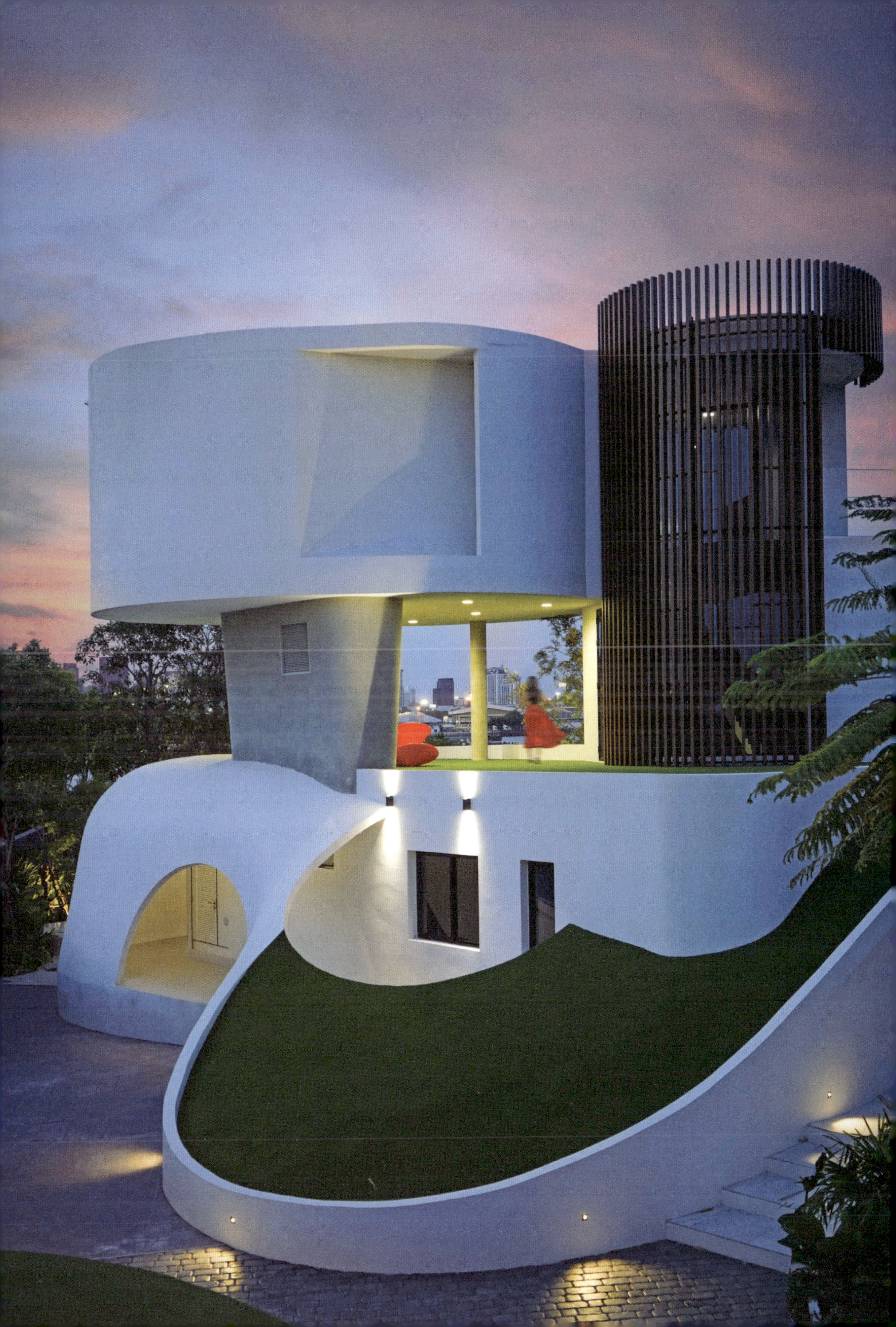

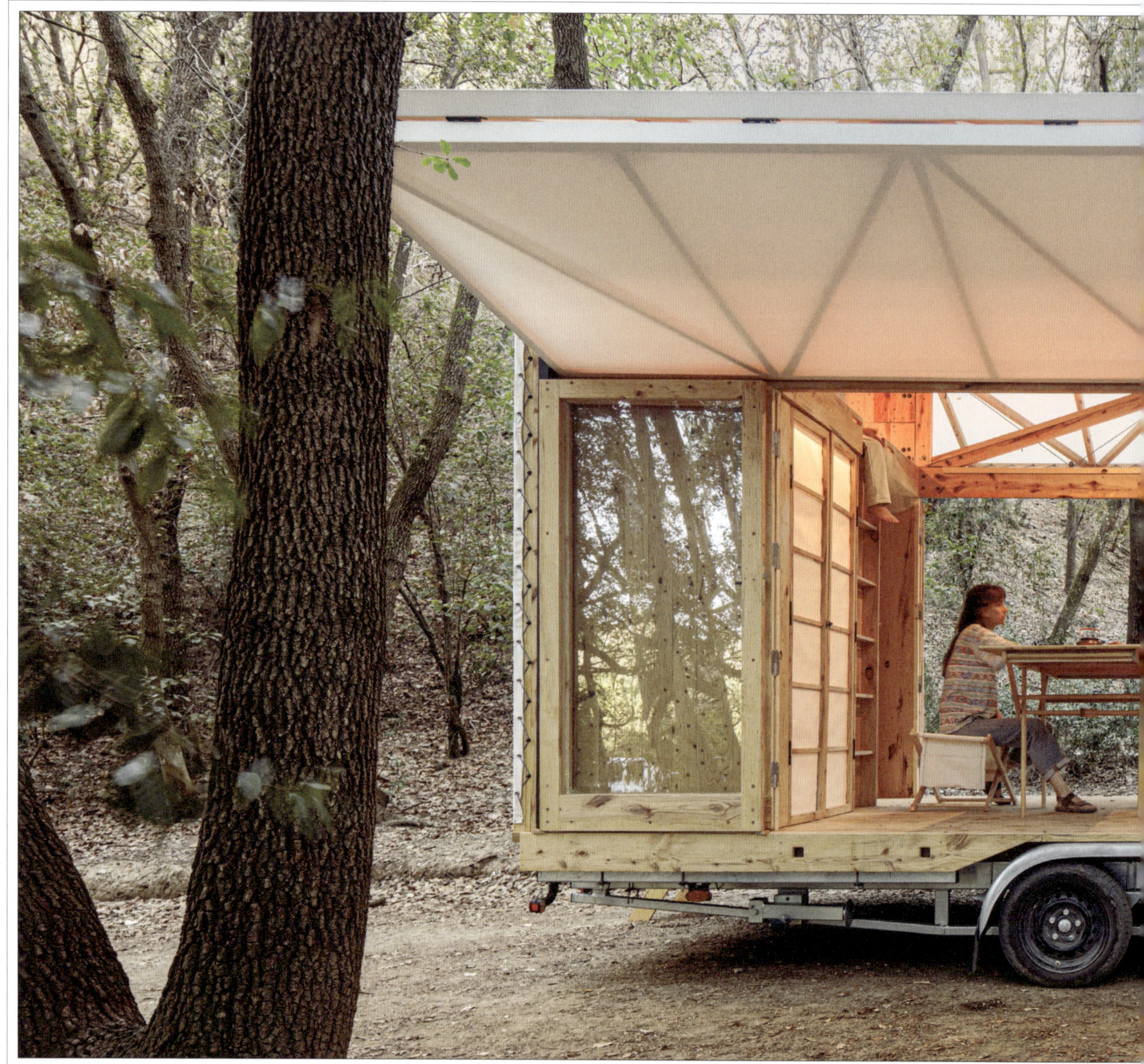

The MO.CA (Mobile Catalyst) project, crafted by the Institute for Advanced Architecture of Catalonia (IAAC), redefines residential design through a lens of sustainability and adaptability. Unveiled in 2024 as part of the Master in Advanced Ecological Buildings and Biocities (MAEBB) program at IAAC's Valldaura Labs, this prototype is a testament to innovative architecture that responds to pressing ecological challenges. Nestled in the Collserola Natural Park near Barcelona, Spain, MO.CA is a 258-square-foot off-grid dwelling designed and built by students and researchers to explore self-sufficiency in food, energy, and material use within a circular bioeconomy framework.

MO.CA's design is a harmonious blend of form and function. Its compact, rectangular structure features a timber frame sourced from sustainably managed local forests, clad in lightweight, breathable panels that optimize insulation. The exterior is punctuated by large, strategically placed windows and a skylight, flooding the interior with natural light

MO.CA IS CENTERED AROUND A FLEXIBLE OPEN SPACE DESIGNED TO BE EASILY ADAPTED INTO AN AREA FOR SLEEPING, LIVING, DINING, OR EVEN EVENTS. **Jon Astbury,** *Dezeen*

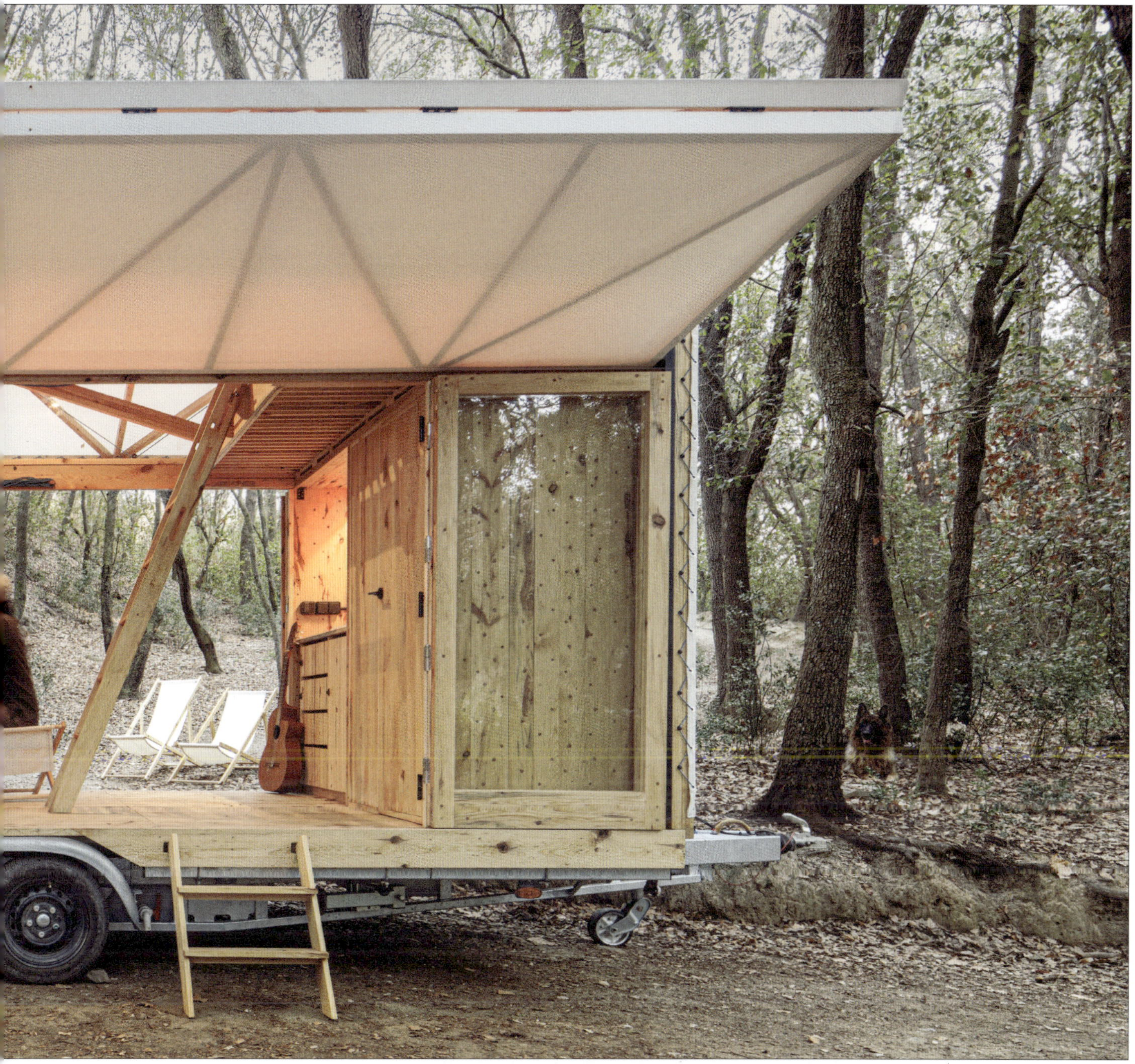

MO.CA

and reducing energy demands. A standout feature is its modular roof, topped with artificial turf and photovoltaic panels, generating renewable energy while mimicking the surrounding landscape. This integration of green technology and natural aesthetics reflects IAAC's commitment to ecological synergy.

Inside, MO.CA is a marvel of spatial efficiency. The open-plan layout includes a living area, a compact kitchen powered by solar energy, and a sleeping loft, all finished with bio-based materials like cork and hemp. A rainwater harvesting system feeds a small hydroponic garden, enabling year-round food production, while a composting toilet closes the waste loop. The design prioritizes passive heating and cooling, with

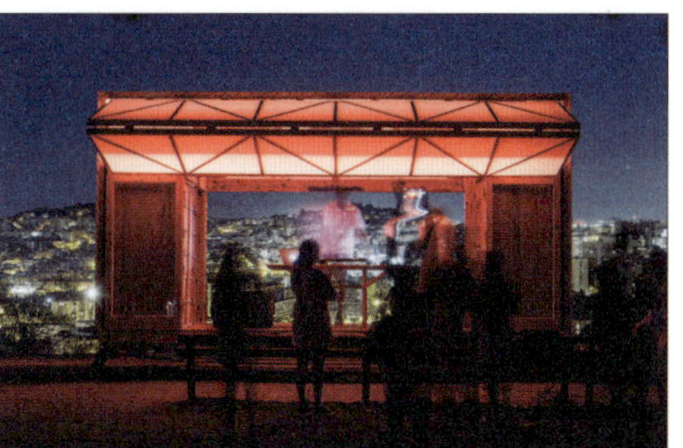

cross-ventilation and thermal mass reducing reliance on mechanical systems, making it a true zero-energy prototype.

What sets MO.CA apart is its mobility. Mounted on a trailer chassis, it can be transported to diverse locations, serving as a catalyst for sustainable living education. Recognized with the 2024 Design Educates Award, MO.CA embodies IAAC's ethos of pushing architectural boundaries. It's not just a house—it's a blueprint for a future where buildings coexist with nature, offering a scalable, replicable model for ecological, self-sustainable, off-the-grid resilience in an era of climate uncertainty.

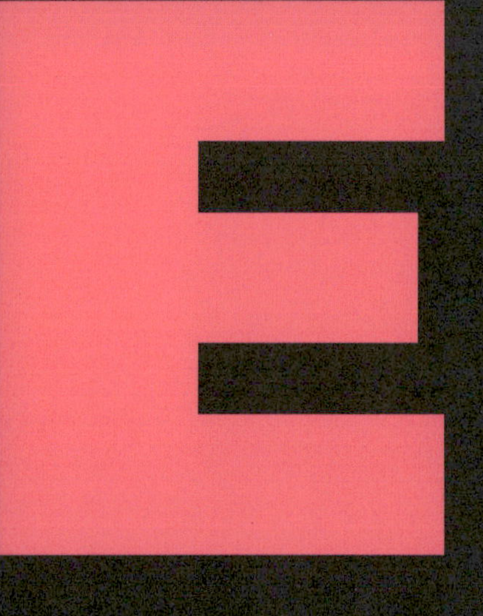

EDUCATION

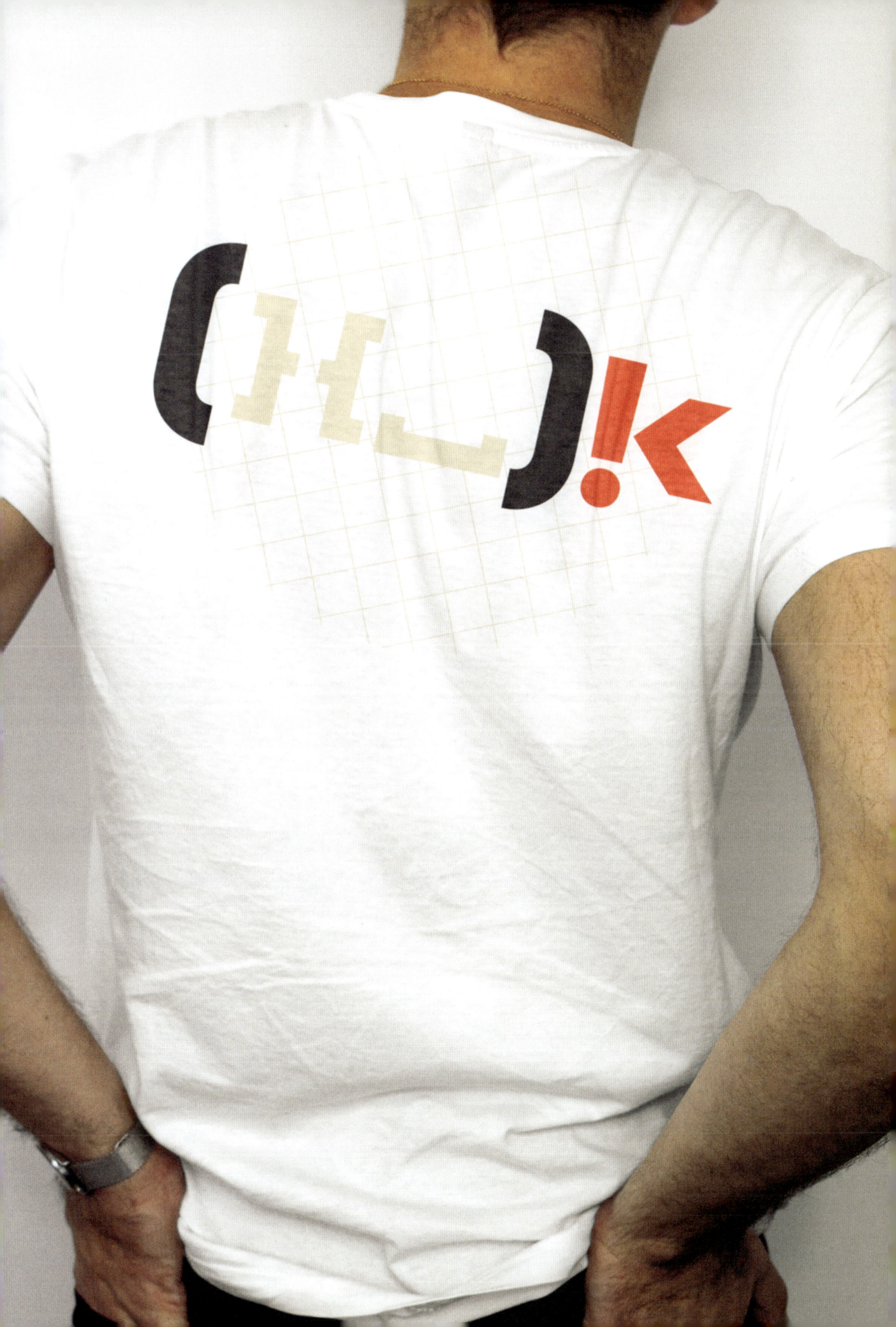

JUSTIN'S CREATIVE BRILLIANCE CONJURES MOTION DESIGN THAT TRANSCENDS THE ORDINARY AND INSPIRES. TCW'S MAGIC STEMS FROM HIS HUMAN-CENTRIC VISION, STRATEGIC THINKING, AND GENEROUS, FREE-SPIRITED CREATIVE PROCESS.

Ada Whitney, *Professor & Curator, School of Visual Arts*

WITH A SHARP EYE FOR DETAIL AND A DEEP UNDERSTANDING OF DESIGN'S EVOLVING LANGUAGE, HE SHAPES IMAGES THAT CHALLENGE CONVENTIONS AND CREATE NEW PERSPECTIVES.

Randy Hunt, *Chair of MFA Design, School of Visual Arts*

A GENERATION OF SVA STUDENTS HAS JUSTIN TO THANK FOR THEIR SHARPENED TYPE SKILLS, DESIGN CONFIDENCE, AND POINT OF VIEW.

Willy Wong, *Professor, School of Visual Arts*

JUSTIN IS AN INCREDIBLE MENTOR WHO TRULY CARES. HIS PASSION AND GUIDANCE AT SVA'S MFA PROGRAM SHAPED HOW A LOT OF OUR COHORT APPROACHES DESIGN.

Tiffany Pai, *Former Student & Senior Art Director of Brand Identity, The New York Times*

JUSTIN COLT IS BOUNDLESS CREATIVITY. HE BREATHES JOY, BRILLIANCE, CARE, CRAFT, THOUGHTFULNESS, BEAUTY, MOVEMENT, AND MAGIC INTO EVERY PROJECT, COLLABORATION, AND VENTURE HE TAKES ON.

Warren Lehrer, *Designer & Professor, School of Visual Arts*

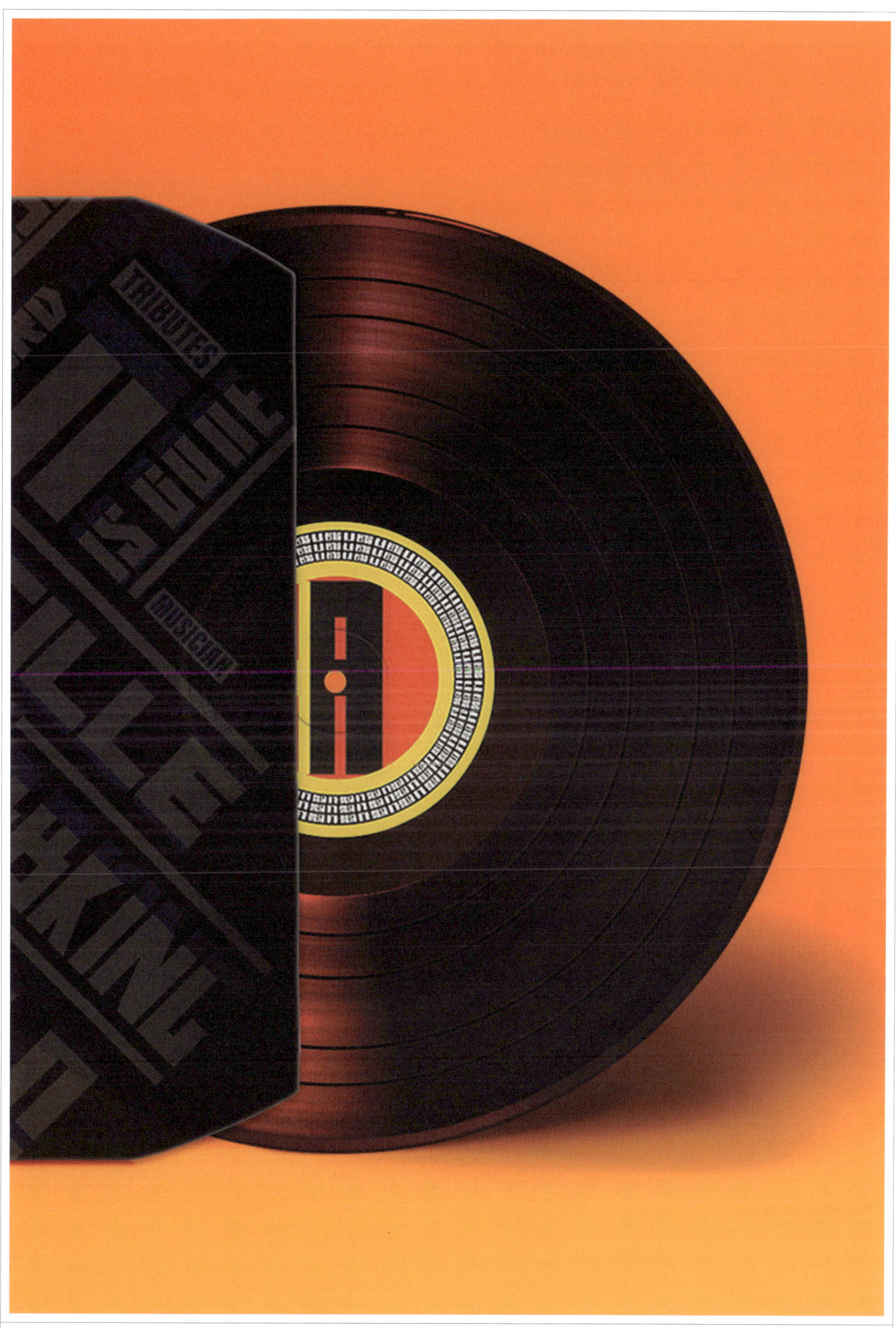

(Page 127) Album Packaging "Chuck", New Talent Annual 2022. Professor: Justin Colt. Gold-winning student: JJ Jung
(Above) Vinyl Cover Design, New Talent Annual 2021. Professor: Justin Colt. Gold-winning student: Junghoon Oh

I first heard Justin Colt's name during the early period of the SVA MFA Design program. I was speaking to a group in State College, Pennsylvania, and ran into my friend Lanny Sommese, a legendary graphic design teacher. "My best student is applying to your program," he said, referring to Justin. "He's our brightest star." So I made a mental note of "Justin," a name that suggests the Wild West, and presumed that he'd live up to Lanny's promise. Justin's work did not disappoint. His evocative typography, combined with conceptual acuity, gave him an edge. Upon graduating, he co-founded a design office, The Collected Works, with classmate Jose Fresneda in a studio space provided by Milton Glaser. Out of the gate, they worked together on prestigious jobs—so impressive was their output that they were made faculty for the Type for Masters class that received some of the highest year-end student accolades. Over the past ten years, The Collected Works has done snappy brand campaigns that transcend trends while exuding contemporary aesthetics. Much of this is Justin's mastery of technique and technology, which says "today" without being slavishly tied to "new."

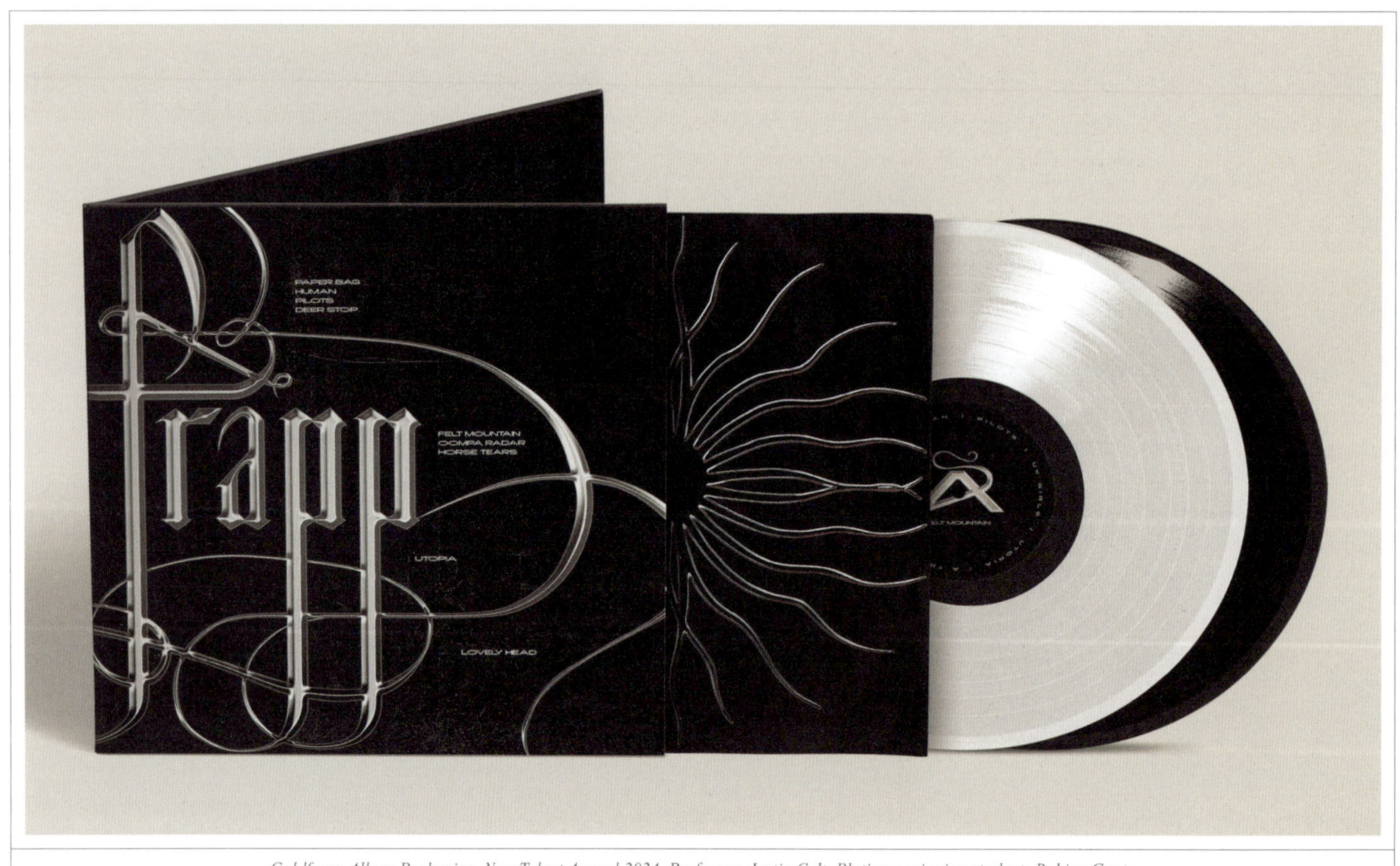

Goldfrapp Album Packaging, New Talent Annual 2024. Professor: Justin Colt. Platinum-winning student: Rabiya Gupta

Q&A: Justin Colt, Professor, School of Visual Arts

What is your process for selecting students for your classes? Are there certain qualifications they have to meet?
I'm lucky that I don't have to go through a strict selection process for my classes. I do start the first class with a very honest rundown of what to expect: This will be the toughest class they take all semester. In my opinion, it's also the most important. For my class, we focus a lot on typography because I believe that to be a successful designer, you need to be a master at it. And let's be honest, typography is challenging.

Have you ever dismissed a student from your class? If so, for what reason?
Yes. Almost every year, there's at least one student who ends up being dismissed from my class. I genuinely believe everyone should have the chance to learn and succeed, but there's a certain baseline that needs to be met. Assignments are due in full every class. If a project isn't finished, it's better for the student to stay home.

Students need to be active participants, supporting each other. It's not enough to just be naturally talented and focus solely on your own work. I expect my students to be generous with their ideas and to provide meaningful feedback and support to their classmates. There also has to be a genuine enthusiasm for the work. Students should be curious, eager to explore new ideas, and willing to challenge themselves. When it becomes clear that someone isn't meeting these expectations, we usually have to

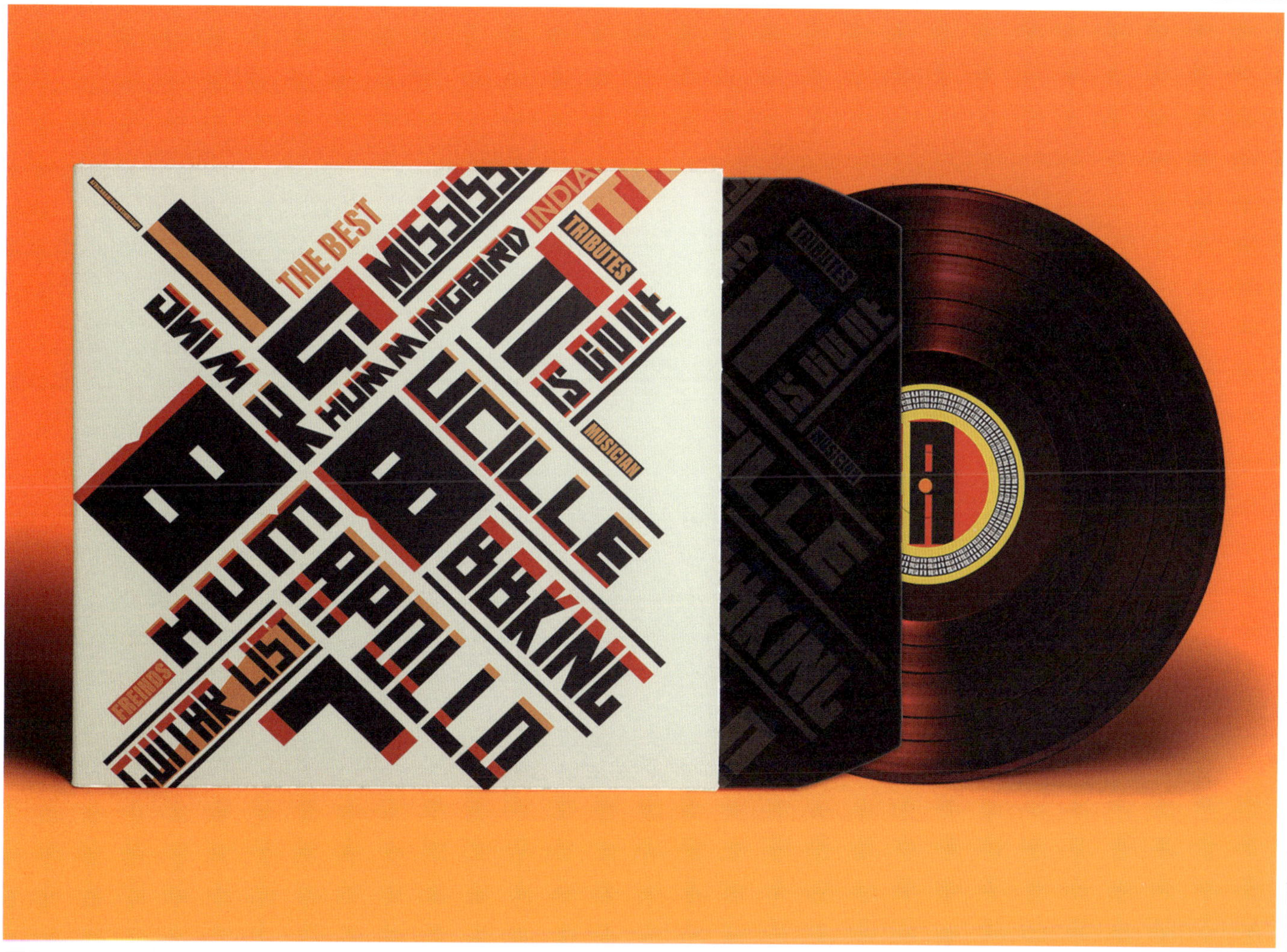

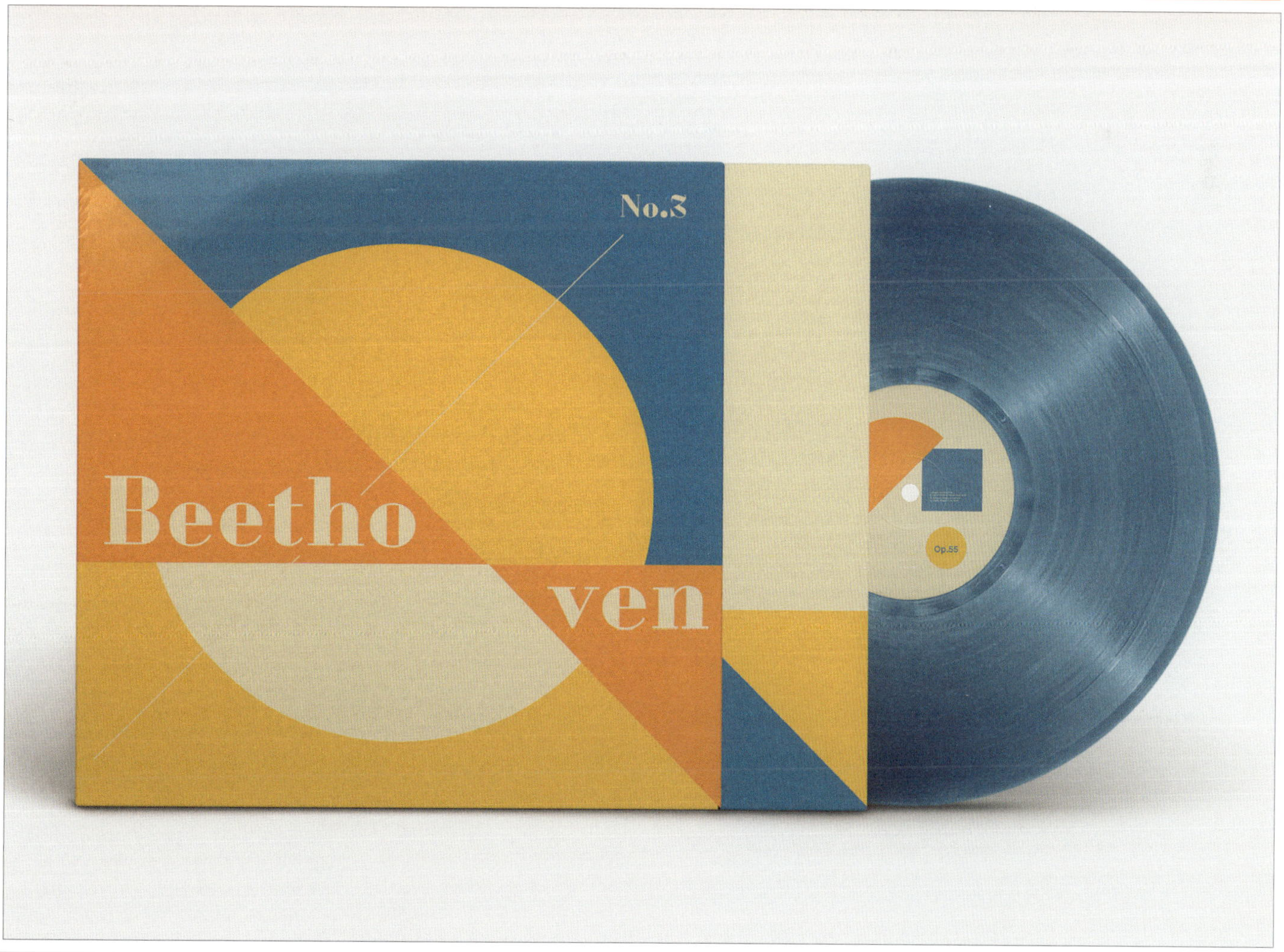

(Top) Vinyl Cover Design, New Talent Annual 2021. Professor: Justin Colt. Gold-winning student: Junghoon Oh
(Bottom) Beethoven Album, New Talent Annual 2022. Professor: Justin Colt. Gold-winning student: Doah Kwon

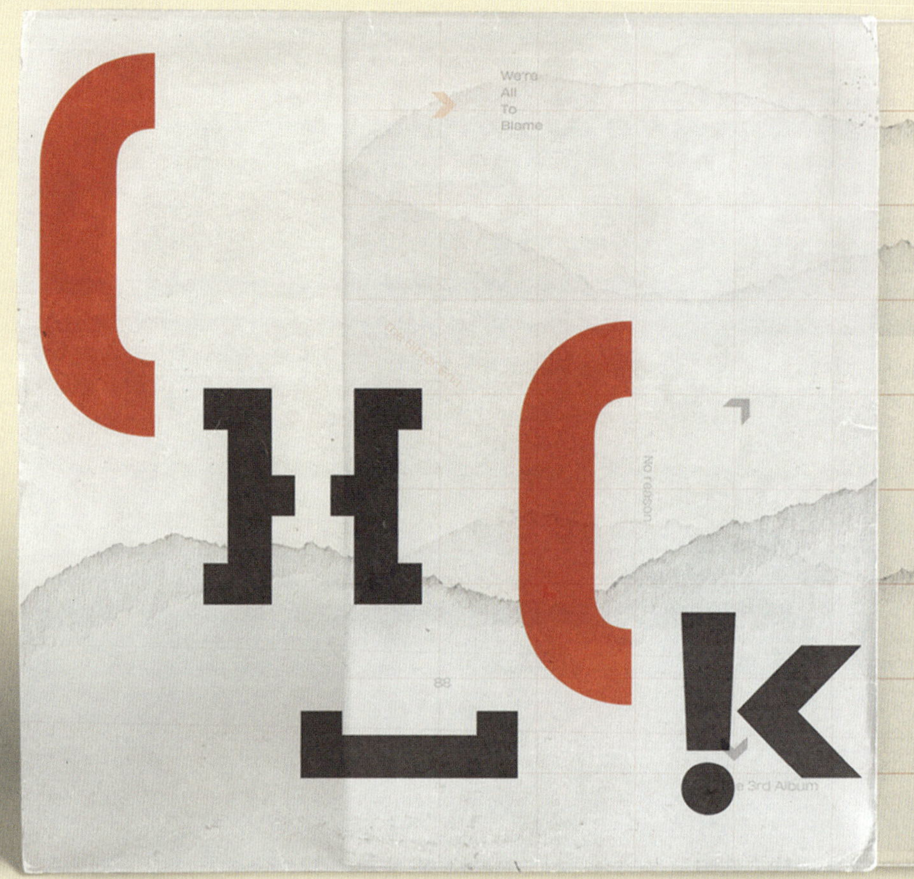
We're
All
To
Blame
No reason
88
The 3rd Album

Tracklist
. Intro
2. No Reason
3. We're All to Blame
7. Open Your Eyes
. Slipping Away
9. I'm Not the One
10. Welcome to Hell
. Angels with Dirty Faces
5. Some Say
6. The Bitter Endt
13. 88
. Pieces
12. There's No Solution

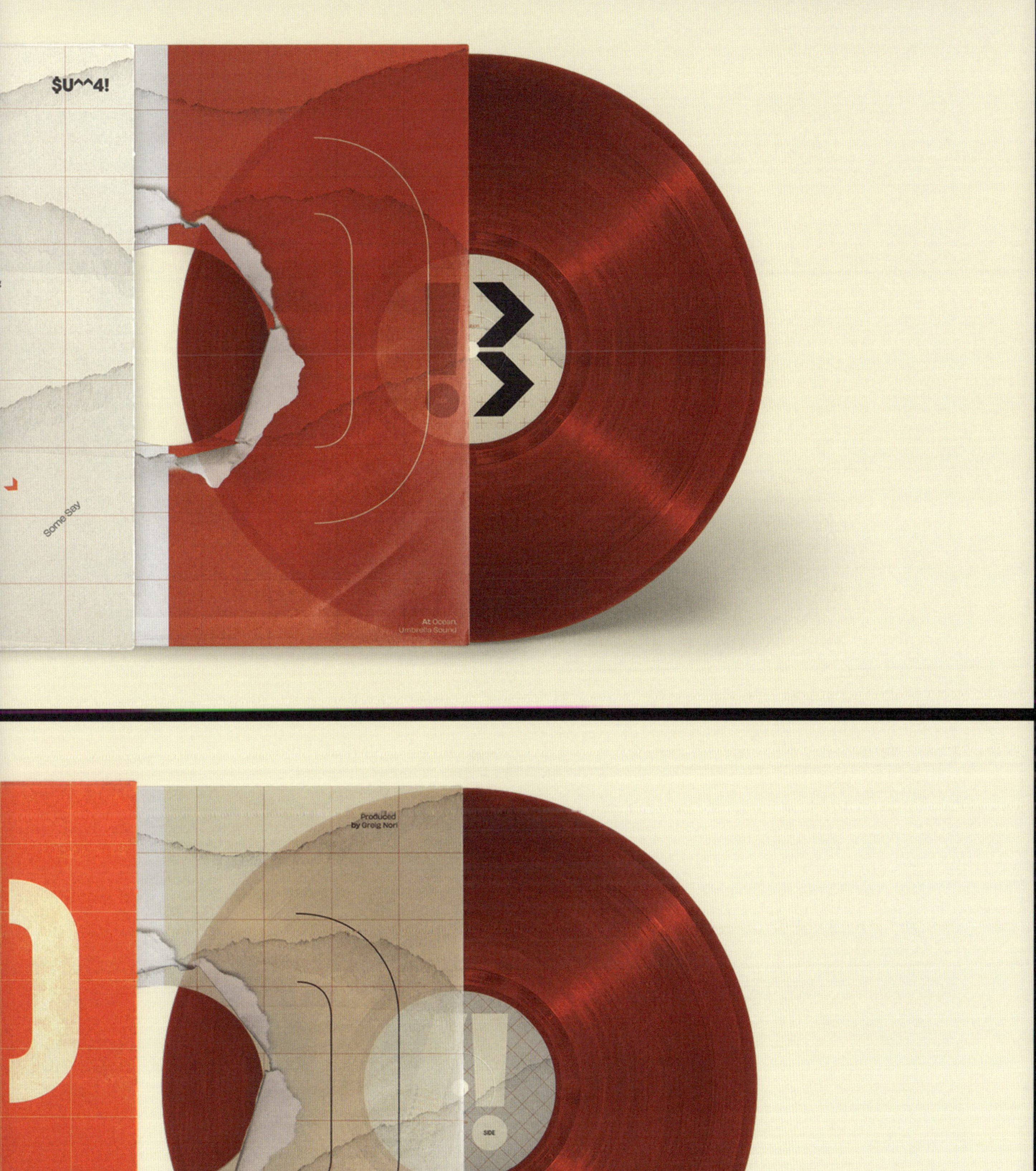

$U^^4!
Some Say
At Ocean,
Umbrella Sound
Produced
by Greig Nori
At Sound City
SIDE

have a conversation about them withdrawing from the class.

This isn't just for their benefit but for the success of the whole class. My goal is always to create a positive, challenging environment where everyone is helping and encouraging each other. If someone doesn't share that spirit, this class is not the right fit.

What might be a typical first assignment?
I usually kick off the semester for both my graduate and undergraduate students with a big festival branding project. We start by passing around a hat. First, each student randomly draws a typographic style like constructivism, Dadaism, or Bauhaus. Then, from a second hat, they pick a festival theme—maybe it's music, art, comedy, etc. Their task is to combine these two elements to create a cohesive identity design system. The combinations are endless and always different each year—imagine a cultural festival inspired by Dadaism or a tech festival with a constructivist vibe. It's a tough design challenge, but that's what makes it so exciting.

In just one week, they have to pitch three different conceptual directions for their unique festival combo. Each direction includes a festival name, a written overview, 30 sketches for the primary logo, ten poster sketches, proposed typefaces, a color palette, and the overall art direction. It's a lot to ask, and with only a week to do it, students have to think deeply and work fast. The results are usually fantastic—full of interesting ideas and an impressive amount of work. It's a real trial by fire, and sometimes it's a bit too much for some students, leading them to bow out of the class, which is totally okay.

Do you ever ask them to include something they're passionate about in their work for your class?
I almost never give students an open brief to create whatever they want. I've tried it in the past, and it almost always leads to predictable ideas and expected outcomes. When they don't have to tackle complex and challenging design problems, the results tend to be pretty average. Instead, I encourage students to bring their personal strengths and interests into the tough assignments I give them. This approach leads to much more interesting results.

Do you work with students individually or in groups?
Both. In grad school, almost every project is a group project. I've noticed that group projects are pretty rare in design school, and I don't really get why. Design is all about collaboration—you'll be working with teams and people with different perspectives throughout your entire career. Working in a group is challenging, and it's a skill that needs to be practiced. There will be conflicts, and students need to learn how to navigate and resolve them while still wanting to be friends at the end of the day.

Plus, group projects are so much more rewarding. Team members can lift each other up, help each other see new approaches, and leverage each other's skills. I always tell my students that they can divide up an assignment in any way that makes sense to them, so they should play to the group's strengths. And honestly, group projects tend to produce more interesting work than solo projects. They often feel more layered, unique, complete, and fascinating.

Do you have group critiques of the students' work?
Always. I never lecture. Class is all about sharing work and giving and receiving feedback. I guide the conversation toward topics and discussions I think are interesting and relevant, but I mostly let the students lead the feedback and ask questions. This is why it's so important for everyone to be active contributors to each other's success.

What percentage of a typical class goes on to create award-winning work?
Every class produces award-winning work—often multiple times over. I also emphasize the importance of getting your work out there and submitting it to competitions and publications. It's not about being egotistical; it's about showing the world that you're a talented designer and attracting the kind of work you want. We're in a visual field, so students need to put their work out into the world. This is a mentality that pays dividends both during their time in school and long after.

At the end of the semester, what kind of advice do you give to the class?
At the end of the semester, I like to take some time just to sit and chat with the class. I do this at the end of every assignment, too. It's a chance to hear what the students thought about the assignment—what they would change if they were to do it over again, where they hit friction points, and where they found success. The end-of-semester chat is similar but reflects on our time together as a whole. I always tell my students that I can dish it out, but I can also take it. So, they should let me know what I should change.

I also like to reiterate a few common themes I've shared throughout the course: Keep pushing yourself and stay out of your comfort zone. Be the kind of person you'd want to work with. Be interesting—this career is so much easier if you're just an interesting person with whom people want to engage. And remember, we're lucky to be doing this for a living. So many people end up in jobs or careers they hate, but that's not us. We're in a challenging but incredibly liberating field where we can make a real impact, connect with people we admire, and be genuinely excited about what we do. That's pretty rare.

Lastly, I remind them that our friendship doesn't end with the semester. I encourage students to stay in touch (and they often do), keep me updated on their successes, and share recent work they've done. I also let them know they're welcome to reach out if they're ever interested in working with me. Many of our interns and designers—paid, of course—at the studio are former students.

Can you name a few of your past students who have gained success? If so, what are they doing now?
Raif Hossain at Time Out Group; Raven Mo at AIGA NY; Soumya Gupta at Notion; Doah Kwon at Google; Ezra Lee and Tiffany Pai at the *New York Times*; Emily Roemer at Amazon; Victoria DeBlasi at MTV; Harbor Bickmore at That That Type Foundry; Sukanya Bose at Interbrand; Huiqi Qiu at KUDOS Design Collaboratory; Vasavi Bubna, Rohan Rege, and Mina Son at COLLINS; and Katherine Killeffer, Bruno Pasi Bergallo, and Renee Freiha at Pentagram.

What do you think of the way so many people in the creative fields now are without any formal, never mind university-level, training?
Maybe it's an unexpected answer, but I think it's great. I don't believe that a person's future success hinges on attending design school. If someone can build a career by being completely self-taught, learning in the field, and just hustling, I think that's fantastic. I tell this to my students, too: Nobody is going to look at your transcript, ask for your GPA, or want to see your diploma. It's your portfolio and the connections you make that will define your trajectory. That could come from your time in design school—but it doesn't have to. And I think that's fantastic.

Justin Colt, SVA www.sva.edu/faculty/justin-colt

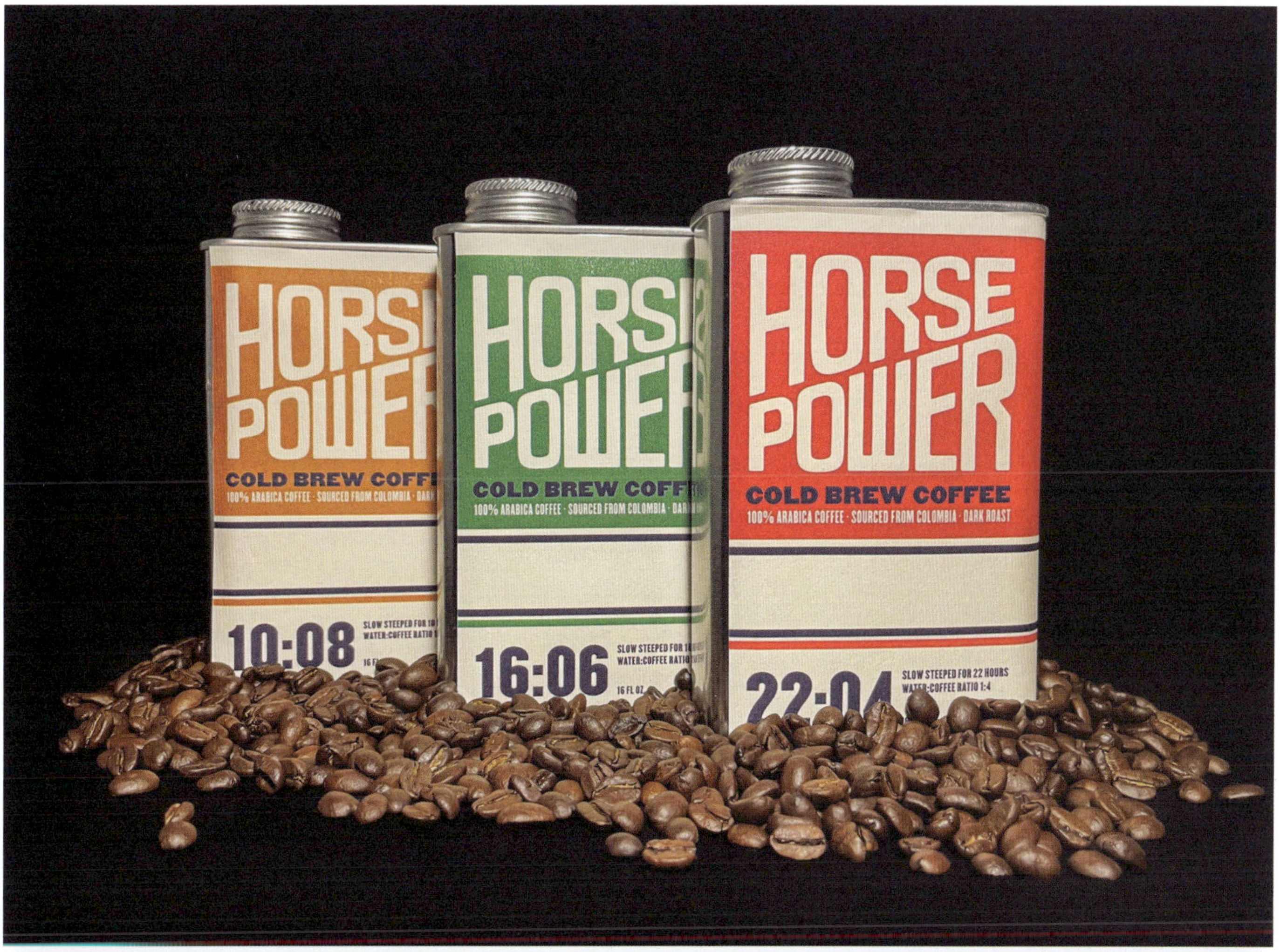

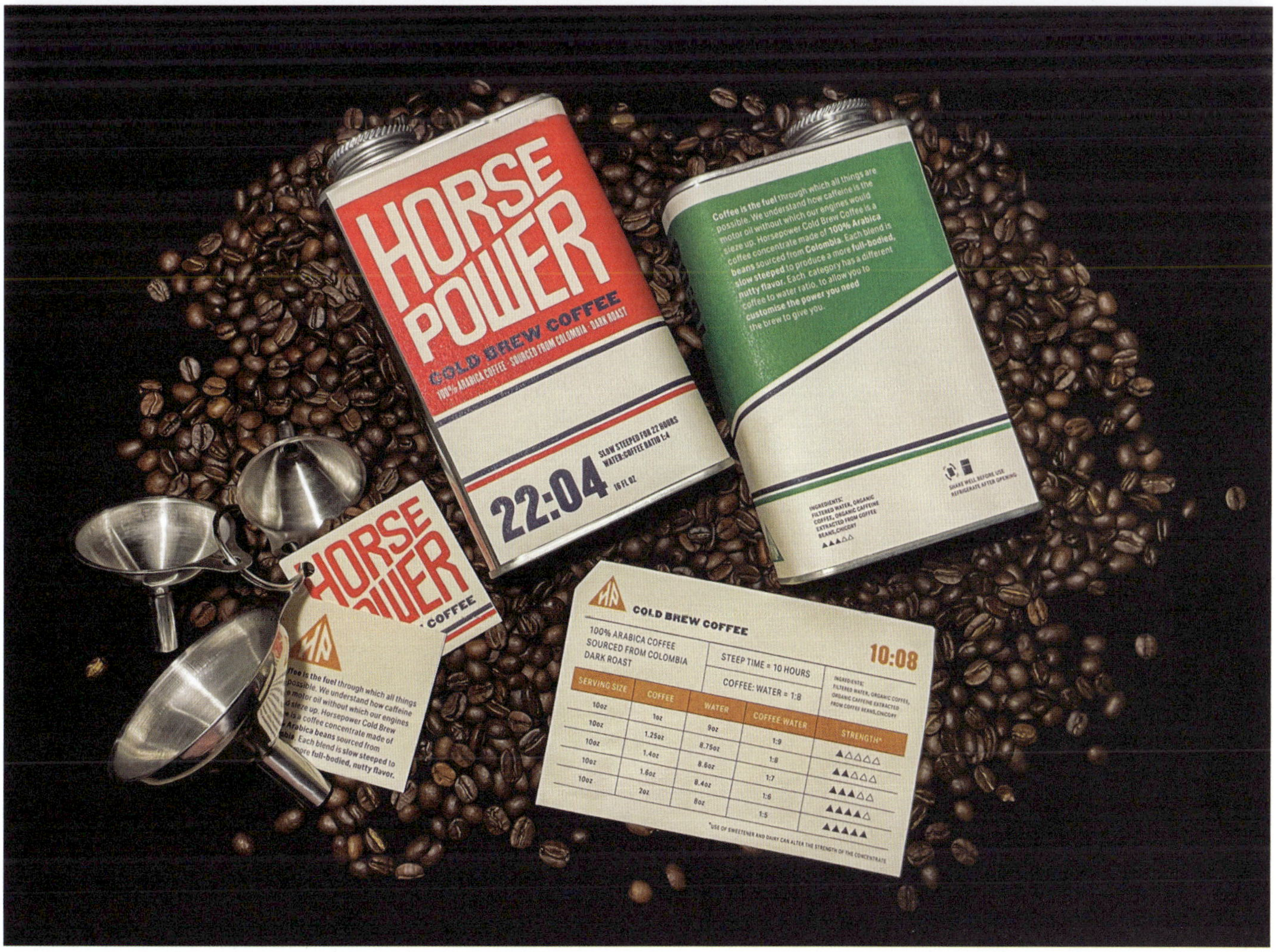

SERVING SIZE	COFFEE	WATER	COFFEE WATER	STRENGTH*
10oz	1oz	9oz	1:9	
10oz	1.25oz	8.75oz	1:9	
10oz	1.4oz	8.6oz	1:8	
10oz	1.6oz	8.4oz	1:7	
10oz	2oz	8oz	1:5	

Horsepower Cold Brew Coffee, New Talent Annual 2024. Professor: Justin Colt. Gold-winning student: Vasavi Bubna

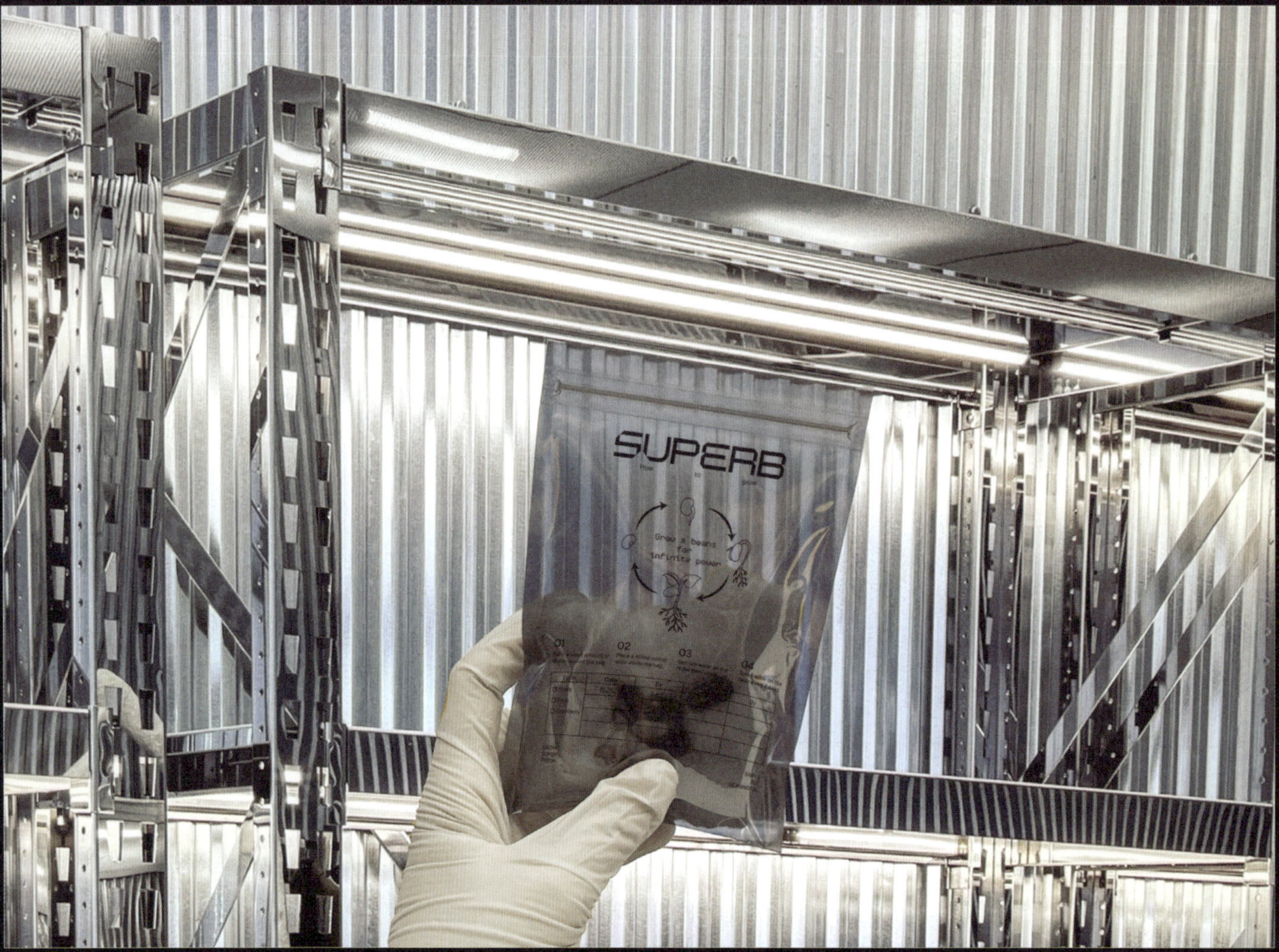

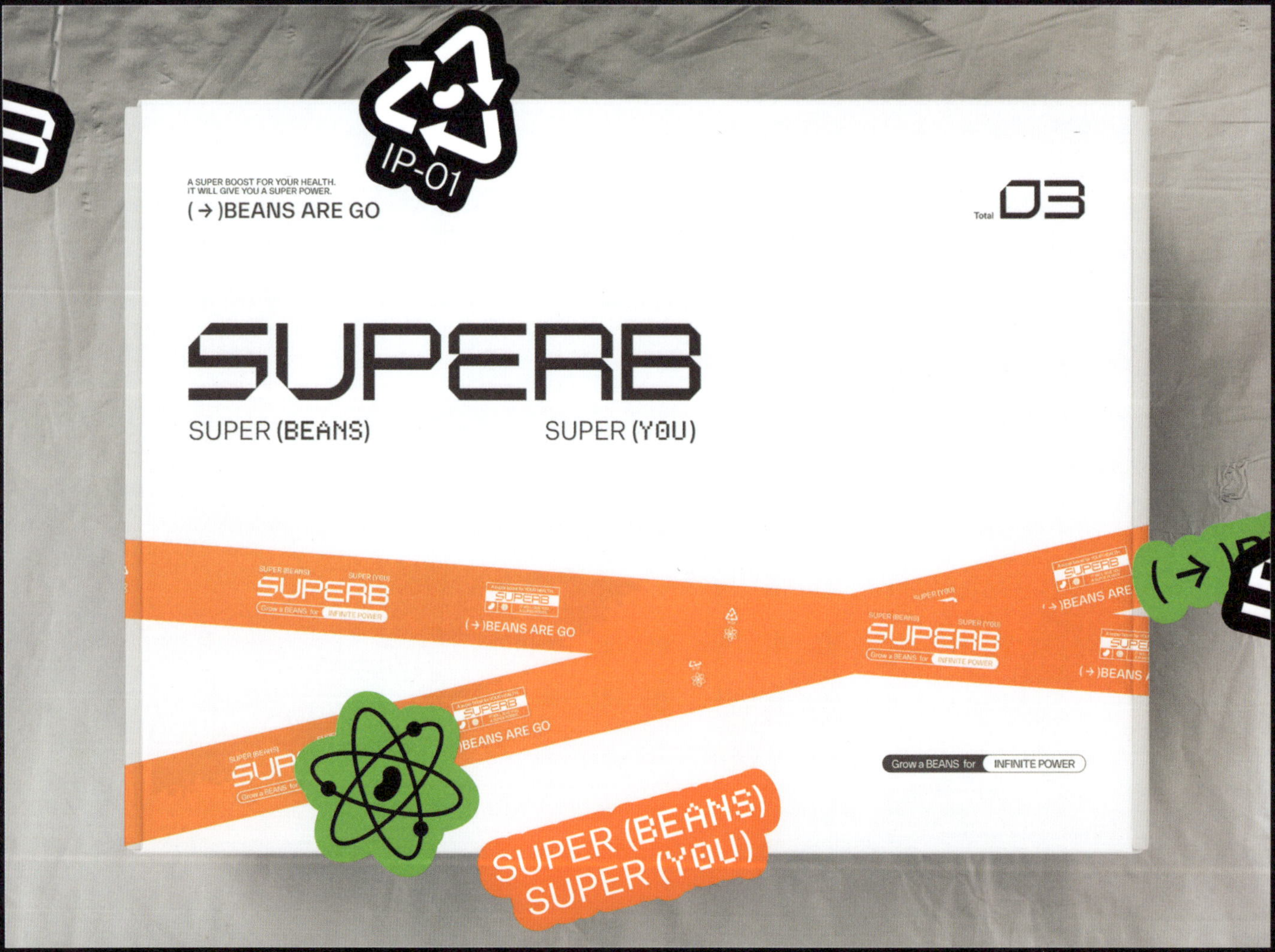

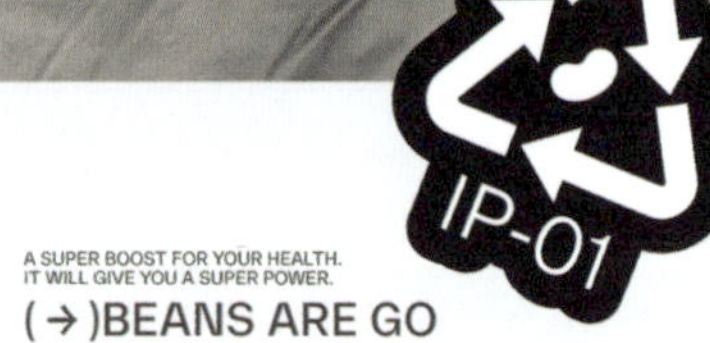

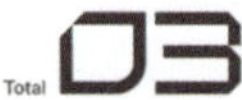

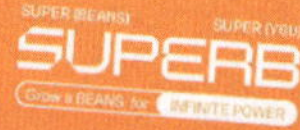
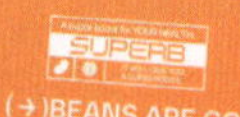

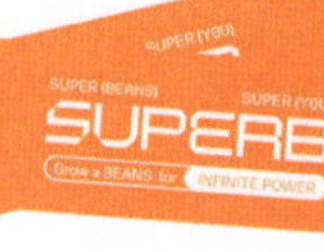
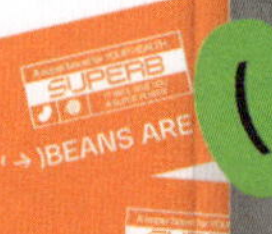

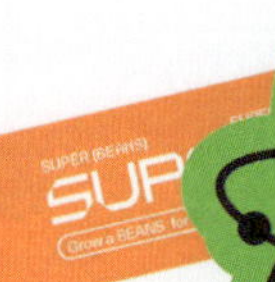
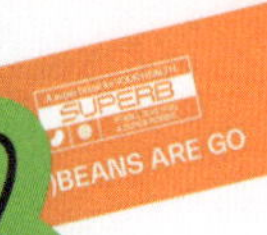

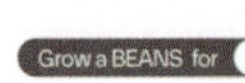
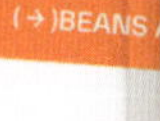
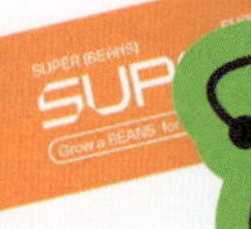

A SUPER BOOST FOR YOUR HEALTH.
IT WILL GIVE YOU A SUPER POWER.
(→)BEANS ARE GO

Total 03

SUPERB

SUPER (BEANS)   SUPER (YOU)

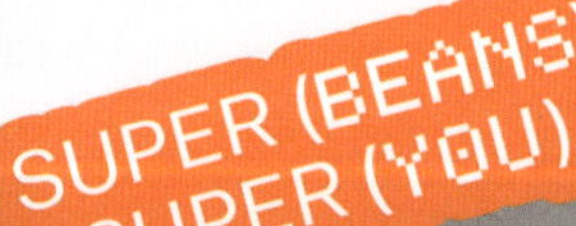

SUPERB, New Talent Annual 2024. Professor: Justin Colt. Gold-winning student: Sungeun Shin

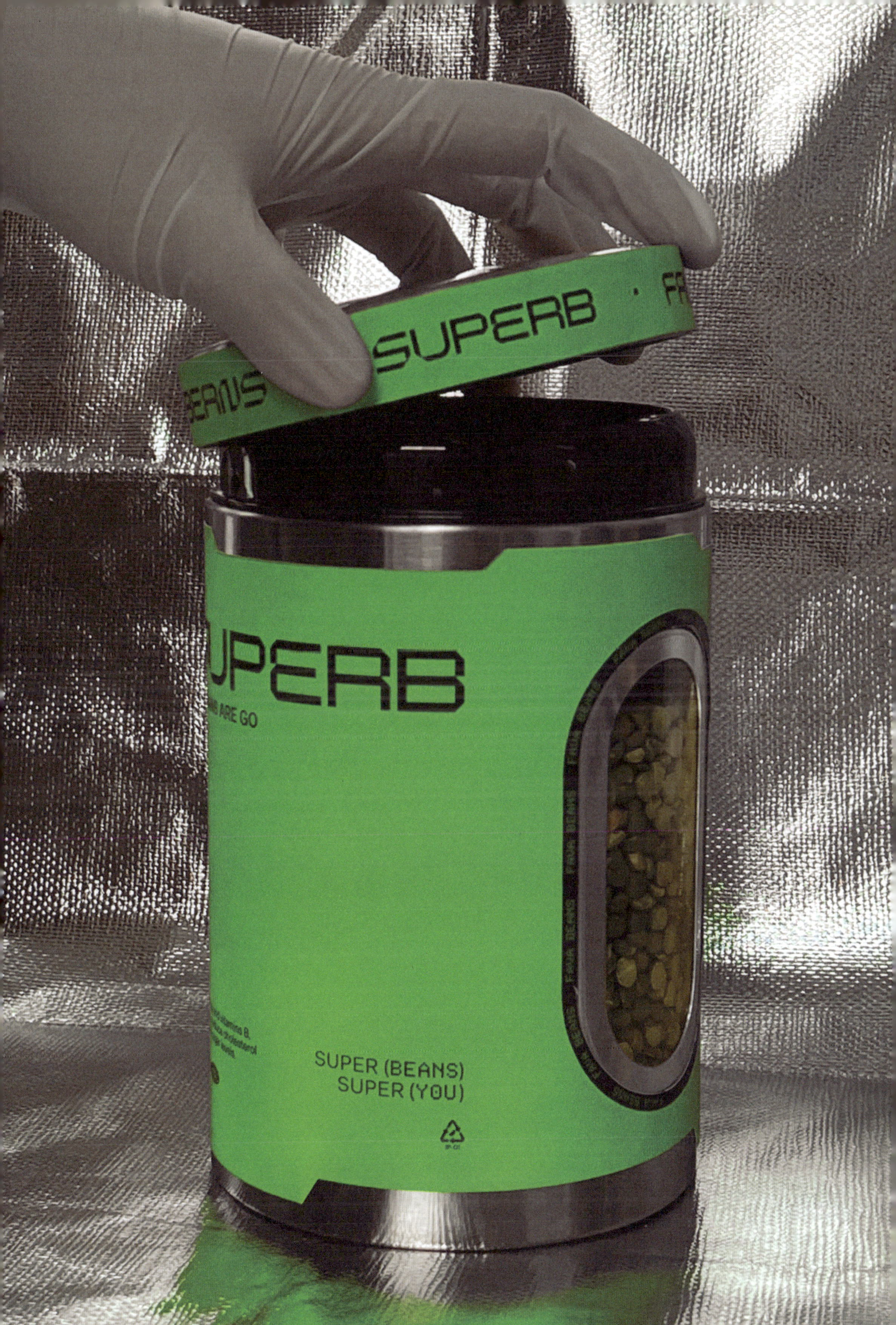

SUPERB
BEANS
FR
UPERB
ARE GO
SUPER (BEANS)
SUPER (YOU)

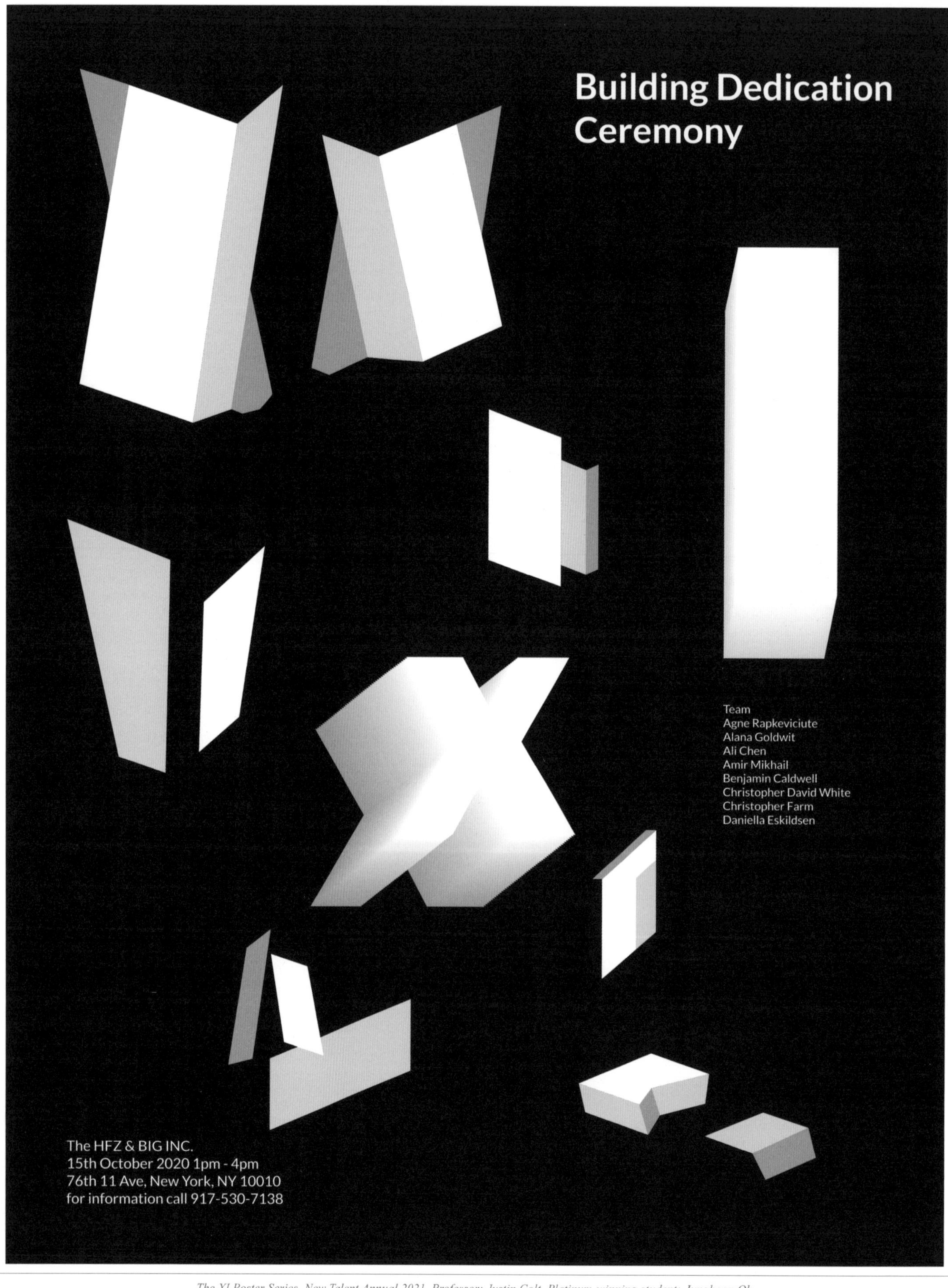

The XI Poster Series, New Talent Annual 2021. Professor: Justin Colt. Platinum-winning student: Junghoon Oh

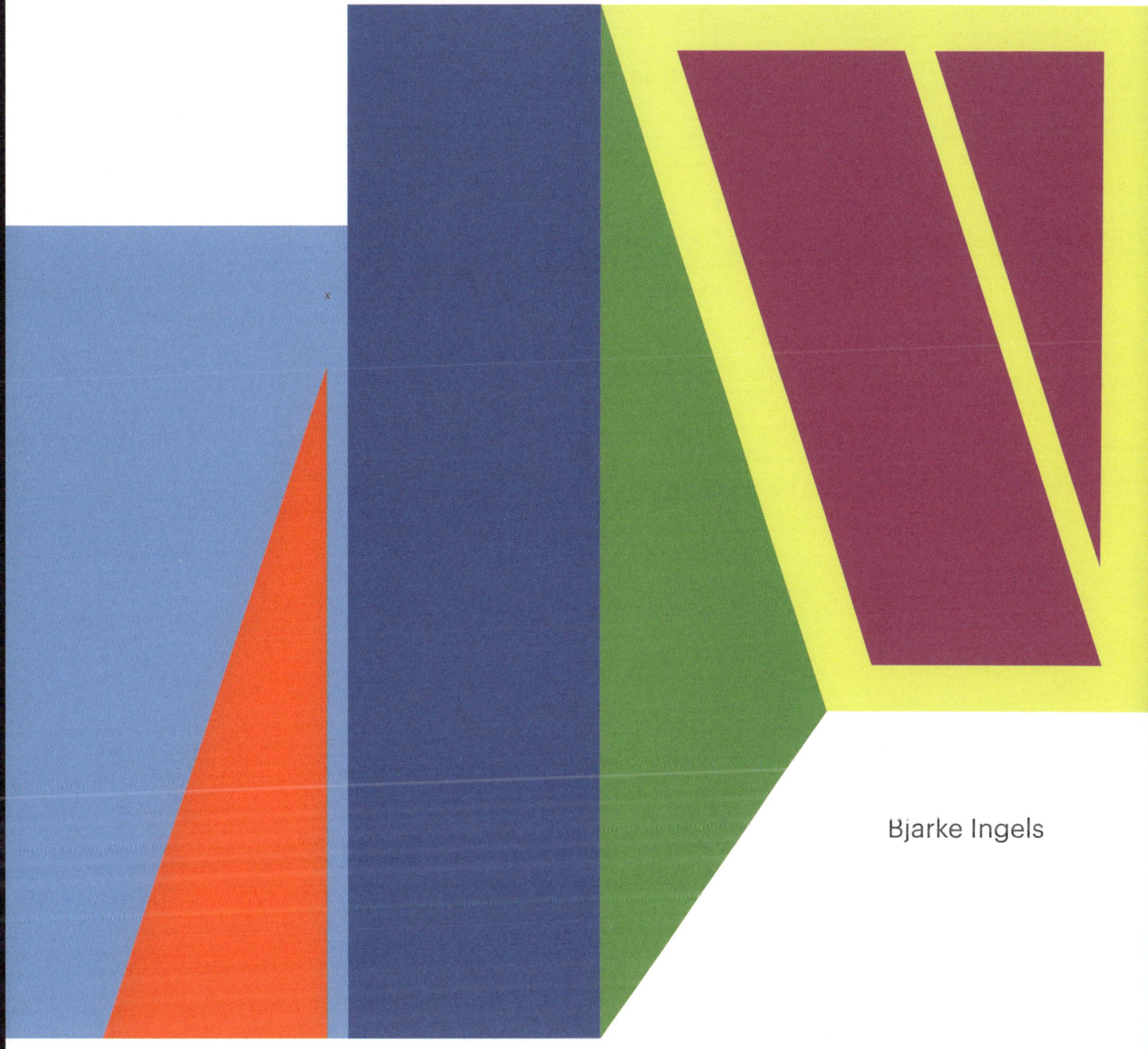

Building dedication ceremony

The HFZ & BIG INC.
15th October 2020 1pm - 4pm
76th 11 Ave, New York, NY 10010
for information call 917-530-7138

Photography Annual 2025

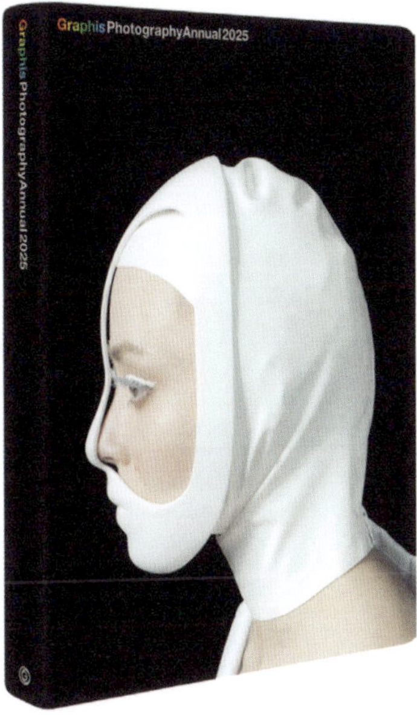

2025
Hardcover: 256 pages
200-plus color illustrations
Trim: 8.5 x 11.75"
ISBN: 978-1-954632-36-3
US $75

Awards: Graphis presents 10 Platinum, 138 Gold, and 181 Silver awards, along with 36 Honorable Mentions.
Winning Entrants: Nick Berryman, Gabriel Cabrera, Jonathan Knowles, Tatsuro Nishimura, Howard Schatz, Allison Smith, Geoff Story, and Michael Winokur.
Judges: Athena Azevedo, Ricardo de Vicq de Cumptich, Colin Gray, Parish Kohanim, and Lindsay Siu.
Content: This book is full of exceptional work by our masterful judges, our Platinum, Gold, and Silver award winners, and our Honorable Mentions. It also includes a retrospective on our Platinum 2015 Photography winners, a list of international photography museums and galleries, and an In Memoriam list of photographers who have passed away this past year. The digital copy has additional pages of work from our series entries for you to peruse.

Advertising Annual 2025

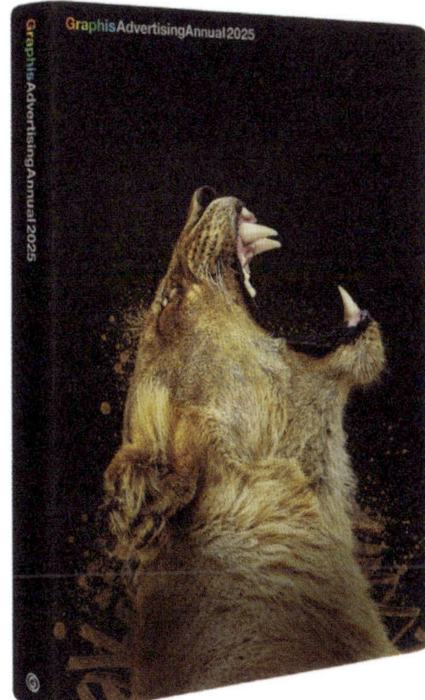

2025
Hardcover: 192 pages
200-plus color illustrations
Trim: 8.5 x 11.75"
ISBN: 978-1-954632-35-6
US $75

Awards: Graphis presents 12 Platinum, 78 Gold, and 68 Silver Awards, along with 19 Honorable Mentions, to many international advertising firms who explored what advertising can do with innovative, creative works.
Winning Entrants: ARSONAL, Barlow.Agency, Canyon, Chang Liu, Darkhorse Design, Eight Sleep, Lewis Communications, Ogilvy Brazil, PETROL Advertising, PPK, and Vanderbyl Design.
Judges: Scott Bucher, Steve Chavez, Quinnton Harris, Mike Kriefski, Dan Magdich, and Courtney Richardson.
Content: This hardcover book displays full-page images of Platinum-winning work from talented advertising firms. Gold and Silver-winning work is also presented, and Honorable Mentions are listed in the physical copy. All work is presented equally on our website. Award-winning work from the judges, an In Memorium list of advertisers who have passed away in the past year, and a section of Platinum-winning works from 2015 are also included.

Design Annual 2025

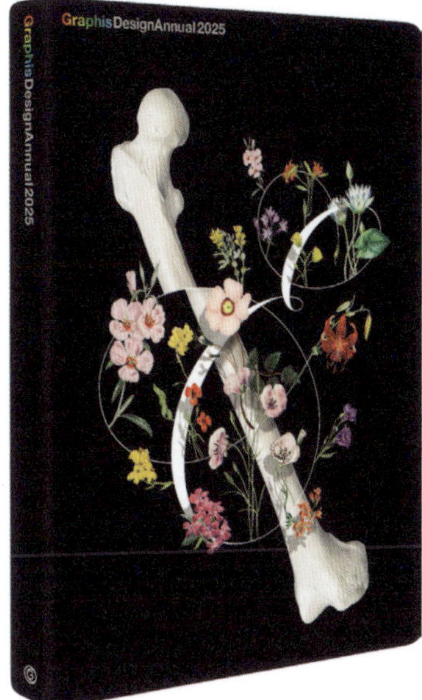

2025
Hardcover: 272 pages
200-plus color illustrations
Trim: 8.5 x 11.75"
ISBN: 978-1-954632-34-9
US $75

Awards: Graphis presents 12 Platinum, 163 Gold, and 401 Silver Awards, along with 118 Honorable Mentions, to many international designers who explored what design can do with innovative, creative works.
Winning Entrants: 33 and Branding, Dankook University, EJ Communication Studio, National Kaohsiung University of Science and Technology (NKUST), Sol Benito, Stranger & Stranger, Studio Del-Rey, Studio Hinrichs, and The Balbusso Twins.
Judges: Eduardo Aires, Toshiaki & Hisa Ide, Jennifer Morla, Brendán Murphy, and Richard Poulin.
Content: This hardcover book displays full-page images of Platinum-winning work from talented designers. Gold and Silver-winning work is also presented, and Honorable Mentions are listed in the physical copy. All work is presented equally on our website. Award-winning work from the judges, an In Memorium list of designers who have passed away in the past year, and a section of Platinum-winning works from 2015 are also included.

Poster Annual 2025

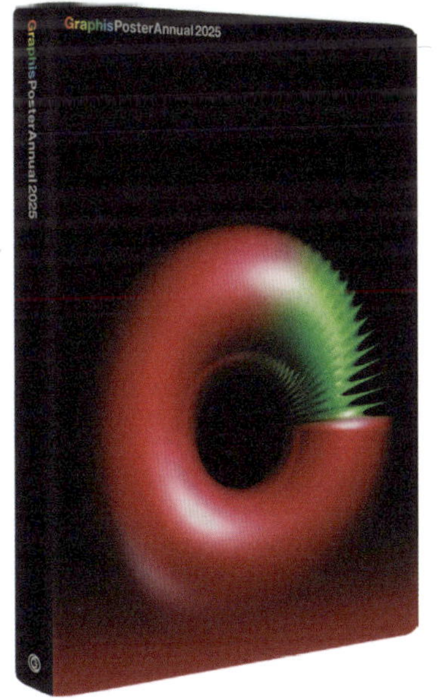

2024
Hardcover: 256 pages
200-plus color illustrations
Trim: 8.5 x 11.75"
ISBN: 978-1-954632-33-2
US $75

Awards: Graphis presents 12 Platinum, 100 Gold, and 328 Silver Awards, along with 90 Honorable Mentions, to many international poster designers who challenged what poster design can be with innovative, creative works.
Winning Entrants: Atelier Bundi AG, CollierGraphica, Dankook University, dGwaltneyArt, Freaner Creative, Gallery BI, João Machado Design, Katarzyna Zapart, Melchior Imboden, Skolos-Wedell, The Union Design Company, and THERE IS STUDIO.
Judges: Liz English, Paul Garbett, Brad Hochberg, Sven Lindhorst-Emme, DaeKi Shim, and HyoJun Shim.
Content: This hardcover book displays full-page images of Platinum-winning work from talented poster designers. Gold and Silver-winning work is also presented, and Honorable Mentions are listed in the physical copy. All work is presented equally on our website. Award-winning work from the judges and a section of Platinum-winning works from 2015 are also included.

New Talent Annual 2024

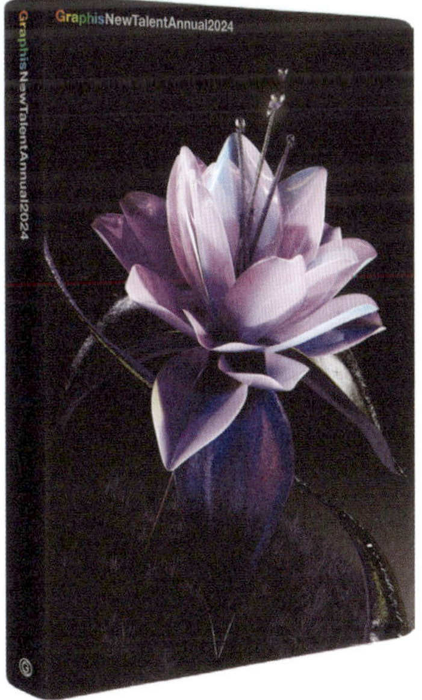

2024
Hardcover: 256 pages
200-plus color illustrations
Trim: 8.5 x 11.75"
ISBN: 978-1-954632-29-5
US $75

Awards: Graphis presents 13 Platinum, 132 Gold, and 587 Silver awards, along with 858 Honorable Mentions.
Winning Entrants: Design: Peter Bergman, Justin Colt, Rob Clayton, Natasha Jen, Simon Johnston, Billy Magbua, William Meek, Richard Mehl, Nathan Savage, Stephen Serrato, HyoJun Shim, Ming Tai, and David Tillinghast.
Judges: David Bernstein, Scott Bucher, Hoon-Dong Chung, Patti Judd, Jim Ma, Kah Poon, Frank P. Wartenberg, Lisa Winstanley, and others listed in the book.
Contents: This book contains award-winning entries in Advertising, Design, Photography, and Film/Video. There are full-page images of Platinum-winning work from talented teachers and students. Gold and Silver-winning work is also presented, and Honorable Mentions are listed. We also present A Decade of New Talent, featuring Platinum-winning works from 2014.

Narrative Design: Kit Hinrichs

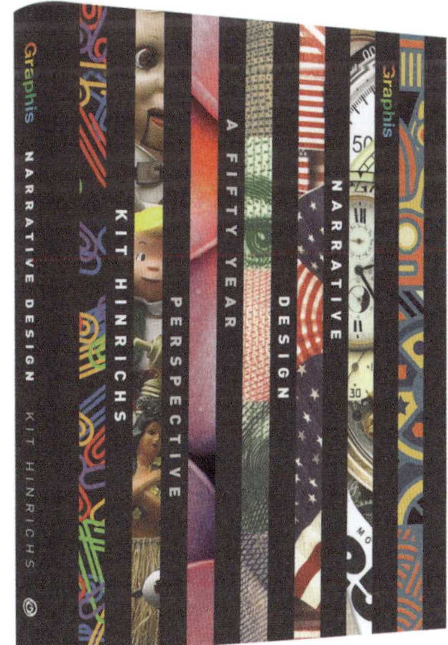

2023
Hardcover: 248 pages
200-plus color illustrations
Trim: 9 x 12"
ISBN: 978-1-954632-03-5
US $65

Narrative Design: A Fifty-Year Perspective is a collection of over 50 years of work from the obsessive graphic designer Kit Hinrichs. To the legendary AIGA medalist, author, teacher, and collector, design is the business of telling a story. It's not just about communicating a product or a corporate ethos—it's about contributing to the collective culture of storytelling. Presented in the book are not individual case studies but rather categories of work and graphic approaches to assignments that have wowed clients and dazzled viewers. The work is arranged to communicate Hinrichs' creative thinking, which always leads to a unique and effective solution to any design conundrum.

Books are available at graphis.com/publications

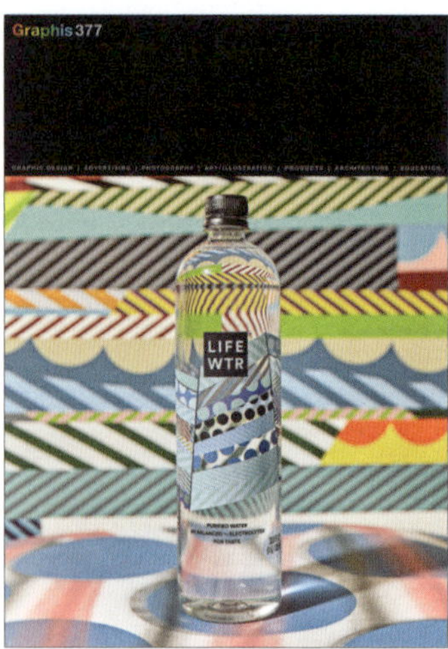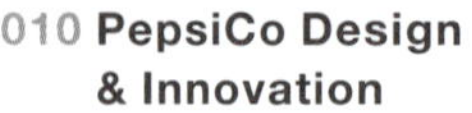

Graphis 377
LIFE WTR

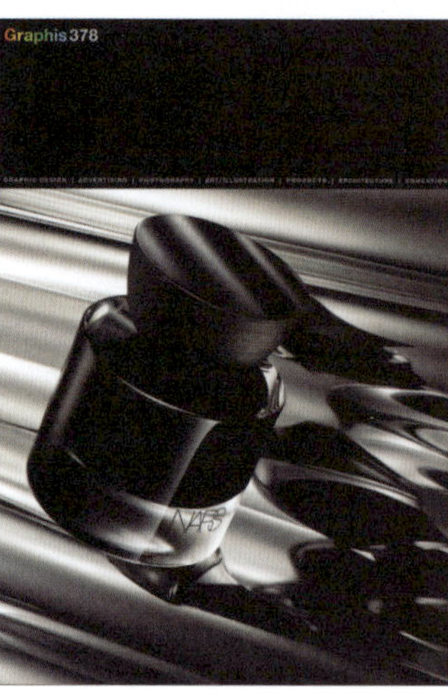

Graphis 378

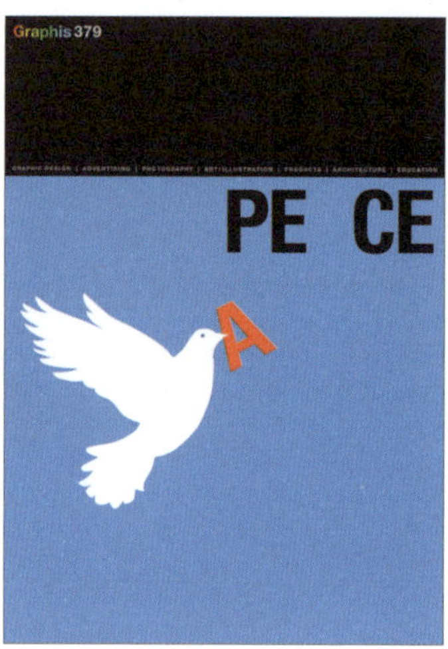

Graphis 379
PE CE
A

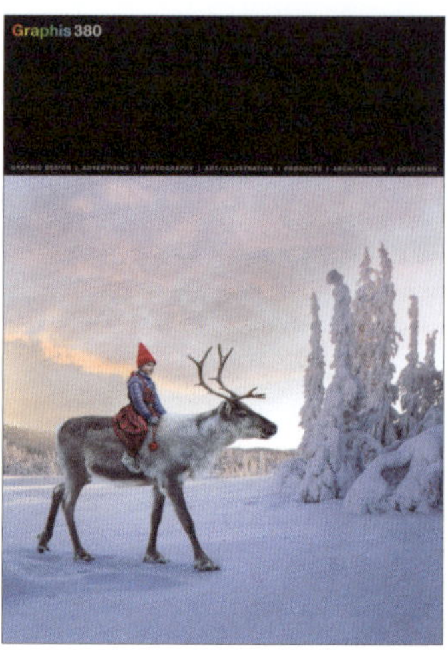

Graphis 380

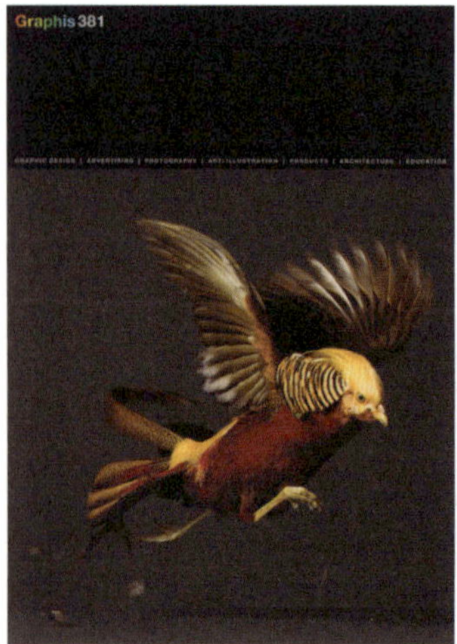

Graphis 381

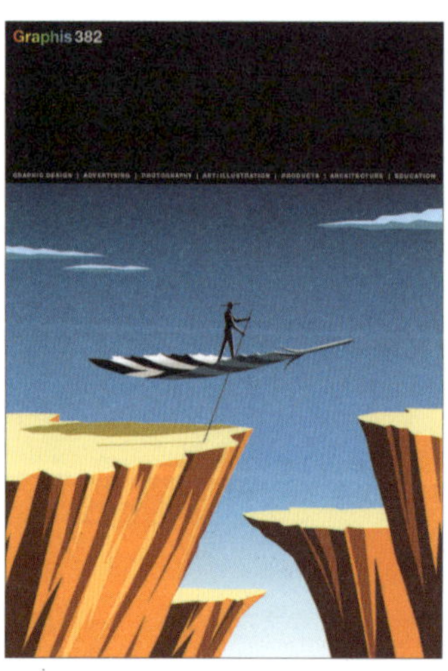

Graphis 382

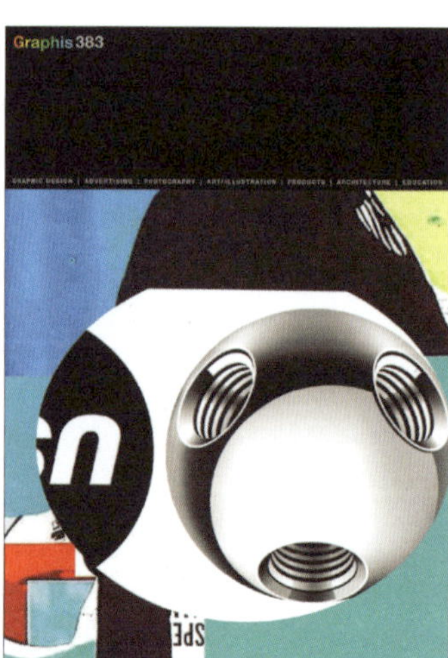

Graphis 383

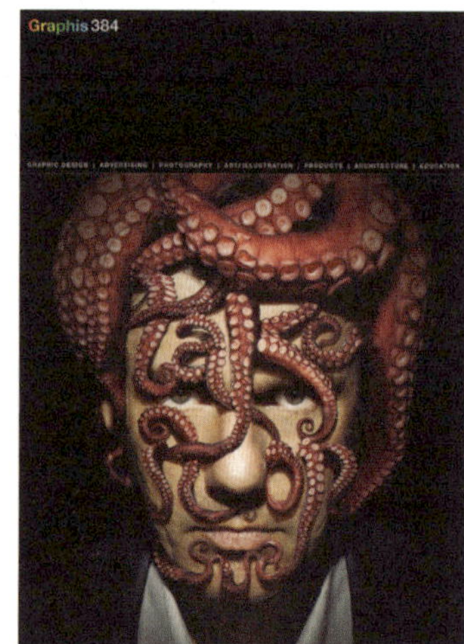

Graphis 384

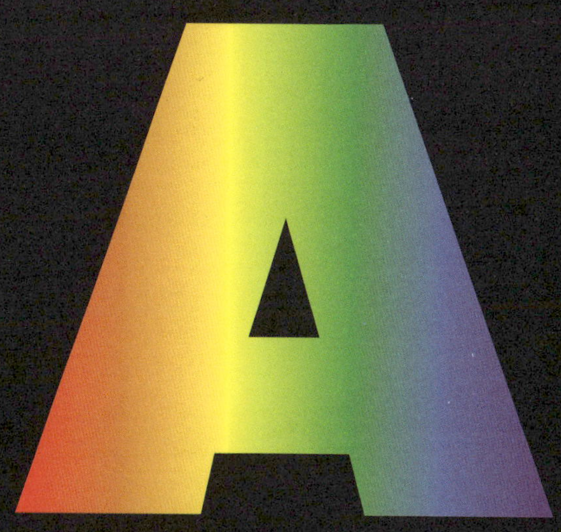

ADVISORY BOARD

QUINNTON HARRIS

PATTI JUDD

MICHAEL PANTUSO

RON TAFT

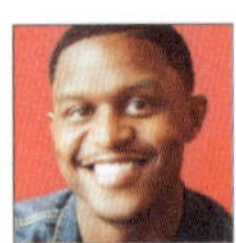

Quinnton Harris

Retrospect co-founder and chief executive officer, Quinnton J. Harris is a creative leader and entrepreneur living in Brooklyn, New York. His new venture focuses on building products and digital experiences that are radical, culturally nuanced, and more accessible for untapped or overlooked market opportunities. Previously, he served as Publicis Sapient Group's creative director within experience design as well as co-leader of global computational design, which focused on evolving the organization's design systems practice. He played a critical role in accelerating CXO John Maeda's vision for fostering a more inclusive, multi-dimensional, and cohesive experience design capability. He also served as head of experience for San Francisco. In early 2020, he completed a short tenure as John Maeda's chief of staff, finding much success in pushing critical CXO initiatives, implementing systems for global collaboration, and enhancing internal communication strategies. Quinnton also led the #hellajuneteenth movement and got over 600 companies committed to observing Juneteenth as a paid holiday for its employees. Prior to joining Publicis Sapient, he served as inaugural creative director at Blavity, Inc., and before that led design at Walker & Company Brands, a startup consumer products and tech company notably acquired by Procter & Gamble. He is an MIT alum, graduating with a SB in mechanical engineering and dual minors in architecture and visual arts.

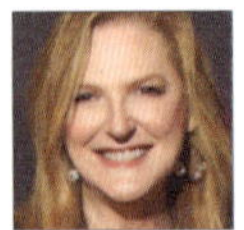

Patti Judd

An award-winning creative director, accomplished marketing and film executive, and co-founder of the San Diego International Film Festival, Patti Judd joined Graphis as chief visionary officer. A key initiative was forming the Graphis Industry Advisory Board to promote greater industry insights and connections globally. Patti blends business savvy gained from 20+ years at her agency with the entertainment biz acumen garnered from working in music and film. Her studio, Judd Brand Media, champions her passion for creating innovative work, receiving over 100 awards in design, advertising, and marketing. Her work includes notable global brands such as WME, Disney, Mattel, the Montreux Jazz Festival, Century 21, Aramark, Service America, and Hilton, alongside numerous emerging brands, recording artists, and filmmakers. Her influence goes from helping launch a major live music venue, where she was a key player in its growth, to one of the top live jazz venues in the world to co-founding the San Diego International Film Festival. She holds two executive producer credits for a children's TV series on Nickelodeon and a feature film in association with the BBC, which premiered at Sundance (acquired by Universal Pictures). Currently, she is in development as executive producer on an exciting new animated children's series. Patti's nonprofit work includes being a foster youth board member and a past president of an arts and culture board benefiting Balboa Park, the largest urban cultural park in the US. Recently, she was awarded as an Altruist Honoree by *Modern Luxury* magazine.

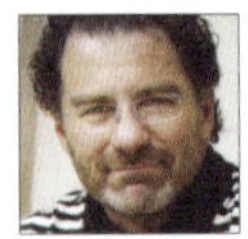

Michael Pantuso

As a multidisciplined graphic designer and artist, Michael Pantuso thrives at the intersection of creative thinking, artistic expression, and strategically inspired ideas. Throughout his career, Michael has managed his own design practice, partnered with the branding agency IDEAS360°, and held positions inside TBWA Worldhealth (formerly CAHG) and Discover Financial. Located in the Chicago area, Michael is focused on creating design and art for clients, collectors, and organizations that make a social impact—these include charities, not-for-profits, NGOs, educational and arts bodies, social enterprises, and for-profit businesses who want to do more good. Michael's practice creates all the usual outputs of a branding agency—design identities, advertising, social media, print literature, websites, email, e-newsletters, photography, etc. But he does so in the context of a bigger picture—a vision for what the brand is, and, more importantly, what it can become. It's a passion that comes from a desire to make things better. Michael's art is an extension of this passion, but it's revealed and expressed in a more visceral way. One example of this can be seen in his "Mechanical Integration" work, where he explores nature and humanity through a series of fine art illustrations that integrate natural life forms with the inner workings of mechanical components. Part of this collection was recently celebrated as a solo exhibition which began in Paris, France, followed by a tour of Europe that concluded in early 2020. Much of that work now remains in galleries and private collections.

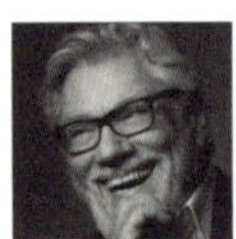

Ron Taft

Ron Taft is a multidisciplinary brand innovation and media arts strategist, creative director, and designer. He is the recipient of 32 Graphis awards and numerous international design and industry awards, including two Emmys for Columbia TriStar Television and two artist award-winning Grammy campaigns. Ron's many disciplines emanate from his background in advertising, network television, film, and the music industry. He has created many celebrated brand identities, product launches, branded events, and advertising and promotional campaigns for such clients as Sony Pictures, HBO, the Emmys, Leo Schachter Diamonds, Hästens, United Recording, Roland, the Berklee College of Music, Microsoft, Nike, Ferrari, Stella Artois, and NASA. He has served formerly as executive vice president/creative director of Dailey Advertising (an IPG company) before founding his own brand innovation and media arts company in 2008. Ron has also served on the boards of the Quincy Jones Musiq Consortium and Mr. Holland's Opus Foundation and has created outreach campaigns and promotional initiatives for NAMM, Music Rising, the NARAS Foundation, the Academy of Television Arts & Sciences, the Kidspace Children's Museum, the ArtCenter College of Design, and the Berklee College of Music.